English grammatical structure

A general syllabus for teachers

L G Alexander
W Stannard Allen
R A Close
R J O'Neill

Longman

Longman Group Limited
London and Harlow

Associated companies, branches and representatives
throughout the world

First published 1975

ISBN 0 582 55325·3

Printed in Great Britain by William Clowes and Sons, Limited
London, Beccles and Colchester

Contents

Contents

Introduction

Aims
This is an inventory of sentence patterns and grammatical structures which has been compiled for purposes related to the teaching of English as a foreign language. It is intended to serve as an aid

in the planning of curricula and syllabuses for particular needs;

in the design and construction of English courses;

in the composition of graded reading material, whether written especially or simplified from existing texts;

in devising diagnostic and qualifying tests;

for prospective and practising teachers of English, so as to give them a survey of the grammatical part of their field;

for other purposes related to the teaching of English, eg to indicate the constructions and phrases that could be used, at different levels, in general classroom dialogue,

as a source of exponents to illustrate language functions when constructing a notional syllabus.

The inventory is not intended to be a comprehensive description of English grammatical structure. On the contrary, it is meant to be limited and selective. Nor is it a textbook, though the authors hope it will provide source material for textbook writers, or for teachers wishing to select examples to illustrate a lesson on a specific grammatical problem.

As a general syllabus, it is bound to need adaptation for particular circumstances. These will vary, for example, according to region and to the age of the learner. They will differ according to whether English is to be taught *a* in a strictly graded sequence; or *b* in situations of interest to the pupils concerned; or *c* as a means of carrying out certain communicative processes, from making and answering simple requests to giving explanations and formulating definitions; or as a combination of *a*, *b* and *c*.

Method of compilation

To compile such a list on the basis of a statistical investigation into the frequency of occurrence of grammatical structures and into the range of styles in which such structures are found would be an enormous task. The results would vary according to the kinds of English investigated, and the relevance of those results would depend on the purposes for which English is needed. The authors have not attempted that task, nor have they pretended to estimate what the results would be. It is rather on the basis of their combined experience of teaching English and of compiling English-teaching materials that they have agreed where the limits of this book should be drawn and in what order individual items should appear. They have taken into consideration such factors as apparent frequency of occurrence, productivity, general usefulness, progression from simple to compound and complex, and pedagogical expediency.

Stages

The syllabus has been divided into six Stages. That division and the sequence of material within each Stage have been decided arbitrarily, in an endeavour to mark steps towards progressive levels of competence. How much of each Stage should be presented within a given period is left to the discretion of the textbook writer, the teacher or those who control the teacher's work; it will naturally depend on a variety of factors, including the number of English lessons in a year, and the number of years in a course. Similarly, the order in which the material is presented is left to the user's own judgement.

Units

Each Stage has been divided into Units. That division, again, is an arbitrary one, and has been made for the sake of tidy arrangement, so as to gather together a collection of items in, as it were, labelled packages of more or less uniform size. Each Unit has been given a general grammatical theme, since there is an obvious advantage in having certain items collected together in one group. But this does not mean that everything in one Unit has to be taught in one lesson or even in two or more consecutive lessons. Indeed, there are sound pedagogical arguments in favour of spreading, say, the irregular plurals of nouns over a number of lessons, and of not teaching, in the same lesson, two similar structures when the learner is likely to confuse one with the other. This syllabus lists material that might be taught. It does not attempt to prescribe *how* it should be taught; that is a question that can no doubt only be answered in the light of each special set of circumstances.

Grading

Variety of circumstances will increase the number of inevitable differences of opinion on whether such and such an item should come earlier in the syllabus, or later. In working towards the final draft of this book, the authors were generally under pressure to introduce an item earlier. When they resisted that pressure, it was because the structure in question was replaceable by a more widely useful one, or because it was known to be a common source of difficulty.

Structures presented in context

Structures have been presented, as far as possible and especially in the early stages, in the context of short conversational exchanges or short dialogues, not only to give them meaning but also to indicate which meaning is intended in cases where a structure or a structural word may be open to different interpretations. It is not intended that these exchanges should be incorporated, as they stand, in the material that a teacher actually presents in class, although there is no reason for not so incorporating them if they happen to fit into a given context. Certain lexical items in the models have been printed in square brackets to indicate that items of the same grammatical class can be substituted for them, provided of course that the resulting substitutions make good sense.

Short answers and contracted forms

The use of dialogue raises the questions of 'short answers', or 'minor sentences', and contracted or reduced forms like *I'll* and *isn't*. Short answers not only play a prominent role in natural conversation but also pick out important features of sentence structure. The Units present 'minor' as well as 'complete' sentences and indicate what is current and acceptable English in both types of sentence. Contractions like *I'll* occur constantly in fluent speech and the learner may need plenty of practice in hearing them. The uncontracted form has been presented first, and then the contracted form has been introduced both for its own sake and to give the dialogue a natural tone. The authors assume

1 that short answers and contracted forms will be widely used in classroom dialogue and in written texts where informal conversation is reproduced; and

2 that complete sentences and uncontracted forms will generally be used in formal composition and in other non-conversational written work.

Style

What has just been said raises the question of style. Where contracted forms have been used it may be assumed that the style is informal while providing raw material for written composition. When a structure is characteristic of informal style on the one hand or of formal style on the other, an indication to that effect has been given in the notes on the right-hand side of the page. In the absence of any such indication and of contracted forms, it may be assumed that the style is neutral and suitable for any general purpose.

Vocabulary

With regard to vocabulary, the choice of structural words has been determined by the structures themselves, and the choice of content words has been conditioned first of all by what lexical items will fit into the structures. Content vocabulary therefore appears in lexical sets appropriate for new patterns presented. It is not intended that all the words in a lexical set should be taught at one time, though it would be reasonable to expect that they would all be learnt, at least passively, at some time during a complete course. *A General Service List of English Words* (compiled and edited by Michael West, Longman, Revised Edition, 1953) has been consulted to ensure both that frequently-used words have been found a place in this syllabus and that less important words have been excluded. Thus, a basic vocabulary of about 600 words has been provided for Stage I. The authors appreciate the fact that the composition of a content vocabulary must depend to some extent on regional and group interests. In any case, what is being recommended in this syllabus is the grammatical structure rather than the lexical item.

Examples are given in the appendixes of lexical items that fit into certain structural patterns. The appendixes are intended as a guide to the material which might be included in a performance test at the end of Stage VI.

Formulas or fixed expressions

Users of this syllabus may find it helpful to distinguish between productive grammatical structures (ie those that can be used for a considerable range of lexical items) and formulas or fixed expressions (eg *How do you do?*).

The models and the notes

The models, given on the left-hand side of each page, may be suitable, with appropriate lexis, for the learner to repeat, practise and imitate. The notes, on the right-hand side, are not explanations to be given to the learner. They are meant neither to give information about usage nor to offer advice on teaching method. Their purpose is solely to indicate to the user—curriculum-planner, textbook writer, teacher, examiner, whoever he may be—why an entry has been made, and to provide cross-references, should they be required.

Active or passive learning

The question of whether a grammatical structure should be practised to the extent that the learner can exploit it creatively, or whether he should merely be able to understand it when it occurs in a context, is another matter that is left to the discretion of the user. Generally speaking, however, the authors would consider it reasonable that everything in the first three Stages should be learnt actively if a firm basis of proficiency in English is to be laid.

Acknowledgements

We are very grateful for detailed criticism made of the typescript of this book by

John Bright
Donn Byrne
Dr Jan A van Ek
Denis Girard
Dr Hans Ulherr

whose expert advice we have done our best to follow in the final draft. They are, of course, in no way responsible for such defects as remain.

Thanks are due also to John A Willis for allowing a copyright photograph to be used on the jacket of the book.

Publisher's note

We wish to record our special thanks to R A Close for his detailed work in revising the manuscript (with the assistance particularly of L G Alexander), and to R A Close and Myint Su for compiling the index of this book. Without the concentration of Mr Close's energies on drawing the work of all the collaborators together, either the book would have been less well-integrated, or completion of the manuscript would have been much delayed.

Conventions used

/θ/, phonetic symbol, as on page x

[camera][4] word(s) in brackets and numbered: lexical item replaceable, in the structure in which it occurs, by one of the items in the numbered part of the Lexicon

[drive] word(s) in brackets replaceable by another word of the same class, so long as a sensible result is produced

(that) word(s) in parentheses optional in the structure

$\text{He} \begin{Bmatrix} \text{'ll} \\ \text{'s going to} \end{Bmatrix} \text{drive}$ word(s) in braces: either 'll or 's going to is acceptable, without change of meaning

/I//you//he/ can word(s) in solidi: either I or you or he is usable in this pattern

= has (approximately) the same meaning as

* before an example indicates unacceptability

The English vowels

Phonetic symbol	Vowel sound as in	Phonetic symbol	Diphthong sound as in
iː	see	ei	day
i	it	əu	go
e	get	ai	fly
æ	cat	au	how
ɑː	father	ɔi	boy
ɔ	hot	iə	here
ɔː	saw	ɛə	there
u	put		
uː	too		
ʌ	up		
əː	bird		
ə	china		

Note : All vowel and diphthong sounds are 'voiced'.

The English consonants

	Voiced		Unvoiced	
Phonetic symbol	Consonant sound as in :	Phonetic symbol	Consonant sound as in :	
b	burn	p	pen, step	
m	moon			
w	we			
v	voice	f	full, roof	
ð	this	θ	thin	
d	day	t	tea, cat	
n	no			
l	look, pull			
r	run			
z (sibilant)	zoo, pens	s (sibilant)	see, books	
ʒ (sibilant)	measure	ʃ (sibilant)	ship, brush	
j	yes			
g	give	k	cat, kick	
ŋ	long			
h	here			

Note : Also sibilant are the combinations /tʃ/ as in *match*, /dʒ/ as in *judge* and /ʒ/ as in *garage*.

Part One

Sentence patterns introduced in the first three Stages

1 Sentence patterns introduced in Stage I

Number	Structure	Example
SP 1	NP^1 + *be* + NP^2, COMPLEMENT	My name is Tom.
SP 2	NP + *be* + ADJ	That pen is black.
SP 3	NP + *be* + ADV-P	He is in the garden.
3a	*Here* or *There* + PERS PRONOUN + *be*	Here I am.
3b	*Here* or *There* + *be* + any other NP	There is the office.
3c	*There* + *be* + NP + ADV-P	There is a dog in the garden.
SP 4	NP^1 + *have* + NP^2, OBJECT	I have two brothers.
SP 5	NP + vi	I am waiting. I understand. (From SP 5 to SP 10a, both the progressive and the non-progressive form of the VERB will be introduced.)
5a	NP + vi + ADV-PARTICLE	I am sitting down.
SP 6	NP^1 + vt + NP^2, OBJECT	He is reading a book.
6a	NP^1 + vt + NP^2 + ADV-P	She is putting the cakes in the oven.
6b	NP^1 + vt + INFINITIVE	I want to go. I want to.
SP 7	NP^1 + PREPOSITIONAL VERB + NP^2	I am looking at this photograph.
SP 8	NP^1 + vt + NP^2 + ADV-PARTICLE	I am putting my coat on.
SP 9	NP^1 + vt + NP^2 + *to* + NP^3	I am giving these books to James.
9a	NP^1 + vt + NP^2 + *for* + NP^3	He is getting a chair for Mary.
SP 10	NP^1 + vt + NP^3 + NP^2	I am giving James these books.
10a	NP^1 + vt + NP^3 + NP^2	He is getting Mary a chair.

Combinations of the above:

I think + SP 1	I think that's the postman.
I think + SP 2	I think you're tired.
I think + PRO-FORM for SP 1 or 2	I think so.

and so on up to SP 10a, but excluding 3a and 3b.

2 Additional patterns introduced in Stage II

SP 6c	NP^1 + vt + NP^2 + INFINITIVE with *to*	I want you to open it. I want you to.
6d	NP^1 + vt + NP^2 + BARE INFINITIVE	I'll let you go.
SP 8a	NP^1 + vt + ADV-PARTICLE + NP^2	I am putting on my coat.

3 Additional patterns introduced in Stage III

SP 2a	NP^1 + *be* + ADJ + PREP-PHRASE	I'm angry with John.
2b	NP^1 + *be* + ADJ + INFIN with *to*	He's afraid to speak.
SP 5b	*Here, there* or ADV-PARTICLE + PERS PRONOUN + vi	Here it comes. In you go.
5c	*Here, there* or ADV-PARTICLE + vi + NP	Here comes the bus.
SP 6e	NP^1 + vt + -*ing*	I enjoy swimming.
SP 7a	NP^1 + vt + NP^2 + PREP-PHRASE	We thank you for your letter.
7b	Same structure, but see III.12	I'll take care of you.

4

Additional combinations
Ask (him) if he is a doctor. Ask (him) what his name is.
I'm sorry I'm late. I'm afraid I must leave you.

See page 107 for a full range of verb patterns recommended for presentation by the end of Stage VI.

Stage I

Contents

16   MASS NOUNS: *Rice is good food ; the tea in this pot is cold ; this is hot tea ; a cup of tea, a piece of cake, a drop of water ; a teapot.*

17 SP 4, with *some* and *any* : *We have some bread, some eggs ; have we any bread, eggs? We haven't any bread, eggs ; there is some milk, there are some eggs, in the fridge ;* Q-*Yes/ No*, NEG; *there is, are some ; there isn't, aren't, any ; some, any big ones.*

18 SP 5, with VERB used intransitively, in PROGRESSIVE ASPECT: *I am waiting ;* Q-*Yes/No,* NEG; Q-*Who,* Q-*Where,* short answers; IMPERATIVE: *Wait, don't go.*

19 SP 5, PROGRESSIVE ASPECT, with VERBS and PREPOSITIONS indicating motion, contrasted with VERBS and PREPOSITIONS of position: *I am staying at home* in contrast with *I am going to the station ; to, (away) from, onto (or on to), into, off, out of, up, down, across, through ; go to bed, go home.*

20 SP 5a, with ADVERB PARTICLES: *Come in, sit down, you are standing up, keep out, wake up, get up, inside, outside ;* time: *one o'clock, half past one,* etc. *Go to sleep ; get dressed.*

21 SP 6 and SP 6a, with TRANSITIVE VERB and DIRECT OBJECT: *He is reading a book ;* Q-*What,* short answers; *she is putting the cakes in the oven ; me, him, her, us, them.*

22 SP 5, SP 6 and SP 6b, with STATIVE VERBS, and ACTION VERBS when not marked for PRO-GRESSIVE ASPECT, in the SIMPLE PRESENT TENSE: *I want some stamps ; I want to post some letters ; I believe you're right. I think so ; Mr Smith is a builder ; he builds houses. Birds fly. Tom gets up at seven.*

23 SP 5 and SP 6, with MODALS *can* and *must*: *I can swim, I can see a cloud ;* Q-*Yes/No,* NEG; Q-*Who,* Q-*What ; we must stop now ; be careful ; I think* + various sentence patterns.

24   Q-*Yes/No,* NEG, Q-*What,* applied to SIMPLE PRESENT TENSE: *Do you like . . .? Do you speak English? Does Tom like . . .? What does he do? I don't, he doesn't. I don't think so. I don't want to. I don't have a car.*

25 SP 7 and SP 8: *Look at this picture ; I'm looking at it ; listen to ; look for ; wait for ; who does this belong to? ; it's his, hers, ours, theirs. Take it away ; put your coat on ; pick it up.*

26   Q-*What* and Q-*Who* applied to SP 7 and SP 8: *What are you looking at? ; who does this car belong to? ; it's my brother's, my brothers' ; which shoes are you putting on? ; I put warm clothes on in winter.*

27 SP 9 and SP 9a: *Give all these books to James ; get a seat for Mary ; I'm giving them all to James, getting a seat for Mary ;* Q-*Yes/No,* Q-*What,* Q-*Who.*

28 SP 10 and SP 10a: *Give James these books ; get Mary a seat ; I'm giving James all these books ; what are you giving (to) James?*

29   Position of ADVERBS OF FREQUENCY and TIME: *Tom is always happy, he isn't often angry, he is still eating ; we sometimes go to the sea ; sometimes we go into the country ; we usually take our holidays in May.*

30   ADVERBS OF MANNER, their form and position: *Some people drive (their cars) (very) badly ; Mr Turner looks at the road carefully ; put your coat on quickly.* Relative position of ADV OF PLACE and ADV OF TIME: *He usually goes to town on Thursday.*

I.1 SP 1, with proper noun as complement; Q-*Yes/No*; neg; Q-*What*; *is, it is, it is not* in full and contracted, short answers

Models	Notes
Your name is Tom.	
1 *A* Your name is [Tom][1].	1 Dialogue between *A* and *B*.
B My name is Tom.	*Your* in *A* = *My* in *B*, and *vice versa*;
A Your name's Tom.	*name is* contracted to *name's* in fluent
B My name's Tom.	speech; *'s* = /z/ after any voiced sound
	except a sibilant (see page x).

2 *A* Hallo. Is your name Tom?
  B Yes, my name's Tom.

2 *Hallo*, informal greeting. Alternative spellings: *hullo, hello.* Q–*Yes/No* applied to SP 1.

3 *A* Is your name John?
  B No. My name is not John.
    a My name's not John.
    b My name isn't John.

3
  NEGATIVE of SP 1.
  Contraction, as above, + *not*.
  NEG with contraction, frequent in informal style.

4 *A* Is your name Tom?
  B Yes, it is Tom.
    Yes, it's Tom.

    Yes, it is.

    No, it is not Tom.
    It's not Tom. It isn't Tom.
    It is not. It's not. It isn't.
    It isn't Tom. It's John.

4
  it, PRO-FORM for specific NP. *It is* contracted to *it's* in fluent speech; *'s* = /s/ after any UNVOICED consonant except a SIBILANT.
  Short affirmative answer. *Is* not contracted when final.

  Short NEGATIVE answers; *'s not* and *isn't* in final position.

5 *A* What is your name?
    What's your name?
    What is your name, please?
  B Tom.
    My name is Tom. My name's Tom.
    It's Tom.

5 Q–*What* applied to Model 1 above.
  Contraction: *'s* = /s/, as in *it's*.

  Short answer, COMPLEMENT only.

Lexicon
1 Any suitable male or female name; *Mr, Mrs, Miss, Ms*+surname
2 *My, your ; name ; it ; is, not ; what ; please ; yes, no*
3 *Hallo*

I.2 SP 1, with *this* and *that* as pronouns; *here, there*; Q–*Who*; *What is that?* *It's a* ... + count noun

Models
This is my brother.
Who is that? It's Tom.
What is that? It's a camera.

Notes

1 *A* This is my [brother][1], Bob.
  B How do you do?
  C How do you do?

1 *This* = person or thing near the speaker. Polite formula, used when people first meet each other.

2 *A* Is this [Tom][2]?
  B No, this is [John][2].
    That is Tom.
    That's Tom.

2 *this* = near speaker A.
  this = near speaker B as well as A.
  That = at a distance from the speaker.
  Contraction: *'s* = /s/. No contraction after *this* or after any word ending in a SIBILANT.

    That's Tom, there.

  there = the speaker indicates some place not near him.

    ([Come][3] here, Tom.)

  ACTIVE use of IMPERATIVE may be deferred: see I.18.1.

    This is Tom, here.

  here = position near the speaker.

3 *A* Hallo, who is that?
   Who's that?
  B Tom. That's Tom. It's Tom.
  A Good morning, Tom.

3 *who* asking for identity of a person.
Contraction: '*s* = /z/.
It = the person indicated.
Good morning : daily greeting, before
noon; more formal than '*hallo*'.

4 *A* What is that, Tom? What's that?

4 *What*, asking for identification of something non-personal.

  B A [camera]⁴.

Short answer, NP only. NP here = IN-
DEFINITE ARTICLE + COMMON COUNT NOUN.
a camera = one unspecified example.

   It's a camera.
  A Is that a camera?
   Is it a camera? Is it?
  B Yes, it is.

Seeking confirmation: stress on *camera*.
Expressing doubt. Stress on *is*.

5 *A* Is that an [aeroplane]⁵?

5 *an*, INDEF ARTICLE before a vowel sound,
as in Lexicon 5 below.

  B Yes, it's an aeroplane.
  A Is that an [aeroplane]⁵?

Stress *that*, in contrast with *that* two lines
earlier.

  B No, it's a [bird]⁴.

Lexicon
1 *brother, sister, father, mother, son, daughter, uncle, aunt, cousin*
2 *any suitable name*
3 *come, sit, stand*
4 *bag, ball, bird, boat, box, bus, camera, car, cat, chair, coat, dog, fire, fish, house, key, knife, pen, pencil,
picture, plant, room, ship, shoe, table, train, watch*
5 *aeroplane, animal, apple, egg, elephant, office, orange*
6 *this, that ; here, there ; who ; a, an*
7 *How do you do? Good morning*

I.3 SP 1, with *he, she* and possessive forms of personal nouns

Models

He is my brother.
She is my sister.
Mr Turner is Tom's father.
His father. Her father.

Notes

1 *A* Who is that?
  B Jack. It's Jack.
  A Who's Jack?
  B My [brother]¹. He is my brother.
   He's my brother.

1

It : as in I.2.3.

He, SUBJECT; person identified as male.
He's, contraction of *He is*; '*s* = /z/.

2 *B* It's Anne. She is my [sister]¹.
   She's my sister.

She, SUBJECT; person identified as female.
She is contracts to *She's*; '*s* = /z/.

3 *A* This is Mr [Turner].
   He is Tom's [father]².

3

Tom's, POSSESSIVE form of Tom; '*s* = /z/.
Use the POSSESSIVE form with PERSONAL
NOUNS and domestic animals only at this
stage. See V.2.

   Tom is Mr Turner's [son]³.

   Tom is his [son].
   This is Mrs Turner.

his = *Mr Turner's* ; cp *He's* in 1 above.

She's Tom's [mother]⁴.
Tom is Mrs Turner's [son]³.
Tom is her [son].

4   Mr Turner is Jane's [father]², too. | *her = Mrs Turner's.*
Jane is Mr Turner's [daughter]⁵. | 4 *too = also.*
She is his [daughter].
Mrs Turner is Jane's [mother]⁴, too. | *his = Mr Turner's; her = Mrs Turner's.*
Jane is her [daughter]⁵. | Use *his* if possessor is male, and *her* if
                                             | possessor is female.
5 *B* Anne is my sister.
   A So Anne is Jack's sister, too. | 5

                                             | *So = therefore. Jack's : 's = /s/*; cp *It's* in
   B George is Tom's cousin. | note to I.1.4.
   A So Jane is George's cousin.
                                             | Pronounce *George's* with an extra syl-
                                             | lable, /iz/. This will apply also to *Charles's*
                                             | and any other short name ending in
                                             | SIBILANT. Cp note on 'no contraction
                                             | after *this*' in I.2.2.

Lexicon
1 *brother*, (male); *sister*, (female); *cousin, friend*, (male or female)
2 *father, grandfather, uncle, teacher*
3 *son, grandson, nephew, pupil, student*
4 *mother, grandmother, aunt, teacher*
5 *daughter, granddaughter, niece, pupil, student*
6 *he, she, his, her*
7 *so, too*

I.4 SP 1, with *this, that* + noun, and *Tom's* as pro-form; Q-*Whose*, with *whose* as
pronoun or premodifier

Models   **Notes**
This is Tom's room.
This room is Tom's.

1 *A* What's that thing?   1 *that* as PREMODIFIER.
       Is it a [basket]²?
   B No, that's [my]³ [hat]².   *that* as PRONOUN.
2 *A* This is a letter.   2 *This* as PRONOUN.
   B This letter is A's.   *This* as PREMODIFIER.
3a *A* Whose [book]² is this?   3a *Whose* + NOUN, probably more produc-
                                                tive than 3b.
                                                John's as PRO-FORM.
   B It's [John]'s ([book]²).
 b *A* Whose is this [book]²?   b *Whose* as PRONOUN.
   B [Jack]'s.
 c *A* Whose is this? Whose is it?   c *this* stressed, *it* unstressed.
   B [James]'s.   See note on I.3.5.
4 *C* That isn't [James]'s [book]².   4
       It's [my]⁴ [brother]⁵'s (book).
                                                POSSESSIVE form of *my brother* used as
                                                PRO-FORM.

5   Who is that [man]⁶?   5 *Who* used only as PRONOUN; *that*
       Who is that? Who is it?   stressed, *it* unstressed.

Lexicon
1 *thing*
2 *basket, book, clock, desk, face, finger, hand, handkerchief, hat, notebook, plate, purse, room, ruler, spoon,* and suitable words from I.2, Lexicon 4
3 *my, a* or *an*
4 *my, your ;* or *his* or *her,* depending on name substituted for James
5 *brother* or suitable word from I.3, Lexicon 1 to 5
6 *man, woman, boy, girl, child, person*
7 *whose*

I.5 SP 1, stating occupation, Q-*Yes/No*, and neg, with contractions and short answers

Models
Tom's father is a [doctor].
His uncle is an engineer.
I am a student.
You are a teacher.

Notes

1 *A* Mr Turner is a [doctor][1].
    Is Mr Turner an [engineer][1]?
  B No, he isn't an engineer.
    He's a doctor.
2 *A* Is Tom's uncle a doctor?
  B No, he's an engineer.
3 *A* I am a [student][1].
    I'm a student.
    You are a [teacher].
    You're a teacher.
4 *B* Am I a teacher?
  A Yes, you are.
  B Am I a student?
  A No, you are not.
    You're not. You aren't.
  B Are you a student?
  A Yes, I am.
  B Are you a [policeman][1]?
  A No, I am not. I'm not.

5 *A* Who is Mr Turner?

  B He's Tom's father.
  A What is Mr Turner?

  B He's a doctor.

1 The INDEF ARTICLE obligatory in this type of sentence.

3 *I* = the speaker.
I am contracted to *I'm.*
You = the person addressed.
You are contracted to *You're.*

4 Q-*Yes/No* applied to 3 above.
are not contracted when final.

NEG applied to 3 above.
Two contractions, as in I.1.3.

am not contracted when final.

No contraction of *I am not* comparable with *you aren't, he isn't.*

5 *Who* asking for identity of SUBJECT, personal.

What asking for occupation of (personal) SUBJECT.

Lexicon
1 *astronaut, builder, detective, doctor, engineer, farmer, lawyer, nurse, pilot, policeman, postman, pupil, student, teacher, worker* or *workman*

I.6 SP 2, SP 1, with adjectives used predicatively and attributively; Q-*Yes/No*, neg; Q-*Which*, pronoun and premodifier

Models	Notes
What colour is this pen?	
That pen is black. It's black.	
It's a black pen.	

1 *A* What colour is this [pen][1]?

   B [Black][2].

     It is [black]. It's [black].

     It's a [black] [pen].

2 *A* What colour is this [flag][1]?

   B It's [blue][2] and [white][2].

     It's a [blue] and [white] [flag].

3 *A* Is this [book][1] [red][2]?

   B No, it isn't (red).

   A Is it a [green][2] [book][1]?

   B No, it's a [black][2] one.

4 *A* Which is my book?

     Which book is mine?

     Which one is mine?

   B Which is your book?

     Which book is yours?

     Which one is yours?

5 *A* My book is red.

     The red book is mine.

     Your book is blue.

     The blue one is yours.

     Which is your book?

   B The blue one.

Notes

1

Short answer, ADJ COMPLEMENT only.
SP 2, ADJ used predicatively.
SP 1, ADJ used attributively.

2

CONJUNCTION *and*.

3 Q-*Yes/No* applied to SP 2.

one replacing NOUN already mentioned and modified by ADJ.

4 *Which*, as PRONOUN and PREMODIFIER, asking for identification from a specified selection; *my*, PREMODIFIER; *mine*, PRONOUN; *one* modified by *which*.

your, PREMODIFIER.
yours, PRONOUN, no apostrophe.

5

The, DEFINITE ARTICLE, signalling a specified, identifiable example.

Lexicon
1 suitable COMMON NOUNS from previous Lexicons; also *blouse, carpet, ceiling, collar, dress, flag, floor, handkerchief, jacket, leaf, shirt, skirt, suit, wall*
2 *black, blue, brown, green, grey, orange, red, white, yellow*
3 *mine, yours*
4 *one*, as in *a green one, the blue one*
5 *colour*
6 *which*
7 *and*

I.7 SP 2, SP 1, with two adjectives in the predicate or used as premodifiers

Models	Notes
Dick is tall and strong.	
He's a tall, strong boy.	

1 [Dick] is [tall][1]. He's [strong][1], too.

   He's tall and strong.

   He's a tall, strong boy.

Notes

1

Two ADJS joined by *and* in PREDICATE, but separated by comma as PREMODIFIERS.

2   [That flag]² is blue and white.
    It's a blue and white flag.

2

    and retained when two ADJS of colour
    are PREMODIFIERS.

3 *A* Is Robert tall?
  B Yes, he's very tall,
     but he isn't strong.
     He's a [weak]¹ boy.

3

    ADJ modified by *very*.
    but introducing a contrast.

4 *A* Which boy is Dick?
     Which one is Robert?
  B Dick is the tall strong boy.
     Robert is the other boy.
     He's the other (one).

4 *Which*, see I.6.4, now referring to a
  person.
  the, as in I.6.5.
  other, PREMODIFIER before NOUN or *one*,
  also used as PRONOUN, SINGULAR.

5 *A* Is Ted tall or [short]¹?
  B He's not very tall, but he's very strong.
  A Is he tall?
  B Not very.

  or joining alternatives.

Lexicon
1 ADJECTIVES, presented as pairs of opposites: (a) describing persons, animals or things: *big, little ;
  large, small ; good, bad ; tall, short ; heavy, light ; quiet, noisy ; quick, slow ; nice, pretty, beautiful,
  ugly ; strong, weak.* (b) describing persons or animals: *old, young ; fat, thin.* (c) describing things:
  old, new ; long, short ; straight, bent/crooked ; thick, thin ; hard, soft ; high, low ; sharp, blunt. All
  these ADJS can be used both predicatively and attributively, and can be modified by *very*
2 *this, that, my, your, his, her* + any suitable COUNT NOUN from previous Lexicons
3 *very ; but, or ; other*

I.8 SP 2, with a variety of adjectives answering questions like *How are you?*
How are you feeling?

Models
I'm (very) well.
I'm hungry. I'm cold.
You're right. I'm wrong.
That's all right.

Notes

1 *A* How [are]¹ [you]² ([today]³)?

  B [I'm] very well, thank you.

    or (I'm) [not very well]⁴.
  A I'm [sorry]⁵.

1 Q-*How* applied to SP 2, enquiring about
  health.
  well as ADJ, PREDIC only. Contrast:
  How are you? which requires an answer,
  with *How do you do?* (I.2.1).

  sorry for something that has been said,
  done or omitted ; PREDIC only at this
  stage; opposite, *glad*.

2 *A* Are you [happy]⁶?

  B Yes, (I'm) very happy.
    Very (happy).
    But I'm hungry.
3 *A* Are you [tired]⁷?
  B That's all right. I'm all right.
4 *A* What's the matter?
  B I'm (very) [cold]⁷.

2 Enquiry about emotional or physical
  state.

  Very, or *Very* + ADJ, can be short answer.

3

  = There's no need to worry (about me).
4 Something is *not* all right.

5 *A* Is this ([answer][8]) [right][9] ?
  B Yes, that's right. No, it's wrong.
  A Is this the right [page][10] ?
  B Yes, that's the right one.
6 *A* This ([question][8])'s [easy][11].
  B You're [right][9]. It's [easy][11].
  or You're [wrong][9], I'm afraid.
  It's (very) [difficult][11].

5 *right* and *wrong*, not usually modified by *very*.

Lexicon
1 *are*, with *you*; *is*, with any third person
2 *you*; *he, she*; *your wife, your husband*; *his wife, her husband*; etc
3 *today, this morning, this evening, tonight*
4 *(very) ill* (PREDIC only); *(very) sick* (PREDIC and ATTRIB)
5 ADJS: *sorry, glad, delighted* (used predicatively only at this stage)
6 ADJS: *busy, comfortable, happy, sad, satisfied* (PREDIC and ATTRIB); *afraid, pleased, well, all right* (PREDIC only)
7 ADJS: *cold, hungry, sleepy, thirsty, tired, wet* (PREDIC and ATTRIB)
8 *answer, question, word*
9 *right* and *wrong* as opposites
10 *address, book, house, name, number, page, room, road, time, way*
11 ADJS: *easy, hard* (= *not easy*), *difficult, simple* (PREDIC and ATTRIB)
12 *thank you*

I.9 SP 2, with a further variety of adjectives

Models
He's kind. He's Swiss.
It's cold today.
This car is expensive.
A mouse is a small grey animal.

Notes

1 *A* What is [Herbert][1] [like][2] ?
  B He's [careful][3].

1 Enquiry about personal characteristics.

2 *A* Is he [Swedish][4] ?
  B No, he's [Swiss][4].

2 What nationality is he?

3 *A* What is it like today?
  B It's [fine][5].

3 = What is the weather like?
  It = the weather.

4 *A* What's wrong with this [watch]?
  B It's [broken][6].

4 For *with*, see I.19.8.

5 *A* Is this expensive?
  B No, it's (very) [cheap][7].

5 Asking the value or price.

6 *A* What is a [mouse][8] ?

6 *a mouse* here refers to the class of thing rather than to one example: cp I.2.4.
  B produces a simple definition.

  B [A mouse] is a [small] [grey] [animal].
7   This is a [clean] [white] [handerchief].

7 Colour ADJ coming nearer the HEAD-WORD.
  ADJ of nationality coming nearer still.

  A [big] [black] [American] [car].
8 *A* What is a [lion]?
  B It's like a very [large] [cat].

Lexicon
1 any suitable name; also: *your friend, your neighbour, the new pupil*
2 *like*, as in *What is he like?*
3 *careful, careless, clever, fat, intelligent, kind, nice, quick, slow, tall, thin*; all PREDIC and ATTRIB

4 any ADJ of nationality. All such ADJS spelt with capital letter
5 *fine, dull ; cold, cool, warm, hot ; wet, dry ;* all PREDIC and ATTRIB
6 *dirty, (very) old ; broken,* if the thing is made of metal, glass, etc; *bent,* if made of metal or wood ; *torn,* of cloth or paper. All these ADJS are used PREDIC and ATTRIB, but *broken, bent, torn* not modified by *very*
7 *cheap, expensive,* PREDIC and ATTRIB ; *dear,* preferably PREDIC only in this sense
8 *cat, cow, dog, elephant, horse, lion, mouse*

I.10 SP 3, with *here, there* and prepositional phrases ; Q-*Where* ; prepositional phrase as adv-p

Models	Notes
I'm here. Where's Tom?	

He's⎰ on the floor.
⎩ in the garden.
⎱ at the door.
⎰ under the table.

1 *A* [Tom!]
  B Yes, I'm here.
  A Where are you?
  B In the [garden][1].
    I'm in the [garden].

1 *A* is calling for Tom.
  here : see note I.2.2.
  Q-*Where* applied to SP 3.
  In, PREPOSITION indicating position in relation to area or 3-dimensional space.
  The [*garden*], a particular garden which *B* assumes *A* can identify. PREP PHRASE can be used as short answer.

2 *A* Is [Jack] there?
    Where's [Jack]?
  B On the [roof][2].
  C He's on the [roof]?
    Is he?

2 Q-*Yes/No* applied to SP 3.
  Where is contracted to *where's.*
  On PREP, position in relation to surface.
  Statement-pattern, with intonation rise, to form an echo question asking for repetition, expressing astonishment, etc.

3 *A* Where's [my] [pen]?
  B It's on the [desk][3].
  A Where's my [note-book]?
  B In [your] [desk][4].
  A No, it isn't here.
  B It's there, under the [table][5].

3

  On the top surface of the desk.

  In (= inside) in contrast with *on.*
  NEG applied to SP 3.
  under : PREP, position, covered by (the table).

4 *A* Listen. That's the bell.
  B It's the [postman].
    He's at the [door][6].

4 Note as for *the garden,* I.10.1.
  Note as for *the garden.*
  at, PREP, position in relation to a point or dimensions irrelevant.

5 *A* Where's the [light][7]?
  B Over your [head][8].
  A Yes, but where's the [switch]?
  B On the wall.

5 Note as for I.10.1.
  Over: PREP, opposite of *under.*

  On a vertical surface.

Lexicon
1 *bath, bathroom, bedroom, dining-room, drawing-room, garage, garden, hall, kitchen, road, street*
2 *floor, first floor, second floor, third floor, roof ; platform*
3 *chair, desk, floor, shelf, table*
4 *car, desk, drawer, cupboard, hand, pocket*

5 *bed, carpet, chair, desk, mat, table, tree*
6 *door, gate, window*
7 *light, picture, switch*
8 *bed, desk, head*
9 *on, in, at, under, over*

I.11 SP 3a, SP 3b, and SP 3c; structures beginning with *Here*, *There* and *There is*

Models

Here I am. There you are.
There is the office.
Look! There's an elephant!
There's a dog in the garden.

Notes

1 *A* Where [are]¹ [you]²?
  B Here [I]² [am]¹.
  A So there [you] [are].

1
  SP 3a. *Here* and *There*, both stressed,
  may begin a sentence, followed by
  PERS PRONOUN + *be*.

2 *A* Where is the [office]³, please?
  B There it is, over there.

    There is the office.
    There's the office.

2 *the office* : see note I.10.1 on *the garden*.
  over there : speaker indicates a position
  not near him.
  SP 3b. *There* stressed. When NP is not a
  PERS PRONOUN, *be* precedes it in this
  variation of SP 3.

3 *A* Look! There's [an] [elephant].
  B Where? Where's the [elephant]?

3 *There* unstressed.
  the [*elephant*], the one just mentioned
  by *A*.

4 *A* There's a [dog] [in] the [garden].

4 SP 3c. This variation of SP 3, with unstressed *There*, is normal instead of
  A + NOUN + *be* + ADV-P, *A dog is in the
  garden*.

5 *B* There isn't a dog in the garden.
   A There is. There is a dog.

   B There isn't. There isn't a dog.
6a *C* Is there a dog in the garden?
   Is there?
 b What is there in the garden?
   What's in the garden?
  A A dog. There's a dog.
 c *C* Where is there a dog?
  A In the garden.
7   Hallo, is [Jack] there, please?

5 NEG of I.11.4.
  Short affirmatives in contrast with NEG;
  is stressed in both these examples.
  Short negatives; *isn't* stressed in both.
6a Q-*Yes/No* applied to I.11.4.
  Short question form.
 b Q-*What* applied to I.11.4.

  Short answers.
 c Q-*Where* applied to I.11.4.
  Short answer, ADV-P only.
7 As in I.10.2. Contrast I.11.6a.

Lexicon

1 *am, is, are* ⎫
2 *I, he, she, it, you* ⎭ with appropriate concord
3 *bank, dining-room, office, station, telephone*

| 4 | *There is*
There isn't
Is there | *a*
an | any suitable common noun from
previous Lexicons + *bottle, glass,*
cup, saucer, plate, fork, spoon,
towel | *in*
on
at
under
over | *the*
your | any suitable common
noun from previous
Lexicons. |

I.12 SP 1 and SP 2, with adverb of place as postmodifier in NP

Models	Notes
The man over there is a doctor.	
The seat over there is free.	
The man at the door is a detective.	
The bottle on the shelf is empty.	

1 *A* Is there a [doctor]¹ here?
  B There's a man over there.
    He's a doctor.
  C Yes, the man over there is a doctor.
    The man over there's a doctor.

1 Q-*Yes/No* as in I.11.6.
  There's a man, as in I.11.4.

  The man over there forms one NP.
  NP + *is* contracted to NP's.

2 *A* There isn't a [seat]².
  B Yes, there's a seat. It's free.
    The seat over there's free.

2 As in I.11.5.
  Yes: positive reply to NEG statement.

3 *A* There's someone at the door.
  B Who is it? A [detective]¹?
  C Yes, the man at the door's a detective.

3 As in I.11.4. *Someone*, INDEF PRONOUN.
  A detective? = *Is it a detective?*
  The man at the door forms one NP.

4 *A* There's something on the shelf.
  B It's an empty [bottle]³.
  C Yes, the bottle on the shelf's [empty]⁴:
    it isn't [full].

4 *something*, INDEF PRONOUN.

5 *A* Is there a [post office]⁵ near here?

5 *post office*: one NOUN modified by
another, forming a compound; stress
first NOUN, as in *bus-stop, letter-box,*
police-station.
near: PREP, position, not far from.

  B Yes, there's one—
    on the right
    on this side of the street
    opposite the bank; beside the bank
    in front of the station
    inside the station
    between the station and the bank.
6   At the [back]⁷ of the [station].

one = a post office.
opposite: *on the left.*
opposite: *on the other side* (of the . . .).
 = facing; = on one side of it.
in front of (one PREP): opposite *behind.*
opposite *outside.*
between two people or things.

Lexicon
1 As in I.5 Lexicon 1
2 *chair, desk, place, seat, table*
3 *basket, bottle, box, cup, glass*
4 *free; full, empty*
5 *bank, bus-stop, chemist, cinema, letter-box, police-station, post office*
6 *behind, between, in front of, near, opposite; inside, outside, beside; (on the) right, (on the) left; on this,*
  that, the other, side of; at the back of
7 *back, front, side; top, bottom*

I.13 SP 1, SP 2 and SP 3, with plural of nouns and personal pronouns; plural of count nouns; *these, those* as pronouns and premodifiers

Models	Notes
We are good friends.	
We're busy. We're in our room.	

1   *A* (to *B*) Tom's my friend. I'm his friend.
    A (to *C*) Tom. You and I are friends.
                 We are friends. We're friends.
    A (to *B*) He and I are friends.
    B Are you good friends?
    A Yes, we are.
         No, we're not. We aren't.

1   *We = you and I* or *he and I*. Put *I* second.
    You and I, he and I and *we* are PLURAL
    NPS, patterning with *are*. *We are* con-
    tracted to *we're*, unless final. COUNT NOUNS
    (eg *friend*) have PLURAL ending (pro-
    nounced /z/ after VOICED non-SIBILANT
    sound, as in I.1.1). No INDEF ARTICLE in
    PLURAL: contrast I.5.1. ADJ (eg *good*)
    unchanged when NOUN is PLURAL.

2   [Tom] is a student. [Jack] is too.
    [Tom] and [Jack] are students.
    They are students. They're students.
    A Are they good students?
    B Yes, they are. They're not. They aren't.
3   *A* Tom. Are you busy?
         Tom? Jack? Are you there?
    B We're in our room.

    C They're in their room.

2   *They = [Tom] and [Jack]*, PLURAL, followed
    by *are*. *They are* contracted to *they're*,
    unless final. PLURAL ending *s* pronounced
    /s/ after UNVOICED non-SIBILANT sound,
    as in I.1.4.

3   *You* = SECOND PERSON SINGULAR.
    You = SECOND PERSON PLURAL.
    We = the speakers; *our* = POSSESSIVE
    corresponding to *we*.
    their = POSSESSIVE corresponding to *they*.
    They're and *their*, pronounced the same.

4   Jane and Mary are nurses.

4   *nurse*, one syllable; NOUNS ending in a
    SIBILANT have extra syllable /iz/, as in
    I.3.5, in PLURAL. See Lex 1 below.

5   This is a watch. This is, too.
    Here are two watches.

    These (two) (things) are watches.
    These watches are very expensive.
    That is a key. That is a key, too.
    Those are keys. Those keys are mine.

5   NOUNS ending in *ch, s, sh* or *x* have
    extra syllable /iz/ in PLURAL, spelt *es*,
    see Lex 2.
    COUNT NOUNS, PLURAL, can be preceded by
    any numeral above *one*, by *these* (PLURAL
    of *this*) and *those* (PLURAL of *that*).
    These, those : PREMODIFIERS and PRO-
    NOUNS.

6   China is a country. Japan is a country.
    China and Japan are countries.

6   SINGULAR NOUN ending in consonant + *y*;
    PLURAL ending *-ies*. Contrast with NOUNS
    ending in vowel + *y*, eg *keys* (I.13.5).

7   [Cars] are expensive.
8   My books are on that shelf.
    The books on that shelf are mine.

7   ie cars in general.
8   DEF ART, *the*, before PLURAL to indicate
    specified examples. *Books* is the head-
    word in the NP *the books on that shelf*
    and determines concord with the VERB.

Lexicon
1 PLURAL formed like *nurse : face, garage, nose, page, place*
2 PLURAL formed like *watch : bus, bush, class, glass, match*
3 PLURAL formed like *country : baby, body, copy, family, factory, lady*

I.14   Irregular plurals, ie not conforming with the rules in I.13

Models   **Notes**
Men, women and children.
The people here are very kind.

1   One man, two men, three men.
    woman, women; child, children.

1   PLURAL *men, women* /wimin/, *children*
    /tʃildrən/. Similar forms in compounds,

	One policeman, two etc policemen.		eg *gentlemen, policemen, postmen, workmen* (SINGULAR and PLURAL pronounced alike in fluent speech).
2	She's a kind person. They're [kind] [people]. [The people]¹ here are very kind.	2	*person :* SINGULAR; *people :* PLURAL.
3	My left foot, my right foot. My feet are on the floor.	3	*foot,* SINGULAR; *feet,* PLURAL.
4	One tooth, two teeth, three teeth. One of my teeth is broken.	4	*tooth,* SINGULAR; *teeth,* PLURAL. *One* is the HEAD-WORD in *one of my teeth.* Cp note I.13.8.
5a b	A mouse is a small grey animal. Mice are small grey animals.	5	*mouse,* SINGULAR; *mice,* PLURAL. Either a or b can be used in definitions.
6	A sharp knife is dangerous. Sharp knives are dangerous.	6	*knife,* ending in /f/. *knives,* ending in /vz/.
7	There is a shelf in my room. There are two shelves in my room.	7	*shelf,* ending in /f/; *shelves,* in /vz/. *There is,* SINGULAR; *there are,* PLURAL.
8	There's a bath in our house. There are baths in modern houses.	8	*bath,* ending in /θ/; *baths,* in /ðz/. *houses* has an extra syllable, like *nurses,* I.13.4, and the first *s,* pronounced /s/ in the SINGULAR, becomes /z/ in the PLURAL.
9	A potato is a vegetable. Potatoes are vegetables.	9	*potato, tomato,* SINGULAR; *potatoes, tomatoes,* PLURAL.
10	A sheep is an animal. A deer is, too. Sheep and deer are animals.	10	*sheep* and *deer* have the same form for SINGULAR and PLURAL.
11	A man's [job]⁶. A child's [game]⁷.	11	The POSSESSIVE (I.3.3) is regular in contrast with PLURAL *men,* etc.

Lexicon

1 Use *the police* as PLURAL, like *the people,* in I.14.2. *Fish* can be SING or PLUR, though *fishes* also occurs to emphasize separate units
2 Like *foot, feet : goose, geese*
3 Like *knife, shelf : life, wife ; half, leaf, loaf, thief*
4 Like *bath : mouth, path*
5 Like *potato : cargo, echo, hero, motto.* However, a number of nouns ending in *o* follow the rules in I.13.1, eg *kilos, photos ;* other examples will be found in a good dictionary
6 *job*
7 *game, toy*

I.15 SP 4, *I have, I have got, I've got;* Q-*Yes/No*; Q-*What*; Q-*How many;* cardinal numbers

Models	**Notes**
I have ⎱ two brothers. I've got ⎰	
1 [Jack] and [Dick] are my [brothers]. I have ⎱ I've ⎬ two brothers. I have got, I've got ⎰	1 *I have* contracted to *I've.* *I've got* commonly occurs instead of *I've* in informal style.
2 You have, you've ⎱ a [nice] [house]. You have got, you've got ⎰	2 Use *have, 've, have got, 've got* also with *you, we* and *they.*

3   Jack has ⎫
     Jack has got ⎬two brothers, too.
     Jack's got ⎭

3 Use *has* with third person SINGULAR only. When contracted, *'s* (for *has*) pronounced as in I.1.

4 *A* Have you (got) a [book]?
       Has John (got) a book?

4 Q-*Yes/No* applied to SP 4. *got* is commonly present in informal British style. See note to I.24.10.
   have, has not contracted when final.

   B Yes, I have. Yes, he has.
        Yes, I have one. I've got one.
        No, I have not. No, he has not.
        No, I haven't. No, he hasn't.
        I haven't got one. He hasn't got one.

5 *A* What have you (got) in your [hand]?

5 Q-*What* applied to SP 4. *Got* can be omitted here, but the result would sound formal.

   B I have (got) ⎫
        I've (got) ⎬a [letter].

6 *A* How many brothers have you (got)?
   B Two. One brother is at home; the other brother is at school.

6 Q-*How many* applied to SP 4; *many* with COUNT NOUNS, PLURAL.
   One brother, instead of *a brother*, to make the contrast *one* versus *the other*, *at home*= in one's own house; *at school*= at the place where one generally studies with other children.

7 *A* You have two sisters.
   B No, I've got one sister.

7

   one sister, instead of *a sister*, to make the contrast *one* not *more than one*.

8   A horse has (got) four legs and a tail.
     A horse is a large animal, with four legs and a tail.

8

   with (*four legs*)= which has (four legs).

9 *A* Who is George Turner?
   B He's the boy with the long hair.
        He's the boy with the camera.
        He's the boy in the white shirt.

   Personal characteristic.
   ie carrying it.
   ie dressed in it.

Lexicon
1 *have, got*
2 *at home, at school*
3 the cardinal numbers

I.16 Mass nouns as NP

Models
Rice is a good food.
The tea in this pot is cold.
This is hot tea.
A cup of tea. A tea-pot.

Notes

1 *A* What is there in that [glass]²?
   B [Water]¹.
        This is only water.

1 Q-*What* as in I.11.6b.
   Short answer; MASS NOUN, no (or 'zero') ARTICLE; *only* indicates 'that is all'.

2 *A* What is rice?
  B Rice is a plant.

     It's very good food.
3 *A* This [tea]¹ is very [good]⁴.
  B My [tea] is [cold]⁴.
     The tea in this pot is cold.
4 *A* What will you have, coffee or tea?

  B [Coffee]¹. A [cup]² of [coffee]¹ and a
     glass of water, please.
  C Tea, with a [drop]³ of [milk]¹ in it.
  D Two slices of bread and butter, and a
     piece of cake, please.

5 *A* Yes, madam?
  B Two kilos of sugar, please.
6   There is hot tea in the tea-pot.

2 Contrast I.9.6 *A*.
  Rice, ie the substance in general; no
  ARTICLE.
  food, ie MASS NOUN, modified by ADJ.
3 MASS NOUNS can be preceded by *the, this,*
  that, my, your, Jack's, etc, but not by
  a, an or *one.*
4 Regard *What will you have?* as a formula
  at this stage.
  MASS NOUNS are frequently preceded by
  the structure *a X of, X* being the name
  of a container (eg *cup, glass, pot, bottle*)
  or a measure (eg *kilo, gallon*). *X* may
  also be *piece, slice, lump,* etc, of something
  solid; *bit,* informal, of solid; or *drop* of
  liquid.
5 Spoken by the assistant in a shop.
  See note on 4 above.
6 Contrast *a pot of tea,* as in I.16.4, with
  a tea-pot, the container, stress as in
  I.12.5.

Lexicon
1 MASS NOUNS
  solid food: *bread, butter, cake, chocolate, food, fruit, meat, rice, salt, sugar*
  liquid food: *coffee, milk, oil, tea, wine, water*
  other substances, liquids, etc: *air, blood, cotton, dirt, dust, earth, fire, glass, grass, hair, ice, iron,*
  money, mud, oil, sand, skin, snow, soap, water, wood, wool
  materials: *cloth, nylon, paper*
2 containers: *bag, basin, basket, bottle, bowl, box, bucket, can, cup, glass, jar, jug, pot, tin, coffee-cup,*
  milk-bottle, rice-bowl, sugar-bowl, tea-cup, tea-pot, tea-spoon
3 *piece, bit, slice, lump* of solid; *drop* of liquid
4 *good, bad ; hot, cold ; fresh, stale*
5 *only*

I.17 SP 4, with *some* and *any*; Q-*Yes/No*, neg

Models

We have { some bread.
         some eggs.

We haven't { any fruit.
           any potatoes.

There is some milk } in the fridge.
There are some eggs

Notes

1 *A* Have we any [food]¹ in the [house]²?
     Have we any [eggs]³?
  B We have (got) } some [bread]¹ and
     We've (got) } some [eggs]³.

     We have (got) } some.
     We've (got) }

1 *any* replaceable by *some* in these questions; *the house,* cp *the garden,* I.10.1.
  some + MASS NOUN or COUNT NOUN PLURAL
  to indicate unspecified quantity, in
  AFFIRMATIVE statement. Pronounce /səm/.
  some, as PRO-FORM for *some* + MASS NOUN
  or *some* + COUNT NOUN. (Pronounced
  /sʌm/.)

We haven't (got)⎱any bread or
We've not got ⎰any eggs.

any + MASS or COUNT, to indicate 'one single quantity', in NEGATIVE statement. Note use of *or* in *B*'s reply.

We haven't (got)⎱any.
We've not got ⎰

any, as PRO-FORM for *any* + MASS or *any* + COUNT.

2 *A* There is some [milk][1] in the [fridge][2].
There is some.

2 Cp I.11.4: *some* /səm/ in fluent speech. *some* /sʌm/.

B Is there any [butter][1] (in the fridge)?
Is there any?

any or *some* acceptable in these questions; but only *any* in the NEGATIVE.

A No, there isn't any (butter).

3 *A* There are some [eggs][3] in the [cupboard][2].
There are some.

B Are there any [apples][3]?

A No, there aren't any.

4 *A* These [potatoes][3] are very [small][4].
Have we (got) any [big][5] ones?

4

B Yes, there are some big ones in that box.

ones replaces the COUNT NOUN, PLURAL, mentioned. *One(s)* cannot replace a MASS NOUN in this way.

Lexicon
1 any suitable MASS NOUN
2 any suitable COUNT NOUN, SINGULAR or PLURAL
3 any suitable COUNT NOUN, PLURAL

There is, There isn't
There are, There aren't   ⎱*any*⎰   ⎧suitable MASS NOUN or COUNT NOUN PLURAL⎫   ⎱*in*⎰ *the* ⎧suitable COUNT NOUN⎫
Is there, Are there   ⎰*some*⎱   ⎩⎭   ⎰*on*⎱   ⎩⎭

4 *small, big, large, bad, old, stale*
5 *small, big, large, good, new, fresh*

I.18 SP 5, with verb used intransitively, in progressive aspect; Q-*Yes/No*, neg; Q-*Who*, Q-*Where*, short answers; imperative

Models
I am waiting.

Notes

1 *A* Jack!
B Yes?
A (Wait)[1]. Don't [go][1].

1

Wait, IMPERATIVE, same form as the stem. *Don't go*, IMPERATIVE. NP[1] (SUBJECT) = *you*, understood.

B I am [wait][1]ing. I'm waiting.

SP 5, with vi used in the PROGRESSIVE ASPECT to indicate action in progress. *be* is here used as an AUXILIARY, followed by PRESENT PARTICIPLE, or the *-ing* form, of VERB *wait*.

B I am not [go]ing. I'm not going.

2 *A* Are you [wait][1]ing?
B Yes, I am.

2 Q-*Yes/No*.
Short answer, NP + AUXILIARY.

3 *A* What are you doing?
B [Wait]ing.

3 Q-*What*, asking for VP.
Short answer, *-ing*, without AUXILIARY.

4 *A* Who is [wait]ing?
  B Jack. Jack is.

4 Q-*Who*, asking for NP SUBJECT.
  Short answer: NP SUBJECT, or NP SUBJECT
  + AUXILIARY.

5 *A* Where is he [wait]ing?
  B Over there.

5 Q-*Where*, asking for ADV-P.
  Short answer, ADV-P.

6   The [sun]² is [rising]³ in the sky.
Similarly

6 *The sun* = the one we all know.

I am	I'm	Am I	I'm not	—	
You are	You're	Are you	You're not	You aren't	
He is	He's	Is he	He's not	He isn't	
She is	She's	Is she	She's not	She isn't	[wait]ing
We are	We're	Are we	We're not	We aren't	
They are	They're	Are they	They're not	They aren't	

Lexicon

1 VERBS used intransitively and readily used in PROGRESSIVE aspect: *come, cry, dance, draw, drink, eat, fall, go, laugh, listen, look, play, read, run, sing, sit, sleep, smile, speak, stand, swim, talk, wait, walk, watch, work, write*
  Spelling rules: (i) if the stem ends in *-e*, omit the *-e* when the ending *-ing* is added, eg *come, coming*;
  (ii) if a monosyllabic stem ends in a single consonant, preceded by a single vowel, double the final consonant when *-ing* is added, eg *run, running*

2 *sun, moon*
3 *rise, shine*

I.19 SP 5, progressive aspect, with verbs and prepositions indicating motion, contrasted with verbs and prepositions of position

Models

He is staying at home.
He is going to the station.
He is walking into a shop.

Notes

1 Tom is not well. He's [at home]¹.
  He's staying at home today.
  He's in his [room]. He's [in bed]¹.

1 *be* and *stay* are associated with PREP PHRASE indicating position, eg *at, on, in, opposite*, etc + NP.
  in bed, cp *at home* (see Lex 1 below).

2 Mr Turner is [wait]²ing on the [platform].

2 *wait* associated with PREP PHRASE indicating position.

3 Mr Taylor is [going]³ to his [office]⁴.

3 *go*, motion, associated with PREP PHRASE indicating motion.

4 Now he is [going] from his [office] to the [station].
  He's [walking] away from his [office].

4 *from*, motion leaving a point, combined with *to*, approaching another point; *away from*, when *to* is omitted.

5 He's walking into a [shop]⁴.
  He's going into the [grocer]'s (shop).
  His friend is coming out of the shop.

5 *walk*, motion; *into*, motion entering a space. Sim. *the baker's, the butcher's* etc; *out of*, opposite direction to *into*.

6 Now he's at the [railway station]⁵.
  He's going onto the platform.

6 *be*, position, with *at* again.
  go, motion, with *onto* (or *on to*), motion in relation to a surface; opposite, *off*.

7 One man is walking up the [steps]⁵.
Another man is running down the steps.

7 *up*, motion to a higher level; opp *down*.
One man, see I.15.6. *Another*, written
as one word.

8 Tom's not well. He's going home.
He's going [upstairs]⁶. He's going
[to bed]⁷.
His mother is going upstairs with him.

8 *Go home*.
upstairs, to or on a higher floor inside
a building; opp *downstairs*. *To bed*,
cp *in bed* (I.19.1). *With* = accompanying.

9 A dog is running across the [street].
It's going through a hole in the [fence].
It's running round the field.

9 *across* a surface.
through a space or hole.
round, in a circular motion.

10 What is happening (in this picture)?
A train is going over a bridge.
A boat is going under the bridge.

10 *is happening*, use with third person only.
motion over.
motion under.

Lexicon

1 on the same pattern: *at home, at school, in bed*, or *in school* if emphasis is on the idea 'inside that space', *at*, or *in*, *church, in hospital, in prison*. Only use these fixed expressions when the appropriate meanings are intended: see, eg, I.15.6
2 *lie*, NB *lying, remain, sit, stand, stay*
3 *come, drive, go, run, travel*, NB *travelling, walk*
4 *office, shop*
5 *the bank, the cinema, the station, the theatre* (cp *the garden*, 1.10)
6 *downstairs, upstairs*
7 on the same pattern: *to bed, to church, to hospital, to market, to prison, to school*
8 *to, from, away from; onto, off; into, out of; across, through; up, down; round; by* or *past* a point; *along* a line, eg a road; *as far as; above* (ie at a higher level), *below* (ie at a lower level)

I.20 SP 5a, with adverb particles; time

Models
Come in. Sit down.
Why are you standing up?

Notes

1 Come here. Come [in]¹ᵃ.
Come on. Go on.

1 vi, eg *come, go, sit, stand, lie* and *be* followed by an ADVERBIAL, eg *here*, or by an
ADV PARTICLE: see Lex 1 below. The
ADV PARTICLE indicates the direction or
position of an action. *On* = forwards.

2 Don't lie on the [ground]².
Get up. Stand up. Sit down.

2 *lie* followed by PREP PHRASE.
Get up, an abrupt command; *get* with
ADV PARTICLE as COMPLEMENT.

3 *A* Why are you standing (up)?
B Because I haven't (got) a seat.

3 Q-*Why*,
answered by a CLAUSE beginning with
because.

4 It's [rain]³ing. Stay here.
Keep inside. Don't go outside.

4
Keep, meaning *stay*.

5 Wait a [minute]⁴. Don't go away.

5 *a minute* is here an ADV of time.

6 Stay there. Don't come here.
Go back. Stay outside. Keep out.

6
back, ADV PARTICLE = to where you came
from.

7 *A* You're tired. Go up to bed.
Lie down. Go to sleep.
B I am lying down. I'm going to sleep.

7 *up to* : ADV PARTICLE + PREPOSITION.
Go to sleep.
Stress the AUXILIARY (eg *am*) to make
the statement emphatic. Note *lying*.

8 *A* Are you still in bed? Wake up.
  B What is the time? What time is it?
  A It's [eight o'clock][5]. [Get up][6].
  B It's all right. I'm getting up.
    I'm getting dressed.

8 *still*, indicating continuance of action or state.
Get up here = get out of bed.

get dressed = put one's clothes on.

Lexicon

1 a. Words used as PREPOSITIONS and ADVERB PARTICLES *in, up, down, inside, outside*	b. as PREPOSITIONS only *to, at, from, into, out of*	c. as ADVERB PARTICLES, not as PREPOSITIONS *away, back, out*

2 *ground* (in the open air), *floor* (in a building)
3 *rain, snow*
4 *minute, second* (ie sixtieth of a minute)
5 */one//two//three/*, etc (*o'clock*); *half past* (*one*) etc; *quarter past* (*one*) etc; (*a*) *quarter to* (*one*) etc; *five* (*minutes*) *past* or *to* (*one*) etc; *ten* (*minutes*) *past* or *to* (*one*) etc; *twenty* (*minutes*) *past* or *to* (*one*) etc; *twenty-five* (*minutes*) *past* or *to* (*one*) etc. The word *minutes* is obligatory for any smaller fraction of an hour, eg *two minutes past* (*one*), *eight minutes to* (*three*)
6 *get dressed, get up, wake up*

I.21 SP 6 and SP 6a, with transitive verb and direct object; Q-*What*, short answers

Models
Mr Turner is reading a book.
Mrs Turner is making some cakes.
She is putting them in the oven.

Notes

1 *A* [Mr Turner] [is] [read][1]ing.
  B Who is reading?
  A Mr Turner (is).
  B What is he reading?
  A A [book]. He's reading a book.
  B What is he doing with the book?
  A Reading it. He's reading it.
2 *A* What is Mrs Turner doing?
  B She's [mak][2]ing [some cakes].

  A What is she making?
  B Some cakes.
3 *A* What is she doing with the cakes?
  B She's taking them off the table.
    She's taking them to the oven.
4 *B* Now she's [put][3]ting them in the oven.
  A Where's she putting them?
  B In the oven.
5   [Touch] your [chin][4].
6   Watch. This [paper] is [burn][5]ing.
    I'm [burn]ing the [paper].

1 *read* used as vi.
Asking for NP SUBJECT.

Assuming *read* used as vt and asking for NP OBJECT.

it as OBJECT.
2 ie what is her activity?
cake may be a MASS NOUN (I.16) or a COUNT NOUN.
ie what (new things) is she producing?
Contrast *What is she doing?*
3
Distinguish *take something off* or *out of* from *take it to . . . .*
4 *they*, SUBJECT; *them*, OBJECT.
put requires SP 6a, ie OBJ + ADV-P.
into unnecessary after *put*.
5 vt, IMPERATIVE.
6 *burn*, used as vi.
burn used as vt.

7 You are my teacher. I am learning.
  You are teaching me.

7 *I*, SUBJECT.
  me, OBJECT. Similarly, *he, him ; she, her ;
  we, us ; they, them. You* and *it* unchanged.

In teaching *put, take* and other verbs, in the PROGRESSIVE aspect, make sure that the learner sees the action in progress and having duration. Do not associate *she's putting*, for example, with one single momentary act.

Lexicon
1 As either vi with an OBJECT understood, or vt with OBJECT stated: *answer, ask, build, catch, climb, cook, count, cut, draw, drink, drive, eat, learn, play, pull, push, read, rub, sing, smoke* (eg a cigarette), *speak* (*a language*), *talk, throw, watch*
2 As vt with OBJECT which must be stated: *bring, do, enjoy, fetch* (= go and get), *get, find, have, hit, make, raise* (contrast *rise*, I.18, Lex 3), *say, send, take, tell, touch, wear* (a garment)
3 As vt in SP 6a: *lay* (contrast *lie*, I.19, Lex 2), *put, place*
4 *arm, ankle, chin, ear, eye, face, knee, leg, neck, shoulder*, etc
5 As either vi with no OBJECT understood, or vt with OBJECT stated: *bathe, break, boil, burn, burst, melt, mix, move, ring, roll, shake, stop, turn, wash*

I.22 SP 5, SP 6 and SP 6b, with stative verbs, and action verbs when not marked for progressive aspect, in the simple present tense

Models

I want some stamps, please.
Mr Smith is a builder; he builds houses.

Notes

1 I [want]¹ [some stamps], please.

1 The VERBS in the Lexicon below are STATIVE, rather than ACTION VERBS like those in I.21. PROGRESSIVE aspect is normally avoided with STATIVE VERBS: see Appendix E. NB It is not suggested that this distinction should be taught to beginners theoretically.

2 I [want]² to [post] [some letters].

2 SP 6b, with INFINITIVE as OBJECT. NB The person who *wants* is the one who *posts*.

3 We want to go home.

3 Use *want* with *I, you, we* and *they*.

4 You're ill. You [need]¹ [a doctor].
   You [need]² to see a doctor.

4 Use *need* with *I, you, we* and *they*.

5 I [like]¹ chocolate.

5 *I* (*you, we, they*) *like*.

6 *A* Where is Vancouver?
   B I [forget]³.
   A Who knows? Who remembers?
   C (*Tom*) I know. I know.
   A Tom remembers.
       He wants to tell us.
       He wishes to tell us.

6 With the third PERSON SING (*he, she, someone* or any SINGULAR NOUN) add /z/, /s/ or /iz/ in pronunciation, as in I.1.1, I.1.4 and I.3.5, and add the same ending in spelling as for the regular PLURAL of NOUNS, I.13.1, 2 and 5. *Who remembers?* question asking for PERSONAL SUBJECT.

7 *A* That's [your friend Tom].
   B I [believe]⁴ you are right.

7 VERBS in Lexicon 4 below can be followed by a NOUN CLAUSE containing its own SUBJECT (*you*) and PREDICATE (*are right*). In 7*B*, *that* is usually absent in short utterances.

8 *A* 'Stay here' means 'Don't go away'.
   B I [understand]⁵.

9 *A* Is that Tom over there?	9
B I [think]⁶ so.	= I think (that) it is Tom.

10 Mr Smith is a builder: he builds houses.   10 In I.18, I.19 and I.21 ACTION VERBS are
People speak French in France.   used in PROGRESSIVE aspect to convey the
Birds fly. Fish swim.   idea of action in progress, having dura-
Tim gets up at (about) [seven o'clock]⁷.   tion. In 1.22.10 ACTION VERBS are used
He washes his hands before [a meal]⁸.   in the simple PRESENT TENSE in making
He goes to bed after supper.   general statements and to say what
He says 'Good night' to his parents.   generally occurs. *Fly, flies* as in I.13.6;
He's Swiss: he comes from Switzerland.   *wash, washes* as in I.13.5; *go, goes* as in
We cut bread with a knife.   I.14.9; *says* (pronounced /sez/).
                                             Note instrumental *with*.

Lexicon
1 With SP 6, *believe, forget, know, like, love, mean, need, remember, understand, want*
2 SP 6b, infinitive as object, *hope, need, want, wish* (polite)
3 With SP 5, *forget, know, remember*, in answer to a question
4 With following NOUN CLAUSE, *believe, hope, mean, think, say ;* also *know*
5 With SP 5, in reply to a statement, *agree, know, understand*
6 On pattern *I think so : believe, hope, think, say*
7 *at* + time, as in I.20, Lexicon 5
8 *meal*, COUNT NOUN; *breakfast, lunch, dinner, supper*, normally without *a*
9 *before, after* a time or event

I.23 SP 5 and SP 6, with modals *can* and *must*; Q-*Yes/No*, neg; Q-*Who*, Q-*What*; *I think* + various sentence patterns

Models	Notes
I can swim.	
George can drive a car.	
You must be careful.	

1 *A* Be careful. [The water's very deep.]	1 IMPERATIVE of *be*, same as the STEM, as I.18.1
B It's all right. I can [swim].	*can* (ability) + STEM (or INFINITIVE) of [*swim*]; *can* = /kən/, unstressed, in fluent speech.
2 George can [swim] too. He can drive a car.	2 The MODAL has no inflexion such as -*ing* (I.18.1) or -*s* (I.22.6). Thus: *I, you, he, we*, etc, *can*.
3 I can [see]¹ a [cloud]. I see a cloud.	3 *can* optionally used before VERBS of perception. If *can* is omitted, such VERBS function as STATIVE VERBS (I.22.1).
4 *A* Can you [swim]? Can you [drive a car]? Can you?	4 Q-*Yes/No* applied to I.23.1; cp I.1.2.
B Yes, I can.	
C I can too.	Short answer: [*swim*] etc, understood; *can* = /kæn/ in the short answers.
or No, I cannot (swim). I cannot (drive).	*cannot* normally written as one word.
No, I can't (swim). I can't (drive).	Cp *isn't, aren't*, etc.
George can't (swim) either.	Contrast *I can too*, 4C above.
5 Can [the boy on your left] swim?	5 The whole NP SUBJECT, with POSTMODI-FIERS, comes between *can* and [*swim*].

6 *A* Who can swim?
  B I can. George (can).
7   What can you see?

8   We must [stop] now.
    It's very late.

9   I [think]² that's the postman.
    I [think]² you're tired.
    I [think]² he's in the garage.
    I [think]² there's someone at the door.
    I [think]² Tom's lying down.
    I [think]² I know the answer.
    I [think]² you can answer that question.

6 Asking for NP SUBJECT.
  can usually included after a PRONOUN.
7 For Q-*Yes/No* and Q-*Wh* applied to
  you see, see I.24.
8 MODAL *must*: same note as for I.23.2.
  Defer INTERROG and NEG with *must* till
  III.21.
9 See I.22.7B. Examples are now given of
  SP 1, 2, 3, etc, used as NOUN CLAUSE,
  OBJECT. In every case, *that* (pronounced
  /ðət/ in fluent speech) is an optional
  CONJUNCTION as in I.22.7B. In *I think
  (that) that's the postman*, the second
  that, pronounced /ðæt/ is an obligatory
  element—a DEMONSTRATIVE PRONOUN, as
  in I.2.2.

Lexicon
1 *see, hear ; feel, smell, taste*
2 as for Lexicon I.22.4
3 *deep*, opp *shallow ; late*, opp *early*

I.24 Q-*Yes/No*, neg, Q-*What*, applied to simple present tense

Models

Do you like Chinese food?
Yes, I do. No, I don't like it.
Tom doesn't like it either.
Who wants to go? I do.

Notes

1 *A* I like Chinese food.
  B Are you hungry?

    Have you (got) any money?
    Can you help me?
  A Do you [like] [Chinese food]?
    Do you [eat] [rice] at home?
    Do you speak [English]?
  B Yes, I do.
  C Do you? Do you really?
2   Do you know that man?
3 *A* Does [Tom] like [chicken]?
  B Yes, he does.
4   Does [the man on your right] smoke?
5   What newspaper does [your father]
    read?
  A What does Mr Smith do?
  B He builds houses.
6   I cannot [drive]. I can't drive.
    I do not [smoke]. I don't smoke.
    Tom does not smoke.
    He doesn't smoke.

1 The normal pattern for Yes/No questions
  is

  be
  have } + NP SUBJECT + rest of VP.
  MODAL

  Yes/No questions with *like* etc are
  formed on exactly the same pattern, viz
  do + NP SUBJECT + rest of VP,
  with *do* as AUXILIARY and the rest of
  VERB in the INFINITIVE.
2 *Do* is used with *I, you, we* and *they*.
3 *Does* /dʌz/ with third PERSON SINGULAR.
  For spelling of *does*, cp *goes*, I.22.10.
4 Cp I.23.5.
5 Q-*What* asking for OBJECT of *read*.

  As in I.22.10.

6 NEG of simple present following the
  same pattern as I.15.4 and I.23.4, with
  don't and *doesn't* as contracted forms.

7 *A* Do you know Mr Pilkington?
    B No, I don't.
    A Does Tom know him?
    B No, he doesn't.

8 *A* René comes from France.
    B Does he come from Paris?
    A No, he doesn't (come from Paris).

9 *A* Look, is that a [snake]?
    B No, I don't [think][1] so.

10   Have you (got) a car? I haven't got one.
    or Do you have a car? I don't have one.

11 *A* Who [want]s to [go home]?
    B I do. I [want] to.
    or I don't. I don't [want] to.

12   What does this mean?

7
Short NEGATIVE answer.

8 ie France is his home.
Contrast the AFFIRMATIVE (*comes*) with
INTERROG and NEG.

9 Cp I.22.9. With *hope*, say *I hope not*
as a short answer.

10 Cp I.15.4. The INTERROG and NEG with
do is also used with *have*, especially in
American English.

11 Cp *Who remembers?* I.22.6.
I do, I want to.

12 *mean*, STATIVE VERB.

Lexicon
1 *believe, think, say*

I.25 SP 7, with a prepositional verb, and SP 8, when the object is followed by an adverb particle

Models
Look at this picture.
It belongs to me.
Take it away.
Put your coat on.

Notes

1 *A* Look.
    B I'm looking.
    A Look at this [photograph].
    B I'm [looking at][1] [it].
    A Can you see it? Do you see it?
    B Yes, I can. I (can) see it.

2 *A* Listen.
    B I'm listening.
    A Listen to that bird.
    B I'm listening to it.
    A Can you hear it? Do you hear it?
    B Yes, I can. Yes, I do.

3 *A* Where is your book?
    B I don't know. I can't find it.
    A You must look for it.

4 *A* Wait. Please wait for me.

5 *A* This is [my][2] book. It's [mine][2].
    It belongs to [me].
    B *Does* it belong to you?
    A Yes, it's my [own]. I own it.

6   Why are these things on [my desk]?
    Take these things [off]. Take them [off][3].

1 *Look*, vi, in SP 5.
ACTION VERB, PROGRESSIVE aspect, SP 5.
Look at, VERB + PREP forming one
lexical unit equivalent to vt: SP 7.
Distinguish between *look*, ACTION VERB,
and *see*, STATIVE.

2 *Listen*, vi, ACTION VERB;

   Listen to, same note as for *Look at*.

3

   look for, action, same note as for *look at*.

4 *wait for*, action, also like *look at*.

5

   belong to, STATIVE VERB, otherwise like
look at: me, him, etc after a PREP.
my own = *mine*. *own*, STATIVE VERB.

6

   take (vt) + NP OBJECT + ADV PARTICLE:
example of SP 8.

7   What is all this [rubbish]?
     I don't want it. Take it [away]³.

7
     Take it away (from here) ; away ADV
     PARTICLE.

8 *A* It's raining. Put your [coat] on.
   B I am putting it on.

8 = put it on your body. vt+ OBJECT is
     often followed by ADV PARTICLE, as vi
     is (see I.20).

9   It's very hot. You're very hot.
     Take your [coat] off. Take it off.

9
     = take it off your body.

10   Your coat is on the ground.
     Pick it up. That's not its place.

10
     Distinguish *it's* (= *it is*) from *its*,
     POSSESSIVE of *it*.

Lexicon
1 *look at, listen to ; look for ; wait for, belong to ; own*
2 *my, mine ; your, yours ; his, his ; her, hers ; it, its ; our, ours ; their, theirs.* No apostrophe in *yours, hers, ours, theirs*
3 *away ; back ; off* a surface; *out of* a space
4 *put* a garment *on, take it off ; pick something up ; take it away*

I.26 Q-*What* and Q-*Who* applied to SP 7 and SP 8

Models
What are you looking at?
Who does this belong to?
Which shoes are you putting on?
I put warm clothes on in winter.

Notes

1 *A* [What]¹ are you looking at?

   B That [photograph].
      I'm looking at that photograph.

1 This follows from I.25.1. Stress on
  look-; PREPOSITION unstressed.
  NP OBJECT of PREPOSITION.

2 *A* [What]¹ are you listening to?
   B That [bird]. I'm listening to that bird.

2 See I.25.2.

3 *A* [What]¹ are you looking for?
   B [My book]. I can't find [it].

3 See I.25.3.

4 *A* [What]¹ are you waiting for?
   B [A bus]. I can see [one].

4 See I.25.4.

5 *A* Who does this car belong to?
   B To Mr Turner. It's Mr Turner's.
      To my uncle. It's [my uncle]'s.
      To my brother. It's my [brother]'s.
      To my [brothers]. It's my [brothers'].

5 See I.25.5. Regard *whom* as formal.

  brother's, POSSESSIVE SINGULAR.
  brothers', POSSESSIVE PLURAL.
  brothers, brother's, brothers' all pronounced
  the same.

   To those men. It's those men's.

  Similarly, *women's, children's.*

6 *A* What are you taking away?
   B This [rubbish]. I'm taking it away.

6 See I.25.7; stress the PARTICLE.

7 *A* Which [shoes] are you putting on?
   B My [black] ones.

7 See I.6.4 and I.25.8.

8 *A* What clothes do you wear in (the)   8 *in (the) winter*, ADV-T.
   [winter]² ?
  B [Warm ones]. I wear warm clothes in
   (the) winter.
  A What clothes do you [put on] in (the)   *put on*, VERB + ADV PARTICLE, replacing
   winter?   *wear. On* stressed, *in* unstressed.
  B I put warm clothes on in (the) winter.

Lexicon
1 *What*, if the OBJECT required is non-personal; *who*, if it is personal
2 *spring, summer, autumn, winter ;* or *January, February, March* etc, but without the option of using
  the

I.27 SP 9 and SP 9a; Q-*Yes/No*; Q-*What*, Q-*Who*

Models   **Notes**
Give all these books to James.
Get a seat for Mary.

1 *A* Take all [these] [books].   1 *all* + *these, those, the, my* + COUNT PLUR.
   [Give]¹ all [these] [books] to James.   SP 9.
   Give them all to James.   *them all*, OBJECT = all these books.
   What are you doing with those books?   Asking for VP.
  B [Giv]ing them to James.   Short answer, progressive aspect indicat-
                                                      ing action in progress.
   I'm giving them to James.   *them*, as OBJECT of vt.
  A Who are you giving them to?
  B James. To James.
  A Are you giving them all to him?   *him*, as OBJECT of PREP.
2 *A* Take all [this] [money].   2 *all* + *this, that, the, my* etc + MASS.
   Take it all.   *it all*, OBJECT = all this money.
  B Are you [giv]ing it all to *us*?   *us*, OBJECT of PREP; *me, you, him, her,*
  A Yes, I'm [giv]ing it all to [*you*].   *us, them*, as in I.21.7.
   Who am I giving it to?
  B You're giving it to George and me.   *George and I*, SUBJECT; *George and me*,
                                                      OBJECT.
3 *A* Say something to Peter.   3 *Say, tell* and *explain* all fit into SP 9.
  B Good [morning]², Peter.
   Tell that story to your father.
   Please explain this word to me.
4 *A* Where's George?   4
  B He's in the [next room].   = the room next to this room.
  A What is he doing there?
  B He's [get]³ting a [seat].   *get*, ie obtain, with OBJECT: see I.21,
  A What is he getting?   Lex 2.
  B A seat.   NP OBJECT of vt.
  A Who is he getting it for?   Who will receive it? Who will benefit?
  B Mary. For Mary.
  A What is he in the [next room] for?   = for what purpose; why?
  B He's getting a seat for Mary.
   Mary, here is a seat for you.

5   Can you make a suit for me, please?

Lexicon
1 *bring, explain, give, lend, offer, pass, pay, read, say, sell, send, show, take, teach, tell, throw, write*
2 *afternoon, evening, night* (regard *good day* as very formal)
3 *bring, build, call, change, fetch, find, get, keep, leave, make, order, save*

I.28 SP 10 and SP 10a

Models   **Notes**
Give James these books.
Get Mary a seat.

1 *B* [I'm] [giv]¹ing [these books] to James.   1 See I.27.1.
   A What are you giving (to) James?
   B All these books.   NP, DIRECT OBJECT of vt.
       [I'm] [giv]ing [James] [all these books].   INDIRECT OBJECT, *James*, precedes DIRECT
                                                     OBJECT; example of SP 10.
       I'm giving him all these books.
2 *A* Give me that knife. Thank you.   2 *me*, INDIRECT OBJ; *that knife*, DIRECT OBJ.
   B Please keep it. It's dangerous.   *keep* + NP OBJECT: cp I.20.4.
3   [Tell] [me] [that story] again.   3 *again*, ADV-T, = a second, or one more,
       [Tell]² [me] (again).   time. *Tell* in a short answer can be fol-
                                                     lowed by INDIRECT OBJ alone.
                                                     say and *explain* do *not* fit into SP 10.
4 *A* [Get]³ a [seat] for [Mary].   4 SP 9a.
   B A [sheet]?   Asking for confirmation of DIRECT OBJECT.
   A No, a [seat]. [Get] [Mary] a [seat].   SP 10a.
5 *A* The tailor is making a suit for me.   5
   B What is he making (for) you?
   A A suit. He's making me a suit.   *me*, INDIRECT OBJ; *a suit*, DIRECT OBJ.
6   Send [Tom] [a book about Africa].   6 *about*, PREP. Prefer SP 10 to SP 9 in this
                                                     example, as DIRECT OBJECT is longer.
       Take [this] to [the manager of the bank].   Prefer SP 9, as *the manager of the bank* is
                                                     longer than *this*.
       Give that man this note.   Prefer SP 10 when emphasis is on DIRECT
                                                     OBJ, and when the two OBJECTS are of
                                                     about equal length.
7   Take this note to the officer.   7 SP 9, *officer* is personal.
       Take this note to the office.   SP 9, *office* is inanimate.
       Take the officer this note.   SP 10, *officer*, personal.
                                                     Exclude SP 10 and SP 10a when recipient
                                                     is non-personal, except as in II.2.8.
8   Can you tell me the time?   8 See I.20.8.
       Can you tell me the way to York?

Lexicon
1 *bring, give, hand, lend, offer, pass, pay, read, sell, send, show, take, teach, tell, throw, wish*, eg *I wish
   you a happy New Year, write*. See also Appendix A3
   SP 10 cannot be used for *throw at*
2 In short answers, the following can have INDIRECT OBJECT only: *pay, show, teach, tell*
3 *bring, build, fetch, call, change, choose, find, get, keep, leave, make, order, save*. See also Appendix A4

I.29 Position of adverbs of frequency and time

Models

Tom is always happy.
He is still laughing.
He always enjoys a joke.

Notes

1   Tom is [always]¹ [happy].
Is he [ever]² angry?
He's [never]¹ very angry.
He isn't [often]³ angry.

1 ADV-F, *always*, in normal position.
Normal position in questions.

Normal position in NEGATIVE.

2   George is [still]¹ eating.
Is Jack [still]² eating?
No, he isn't [still]³ eating.

2 ADV of relative time, with PROGRESSIVE.

ie He has stopped eating.
Defer *he still isn't* . . . till VI.15.

3 *A* We [sometimes]¹ go to the [sea]⁴.
B Do you [ever] go into the [country]?
A We don't [often] go into (the) town.
We never go there.

3 Normal position of ADV-F with SIMPLE
PRESENT, AFFIRM and INTERROG.
the sea (in contrast with *the land*);
the country, contrast *(the) town*.

4 *A* We [usually]¹ go for a [walk]⁵ on
[Sunday(s)]⁶
B What do you [usually]¹ do on Monday(s)?
A On Monday(s), we [always]¹ go to work.

4 *go for a walk*, for pleasure.
on Sunday or *on Sundays*.
Q-*Wh* with ADV-F.
ADV-T at beginning for contrast with *A*'s
previous statement.

5   Tom [always]¹ gets up at [six o'clock].
[The New Year] begins on [January]
[1st]⁷.

5 *at* an hour, ADV-T.
on a day. Say *January the first* or *the first
of January*. Write *January 1st* or *1st
January*.

6   We usually take our holidays in May.
We generally go away on May 1st.

[Sometimes]⁸ we go away in June.

6 *in* a month.
go away used literally in I.20.5. Now as
an idiom meaning *go for a holiday*.
ADV-E at beginning for contrast.

7   He isn't hungry any more.
We go to school five times a week.

7 *any more* or *any longer*; ie he has stopped
being hungry. ADV-F and ADV of relative
time in the form of phrases, eg *any more*,
three times a week, normally have end
position.

Lexicon

1 *always, frequently, generally, often, never, sometimes, still, usually* : exclude *ever*
2 Lexicon 1, including *ever*
3 *always, ever, generally, often, still, usually* : exclude *never, sometimes*
4 *city, country* (= not town), *hills, mountains*
5 *bathe, drive, run, swim, walk*
6 *Monday, Tuesday*, etc
7 *first, second, third*, etc
8 *generally, often, sometimes, usually*
9 *holiday, go away*
10 *any more, any longer*

I.30 Adverbs of manner, their form and position; relative position of adv of place and adv of time

Models	Notes

Models

Mr Turner drives his car carefully.
He generally goes to town on Thursday.

Notes

1 Many people [drive] [cars];
they are all [drivers]¹.

1 *Many* before COUNT NOUNS PLURAL.
all coming after *be*.
-(e)r suffix indicating doer.

Some people are bad drivers:
they [drive] [badly]².

Some /sʌm/ in contrast with *many*.
-ly suffix forming ADV-M from ADJ.
Note position of ADV-M in SP 5.

Other people are good drivers:
they drive [well]².

Other in contrast with *some*.
well, as ADV-M corresponding to *good*.
See I.8.1.

They drive their cars well.

ADV-M in SP 6. Do not allow ADV-M to
come between vt and OBJECT.

2 *A* Mr Turner drives (his car) carefully.
 B How does he drive?
 A He drives very carefully.
 B How carefully does he drive?
 A Very. Very carefully.
 B How often does he drive?
 A Often. Very often.

2 ADJ *careful*; ADV *carefully*.
Q-*How* asking for ADV-M.
very modifying ADV-M.
Q-*How* asking for MODIFIER of ADV-M.
Short answers.
Q-*How often*, asking for ADV-F.
very can modify *often* and *frequently*,
but not other ADVS in I.29 Lex 1.

3 Tom is always happy.
He does everything happily.

3 ADJ *happy*; ADV *happily*.
everything, cp *something*, I.12.4.

4 Mr Turner looks at the road carefully.

4 ADV-M with SP 7.

5 It's cold. Put on your coat quickly.

5 ADV-M with SP 8.

6 Mr Turner goes to town.
He goes to town on Thursday.
He usually goes to town on Thursday.
On Thursday, he goes to town.
 A When does he usually go to town?
 B On Thursday.
 A Where does he usually go on Thursday?
 B To town.

6 vi+ ADVERBIAL, as in I.20.
ADV-P normally precedes ADV-T.
Previous sentence, with ADV-F added.
ADV-T at the beginning, as in I.29.4.
Q-*When*, asking for ADV-T.

Q-*Where*, asking for ADV-P.

Lexicon

1 *builder, climber, driver, farmer, learner, player, reader, runner* (cp I.18, Lex 1), *singer, smoker, speaker, swimmer* (cp *runner*), *teacher, worker, writer*
2 *badly, carefully, happily, well*

Summary of Stage I

This summary is provided especially for guidance in the composition of reading material for learners who have already been taught the structures and the kind of lexicon presented in Stage I. For further details see the Index, pages 233–245.

SENTENCE PATTERNS
as listed on page 3. Simple sentences only.

NOUN PHRASE
1 PROPER NOUNS
   names of persons and familiar places
2 COMMON NOUNS
   COUNT NOUNS, personal and non-personal, SINGULAR and PLURAL
   frequently-used IRREGULAR PLURALS
   CONCRETE MASS NOUNS
   COMPOUND NOUNS OF THE TYPE *tea-cup*
3 PRONOUNS
   PERSONAL, SUBJECT and OBJECT
   INDEFINITE, eg *someone, something*
   DEMONSTRATIVES used as PRONOUNS
   mine, yours, etc
   OTHER PRO-FORMS *-one(s)*, as in *the red one(s)*
4 PREMODIFIERS
   DETERMINERS etc
   DEMONSTRATIVES, SINGULAR and PLURAL
   INDEFINITE ARTICLE, as in *This is a camera, he is a doctor,*
   a mouse is a small grey animal
   DEFINITE ARTICLE, as in *The red book is mine, he's on the roof,*
   where's the elephant? (the one mentioned)
   ZERO ARTICLE, as in *rice ; cars are expensive ; at home*
   POSSESSIVES, eg *my, your*, etc, *Tom's; my brother's, my brothers'*
   some, any ; other
5 ATTRIBUTIVE ADJECTIVES, as in *a black pen ; a tall, strong boy ; a blue and white flag*
6 POSTMODIFIERS, as in *the man over there ; the man at the door ; a cup of tea*

VERB PHRASE
1 VERBS
   PRESENT TENSE of full VERBS, including *be* and *have*
   PRESENT PROGRESSIVE of ACTION VERBS
   can and *must*, used only as in I.23
   PREPOSITIONAL VERBS, eg *look at, listen to*
   VERB+ OBJECT+ ADV PARTICLE, eg *put your coat on*
   Q-*Yes/No*, Q-*What*, Q-*Who*, Q-*Where*, Q-*Why*, Q-*How ;* and NEGATIVE
   IMPERATIVE (AFFIRMATIVE and NEGATIVE)
2 ADJECTIVES
   used PREDICATIVELY
   PREPOSITIONAL PHRASES
   with PREPOSITIONS expressing clearly definable relationships in space and time
3 ADVERB PARTICLES
   as in *Come in. He's out*
4 SIMPLE ADVERBS
   of place (eg *here, in the garden*), time (*today*), relative time (*still*), frequency (*often*),
   manner (*badly*)
   OTHER ADVERBIALS
   too and *either*, as in *X drives too. X doesn't drive either*

OTHER ELEMENTS
   INTENSIFIERS
   very, modifying ADJECTIVES and ADVERBS
   CONJUNCTIONS
   joining parts of sentences: *and, but, or*; also *because*, used as in I.20.3

Stage II

Contents

18 GRADABLE ADJECTIVES. ADJECTIVES and ADVERBS modified by ADVERBS of degree: *It's quite hot ; (not) (quite) hot enough ; quite well ; quite often. This chair is quite heavy ; I can only just lift it. This table is too heavy ; I can't lift it at all ; it's too heavy to lift ; it's too heavy for her to lift ; she's too weak to lift it ; she's not strong enough to lift it. You're quite right.*

19 *How*+ ADJECTIVE in questions: *How old is John? ; he's twelve (years old) ; that tree is twelve years old ; how heavy is this parcel? ; how much does it weigh? ; what weight is it? ; how tall, high, long, wide,* etc. *How far is it? Not very far ; quite a long way.*

20 Comparison of ADJECTIVES with *-er* and *-est: Jim is as tall as Ron (is) ; he is not as tall, not so tall, as Tom. This is bigger, nicer, tidier, stronger, narrower, than that. Tom is (the) taller ; he's much taller ; he's the tallest in the class.*

21 IRREGULAR comparisons: *good, better, best ; bad, worse, worst ; well, better ; ill, worse ; little, smaller, smallest ; elder, eldest ; (much) more, the most ; any more, some more,* etc; *too much, too many ; so much, so many ; such a lot.*

22 Comparison of longer ADJECTIVES: *This car is more, less, expensive than that (one) ; this one is not so comfortable ; that is the most expensive, life is pleasanter, more pleasant, in the country ; Jane is more careful than Elizabeth ; is my book the same as yours? ; no, it's different (from yours).*

23 Comparison of ADVERBS; and ADVERBS with the same form as ADJECTIVES: *John drives more carefully than Dick ; he drives better than Dick ; Dick doesn't drive as carefully as John ; Dick drives too fast, faster than John ; you're working too hard ; I can hardly keep awake ; oftener, sooner ; very much better.*

24 The AUXILIARY used as a PRO-FORM for a whole VP: *Tom's faster than I am ; he runs faster than I do ; you wear a hat but I don't ;* question tags: *you're tired, aren't you? Let's go, shall we?*

25 Repeat patterns: *Tom is ready : so am I. He's not waiting : /I'm not either//nor am I/ /neither am I/.* Emphasis: *Who's coming with me? I am. A. You're not ready. B. I am. You go. Don't you wait. Do go.*

26 *Such a*+ NP and *so*+ ADJECTIVE: *I can't afford such an expensive car ; I don't want a car as expensive as this ; why is it so expensive? ; you've been so kind. How kind you are! ; what a nice day! ; what bad luck! ; what interesting people.*

27 PREDETERMINERS: *Some of these cups are broken ; /both//all/ of them are white. /Every/ /Each/ house has a white door ; /Each (one)//every one/ has a bathroom.* Various positions for *all, both, each. They are all hungry ; they're all waiting ; they all want some food ; you've broken them all, all of them. Whole, half.*

28 INDEFINITE PRONOUNS: *Everyone, everybody, everything ; no one, nobody, nothing ; anyone, someone,* etc; *everyone's ; everyone else, everyone else's.* Also *everywhere, nowhere.*

29 Combining simple sentences with *and, so, but, or ; He speaks and writes English ; he speaks English but doesn't write it. Come and open the door ; no one heard me, so I went away. He went to the library, chose a book and sat down.*

30 Combining simple sentences with *both . . . and, either . . . or, neither . . . nor, not only . . . but also, not only . . . but . . . as well;* with *when* and *than;* and with the construction *the prettiest . . . I've ever seen.*

II.1 Verbs replacing *be* in SP 2 and SP 1

Models	Notes
Tom seems nice.	
He seems a nice boy.	
He looks like his father.	

1 *A* What is Tom like?   1 Asking for characteristics, as in I.9.

B I don't know him well.
He [seems]¹ (very) [nice].

2 A What does John /look/¹ like?

B He [looks]¹ [tall and strong].

3 A How does he [look]²? How is he?
B He [looks]² (very) [well]³.

4 A What's the matter (with you)?
B I feel ill. I don't feel well.

$$I\begin{Bmatrix}\text{have}\\\text{'ve got}\end{Bmatrix}[\text{a cold}]^4.$$

5 A What is the weather like?
B It [feels]⁵ [warm]⁶.

6   This plate looks dirty.

7 A What is [that cake] like?
B It [tastes]⁷ (very) good.
It has a (very) good [taste]⁸.

8 A How does this [shirt] [feel]⁷?
B It [feels] [soft].
A Yes, it's made of [silk].

It's a [silk shirt]⁹.

9 A Tom seems a [very nice] [boy].
His cousin seems [a fool].

They seem very [nice] [boys].

10 A Who does Tom look like?
B He looks like [his father].

11 A Who is that?
B I don't know. It looks like [Dick].

12 A What is that?
B It looks like [ink].
Those look like [ink] [stains].

Uncertainty, context for *seem*: *well* = ADV.
SP 2, with *seem* + ADJ. STATIVE VERB.

2 Asking for somebody's impression of John.
SP 2, with *look* + ADJ. STATIVE VERB.

3 Asking about state of health or mood.
well = ADJ, as in I.8.1. Allow *is looking* in this sense.

4 What is wrong?
Allow *am feeling* in this sense.

5 Asking about the state of the weather.
A different use of *feel*. *It* = the weather.
B feels warm in this weather.

6 Many ADJS are formed from MASS NOUNS
thus: *dirt, dirty; mud, muddy; stone, stony.*

7
STATIVE VERB.
See limited Lex 8 below.

8
STATIVE VERB in this sense.
The substance *silk* can be identified in it.
A shirt made of silk, stress both *silk* and *shirt*, in contrast with *postoffice* (I.12.5).

9 SP 1, with NP² personal = He seems nice.
SP 1, with NP² personal = He seems foolish.
NP¹ and NP² agreeing in number.
STATIVE.

10 Cp *What does he look like?* in 2 above.
looks like = isn't, but resembles. STATIVE.

11
Here, *It looks like* = I think it is (somebody). STATIVE.

12
I think it is (something).
NP¹ and NP² agreeing in number.
STATIVE.

Lexicon

1 *look, seem, sound*
2 *feel, look, seem*
3 *ill, happy, cheerful, sad, angry*
4 *flu* (or *influenza*), *a headache, toothache*
5 *feel, look, seem*
6 *(very) cold, (very) cool, (very) warm, (very) hot; fine*
7 *feel, look, seem, smell, sound, taste*
8 *smell, taste*
9 similarly *a cardboard box, a paper bag, a cotton dress, a fur coat, an iron box, a brick wall*

II.2 SP 6 with *have* as an action verb

Models	Notes
We're having breakfast.	
Do you have breakfast at eight?	
I'm having a wash.	
He's giving his car a wash.	

1 *A* What [are you] doing?

    B [We're] having [breakfast]¹.
       We're having a party.
       We're having { fun. / a good time.

2 *A* Are you having breakfast?
    B Yes, we are.
    A Do you [always] have breakfast at 8?
    B Yes, we do.

3 *A* What do you [usually] have?
    B [Tea] and [toast].

4 *A* Have { some / a cup of } [tea].

    B Thanks. Thank you. Yes please.
    or No thanks. No thank you.

5   I'm [drink]ing [some water].
    I'm having a [drink]² (of water).
    I'm having a look at the paper.

6 *A* Are you having a bath?
    B No. I'm having a wash.

7 *A* We're learning [English].
    We're having a(n) [English] lesson.
    B I'm teaching (you) (French).
    I'm giving (you) a (French) lesson.

8   Tom is [wash]ing. He's having a [wash].
    Mr Turner is [wash]ing his [car].
    He's giving his [car] a [wash]³.

Notes

1 Contrast this stimulus question with *What have you got?* in I.15.5.
   = taking breakfast, no ARTICLE.
   = taking part in it.
   = enjoying ourselves.

2

   Used in this way, *have* only takes the Q-*Yes/No* form with *do*, as in I.24, not I.1.

3 For ADVERB OF FREQUENCY, see I.29.

4 IMPERATIVE; speaker is offering.

   These are all forms of acceptance.
   These are refusals. *Thank you* more formal than *Thanks*.

5

   Cp *go for a walk* (I.29.4).

6 As in 5. See Lexicon 2 below for other examples like *drink*, *wash*, VERB and NOUN.

7 Here the VERB *learn* and the NOUN *lesson* are different. Cp *We're playing*, *We're having a game* (of cards etc).
   A is having a lesson, *B* is giving it.

8 One can give someone or something a look, a push, a pull, a wash, etc. Lex 3.

Lexicon

1 *a meal*: lunch, dinner, tea, supper, normally no ARTICLE before names of meals; *fun, a game, a good time, a haircut, a lesson, a party*

2 Words used either as VERBS or as NOUNS: *bath, bathe, dance, drink, fight, look, rest, ride, sleep, swim, wash*

3 Words used either as VERBS or as NOUNS: (*a*) Give someone *an answer, a bath, a call, some help, a kick, a kiss, a look, a push, a pull, a ring*, ie call by telephone, *a shake, a wash*; (*b*) give something *a kick, a look, a polish, a pull, a push, a rub, a shake, a wash*

II.3 Simple past tense of *be*; *in* or *during* a period of time; and other adverbials of past time

Models	Notes
I was at home yesterday.	
You were ill last week.	
He was a student in 1970.	

1   I am at school today.
     [Yesterday]¹ I was at home.
     I was at home then.
     You were at home [yesterday]¹, too.

2   *A* [Were you] ill last week?
     B Yes, [I] was, /[we] were.
          or No, I was not/ we were not.
             I wasn't/ we weren't.

3   *A* Who was a [student] [in 1970]?
     B [Mr Turner] was. [He] was.
          We were. [Tom and Mary] were.
          Was your father [ever] a student?

4   *A* Where were you [yesterday]?
     B [At home]².
          [At the cinema]³.
          At Number Four, North Street.
          [In bed]⁴. [In the country]⁵.
          In [North] Street.
          In [Washington]. In [Asia].

5   *A* When were you there?
     B [Yesterday¹].
          At [ten to eight].
          On [Sunday]. Last [Sunday].
          In the [morning].
          In [June]; in summer; in 1972.
          During the summer.
          During the holidays.

6   *A* How long ago were you there?
     B About [two hours]⁶ ago.

7   *A* When was the accident?
          When was it?
          What time was it?
     B It was at 7.50 a.m.

1   ADV-P, *at school* before ADV-T *today*;
     ADV-T, past, *yesterday*, at beginning for
     contrast. /I/ /he/ /she/ /it/ *was*, no contrac-
     tion; /you/ /we/ /they/ *were*, no contraction.

2   Q-*Yes/No*.
     Short answers, PRONOUN + *be*.
     Short answers, PRONOUN + *be* + *not*.
     NEGATIVE contractions.

3   Q-*Who* ; cp I.5.5
     Short answers, NP + *be*.

4   Q-*Where*.
     Short answer, ADV-P.
     Contrast (*at home*) with (*at the cinema*)³.
     At an address, written (*No.*) *4, North
     Street*. Contrast (*in bed*)⁴, (*in the country*)⁵.
     In a road /street/, no specific address.
     in a village, town, city, country or conti-
     nent.

5   Q-*When*, asking for past time ADV.
     Short answer, ADV-T.
     At an hour.
     On a day; *in* a part of the day.
     In the /afternoon//evening/ ; *at night*.
     In a month, a season, a year.
     During a period or event; while the
     period or event was in progress.

6   *How long* = what period of time,
     ago = measured back from now.

7

     = At what time did it happen?
     The time of the day can be expressed
     normally as *ten to eight*, etc, see I.20,
     Lex 5; or in referring to a timetable, as
     seven fifty, etc; *a.m.* = before noon,
     p.m. = after noon.

Lexicon
1 adverbs of past time: *on* [*Sunday*], *in the* [*morning*], *in* [*June*], *yesterday*, *yesterday morning/afternoon/
   evening*; *last night*, *last Tuesday*; *last week//month//spring//summer//autumn//winter//year/*; *the day
   before yesterday*; *the night//week before last*
2 *at* or *in church*, *at home*; *at* or *in school*, *at work*: see Appendix G
3 *at the /bank//cinema//library//post office//station//theatre//doctor's etc* : *in* can be used in all these
   examples if emphasis is on the idea 'inside the premises'
4 *in bed, in class, in hospital, in town*: see Appendix G
5 *in the country//garden*, etc; see I.10.1 and I.29.3
6 *a minute, two minutes*, etc; *an hour//a week//a month//a year/* ; *two days*, etc; *a /short//long/ time*

II.4 SP 3c in the simple past. Also indefinite quantifiers

Models	Notes

There was a book ⎫
There was some paper ⎬ on the table.
There were some books ⎭

1 *A* I can't find [my book].

1

   B There was a [book] on the [table].
     Was that the one?

There was + *a* or *an* + COUNT NOUN.
Was that the book you meant? PAST TENSE
was, conveying the idea of *a* (*little*) *time ago*.

2 There was some [milk] in the [fridge].

2 *There was* + *some* + MASS NOUN.

3 There /is//was/ a lot of [milk] + ADV-P.
    There /is//was/ *lots of* [milk] + ADV-P.
    There /is//was/ a little [milk] + ADV-P.
    There /is//was/ only a little [milk] + ADV-P.
    There /is//was/ very little [milk] + ADV-P.
    There /is//was/ no [milk] + ADV-P.

3 *a lot of* + MASS.
lots of + MASS, informal.
= a small positive quantity.
= no more than that small quantity.
= a small NEGATIVE quantity, almost none.
There is no milk = there isn't any at all.

4 *A* Was there a towel in the bathroom?
     Was there any soap in the bathroom?
     Was there some soap in the bathroom?
     Was there much water on the floor?

4 Q-*Yes/No*; *a* or *an* + unit.
any + mass = any at all.
some + mass = an amount of.
much + mass, in questions.

   B Yes, there was. No, there wasn't.
     There was a towel. There was one.
     There was some (soap)/a lot (of water).
     There wasn't a towel. There wasn't one.
     There was no towel, no soap.
     There wasn't any (soap).
     There wasn't much (water).

Short answers.
Exclude *any* and *much* from these
AFFIRMATIVE sentences. *One* = a towel.

Exclude *some* in this NEGATIVE sentence.
Allow *much* in this NEGATIVE answer.

5 *A* What was there on the floor?

5 Q-*What*.

   B A lot of water.

6 *A* I can't find my glasses.

6

   B There were some glasses on the table.
     Were those the ones?

There were + *some* + COUNT NOUN
ie were those the glasses you meant?

7 There /are//were/ a lot of books + ADV-P.
    There /are//were/ *lots of* books + ADV-P.
    There /are//were/ a few books + ADV-P.
    There /are//were/ only a few books +
    ADV-P.
    There /are//were/ very few books + ADV-P.
    There /are//were/ no books + ADV-P.

7 *A lot of* + COUNT NOUN PLUR.
lots of + COUNT NOUN PLUR, informal.
= a small positive number.
= no more than that small number.

= a small NEGATIVE number, almost none.
There are no books = there aren't any books.

8 *A* Were there any books + ADV-P?
     Were there some books + ADV-P?
     Were there many books + ADV-P?

8 Q-*Yes/No*; *any* + units = any at all;
some + units = a number of;
many + units, in questions.

   B Yes, there were (some).
     No, there weren't (any) /(many)/.

Exclude *any* and *many*.
Exclude *some*.

9 How much milk was there?
    How many books were there?

9 Q-*How much* or *How many*, asking for
quantity or number.

Lexicon
1 DETERMINERS indicating indefinite quantity of a mass: *some, a lot of, lots of, a little, very little ;* in questions and negations: *any, much*

2 DETERMINERS indicating indefinite number of units: *some, a lot of, lots of, a few, very few*; in questions and negations: *any, many*

II.5 Determiners used with mass nouns and count nouns, as noun modifiers and pro-forms

Models	Notes
How much soup is there in the saucepan?	
There's a lot.	
How many sweets are there in the jar?	
There are a lot.	

1 *A* How much [soup] is there in [that] [pot]?

   1 *How much* + MASS NOUN.

  B There's plenty (of soup).

     plenty of + NOUN; *plenty*, PRO-FORM.

    There's a lot (of soup).

     a lot of + NOUN; *a lot*, PRO-FORM.

    There's lots (of soup).

     lots of + NOUN; *lots*, PRO-FORM (informal).

    There's a $\begin{Bmatrix} good \\ great \end{Bmatrix}$ deal (of soup).

     a $\begin{Bmatrix} good \\ great \end{Bmatrix}$ *deal of* + NOUN; *a good deal*, PRO-FORM.

    There's enough (soup).

     enough + NOUN; *enough*, PRO-FORM.

    There's a little (soup).

     a little + NOUN; *a little*, PRO-FORM.

    There's not (very) much (soup).

     not much + NOUN, *not much*, PRO-FORM.

    There's not enough (soup).

     not enough + NOUN; *not enough*, PRO-FORM.

    There's very little (soup).

     very little + NOUN; *very little*, PRO-FORM.

    There's hardly any (soup).

     hardly any + NOUN; *hardly any*, PRO-FORM.

    There's no soup (at all).

     no + NOUN.

    There's none (at all).

     none, PRO-FORM.

2 *A* How many sweets are there in that jar?

   2 *How many* + COUNT NOUNS, PLURAL.

  B There are plenty (of sweets).
    There are a lot (of sweets).
    There are lots (of sweets).
    There are a good many (sweets).
    There are a great many (sweets).
    There are enough (sweets).
    There are several (sweets).
    There are a few (sweets).
    There are not many (sweets).
    There are very few (sweets).
    There are hardly any (sweets).
    There are no sweets (at all).
    There are none (at all).

As in 1 above, DETERMINERS used with or without a NOUN. Note the difference between DETERMINERS used with MASS NOUNS and those used with COUNT NOUNS.

3 *A* This /pot//jar/ is full of /soup//sweets/.
  B I'm putting more soup/sweets in.
  A Stop. Now it is too full.
    There is too much (soup in the pot).
    There are too many (sweets in the jar).

3 *full of.*
  put in, ADV PARTICLE, as in I.26.7.
  is too full = contains more than enough.
  too much = more than enough.
  too many = more than enough.

4 The pot is quite full.	4 *quite* here = 100%, intonation falls on *full*.
It's $\begin{cases} almost \\ nearly \end{cases}$ full.	*almost*, *nearly*, are here interchangeable.
It's half full, about half full.	
It's not nearly full.	exclude *almost* after *not*.
It's $\begin{cases} almost \\ nearly \end{cases}$ empty.	
It's quite empty.	*quite* here = 100%, intonation falls on *empty*.
5 There are $\begin{cases} very\ many \\ many\ many \end{cases}$ people in the world.	5 *very many ; many many*.

II.6 Simple past of *do*, *have* and *get*, including questions and negative

Models

I did this yesterday.
He had some money.
He had a haircut.
I got a letter this morning.

Notes

1 *A* Look at [my picture].
   [I] did this [yesterday].
 B Did [you] do this?

1
did, simple past of *do* for all persons.
Q-*Yes/No* ; *did* as SIMPLE PAST TENSE
AUXILIARY for all full VERBS except *be*:
cp I.24.

 A Yes, [I] did.
   or No, I didn't (do it).

Short answer: NP + AUXILIARY.
Short answer: NP + AUXILIARY + -*n't*.

2 *A* Who did this?
 B [I] did. [Mary] did.

2 Q-*Who*, asking for PERSONAL SUBJECT.
NP + AUXILIARY.

3 *A* What did [you] do last night?
 B [I] did [my] homework.

3 Q-*What*, asking for NON-PERSONAL OBJECT.
do work, *do homework*—see Appendix D.

4

4

a *A* Did [Tom] have a [haircut]?
 B Yes, he did. No, he didn't.
   He had a haircut.
   He didn't have a haircut.

a *Did* + *have*, preparing for PAST TENSE of
have as used in II.2.
had, SIMPLE PAST of *have*, all persons.
NEG.

b *A* Did [he] have [any money]?
 B Yes, he did. No, he didn't.
   He had some money.
   He didn't have any money.

b *Did* + *have*, preparing for PAST of *have*,
possession.

c *A* Had [he] [any money]?
 B Yes, he had. No, he hadn't.
   He had some money.
   He hadn't any money.

c British alternative to construction in 4b.
Cp I.15.

5 *A* What did [Tom] have?
 B A [haircut]. Some [money].

5 Q-*What*, applicable whether *have* means
possess or otherwise.

6 *A* You haven't (got) a [book].
   Get one.
 B I'm getting one.
 A (*later*). What did you get?
 B I got a [book].

6
Get = obtain; *one* = a book.

Q-*What*, *did* + *get* preparing for *got*.
SIMPLE PAST, all persons.

7 *A* I got a [letter] this morning.
   Did you get one this morning?
 B No, I didn't (get one).

7 I got it a little time ago.
  Q-*Yes/No*.

Lexicon
1 *did, had, got*
2 *haircut, homework*

II.7 Simple past of regular verbs and of *go* and *come*

Models	Notes

I stayed at home
I worked in my office
I posted your letter   } on Monday.
I went to town
I came from London

1 *A* I was not very well on Monday.
 B Did you [stay]¹ at home?
 A Yes, I did. I [stayed] at home.

 or No, I didn't. I didn't stay at home.
2 *A* What did you do this morning?
 B a I [played]¹ a game.
   b I [carried]² some parcels for my mother.

   c I [worked]³ in my office.

   d I [stopped]⁴ a car.

   e I [posted]⁵ [your letter].
     I [mended] [my bicycle].
3 *A* Who telephoned [the doctor]?
 B [I] did. [Mary] did.
 A Who(m) did she telephone?
 B [The doctor].
 A What did you [post]?
 B [Your letter].
 A When did you [post] it?
 B [On Monday].
4 *A* Where did you go on Monday?
 B I went to town.
 A When did you arrive at the station?
 B I arrived at the station at eleven
     twenty-five.

 A Where did you come from today?
 B I came from London (today).

1

Did + stay, preparing for PAST of *stay*.
stayed REGULAR PAST; add sound /d/ to
STEM ending in any VOICED sound except
/d/, no extra syllable; add *-ed* in spelling.

2

B gives various REGULAR forms in reply:
a *played*, note as for *stayed* above;
b *carried*: pronunciation as for *stayed*,
but spelling *-ied* when STEM ends in
consonant + *y*: cp *countries*, I.13.6.
c *worked*: add sound /t/ when STEM ends
in any UNVOICED sound except /t/: no
extra syllable.
d *stopped*: double the consonant in
spelling when STEM ends in single consonant preceded by single vowel.
e *posted, mended*: add extra syllable /id/,
when stem ends in /t/ or /d/.
3 Q-*Who*, asking for SUBJECT.
did-tag, PRO-FORM for tense of VERB.
Q-*Who(m)* asking for PERSONAL OBJECT.

Q-*What*, asking for NON-PERSONAL OBJECT.

Q-*When*, asking for ADV-T.

4 *did + go*, preparing for PAST of *go*.
went, IRREGULAR PAST.
did + arrive; *arrive at* (a place).
arrived: add *-d* in spelling when STEM
ends in e. *Eleven twenty-five* would be
normal in a timetable. See I.20 Lex 5.
did + come.
came, IRREGULAR PAST.

Lexicon
REGULAR VERBS
1 *arrive, borrow, clean, climb, fill, listen (to), open, play, pull, sign, smile, stay, telephone*
2 ending in /ai/: *cry, try ;* ending in /i/: *carry, hurry, study*
3 *ask, fetch, finish, laugh, look (at), help, kick, pick, push, wash, watch, work*
4 VOICED, *rub ;* VOICELESS, *drop, stop*
5 *count, mend, paint, post, taste*
IRREGULAR:
   came, went

II.8 Present perfect of regular verbs, and of *have* and *do*, contrasted with simple past

Models
They have arrived.
They've already arrived.
Have they arrived yet?

Notes

1 *A* Are John and Mary here yet?

  B Yes, they have arrived.
    They have arrived by now.

    They've arrived (by now).
2 *A* Have they arrived (yet)?
  B Yes, they have/No, they haven't (yet).
  A Have they arrived already?
  B Yes, they're already here.
    They've already arrived.
3 *A* Do you want to wash your hands?
  B No, thank you. I've (just) washed them.
  A When did you wash them?

  B I washed them two minutes ago.
4 *A* Is it still raining?
  B No, it has stopped.
    It's stopped.

5 *A* Have you posted my letter?
  B Yes, I've posted it.
  A What have you done?
  B I've posted your letter.
  A When did you post it?
  B [After breakfast].
6 *A* I've finished my breakfast.
a
  B What have you had?
  A I've had [a cup of coffee].

1 *yet*= up to the moment of speaking;
normal in questions and NEGATIVES.
Their arrival took place at some time,
unspecified, before now. *have*, as in I.15,
but now used as an AUXILIARY;
arrived : PAST PARTICIPLE in all REGULAR
VERBS is the same as SIMPLE PAST (II.7).
Contraction of *have*, as in I.15.1.

2 Q–*Yes/No.*
have not contracted when final.
already= as early as now.
Normal position for *already* in AFFIRM-
ATIVE statements, as for ADV-F, I.29.

3 See I.22 and I.24.
just= in very recent time before now.
Q–*When*+ SIMPLE PAST, asking for
specific time of PAST action.
SIMPLE PAST+ ADV-T, PAST: see II.3.6.

4 *still*= as late as now.
has for third PERS SING as in I.15.3.
AUXILIARY *has* can be contracted. Here
it's= *it has :* cp *it's* in I.1.4.

5

have contracted to /v/ in fluent speech;
done PAST PARTICIPLE of *do*.

ADV-T, PAST, with SIMPLE PAST TENSE.

6

PRESENT PERF of *have* as used in II.2.

b *A* Have you got any money?　　　As in I.15.4.
  B I didn't have any yesterday,　　As in II.6.4b.
    but I've got some now.　　　As in I.15.1.
c *A* What have you got there?　　　As in I.15.5.
  B I've got a new coat.　　　　As in I.15.1.
d *A* When did you get that?　⎫
  B I got it yesterday afternoon.⎭　SIMPLE PAST of *get* = obtain, as in II.6.6.

Lexicon
1 REGULAR PAST PARTICIPLES: same as PAST TENSE of REGULAR VERBS
2 (*I have*) *had*, (*I have*) *done*

II.9 Present perfect of *be* and *go*

Models　　　　　　　　　　　　**Notes**
You've been very kind.
Have you (ever) been to Paris?
There has been a fire.

1 *A* Mr Turner has been away.　　1 He has been away (I.29.6) at some
    He's been in Switzerland.　　　unspecified time before now.
  B When was he there?　　　　Q-*When*, asking for specified time, as in
                     II.3.5.
2 *A* Have you had a good time?　　2 See II.2.1.
  B Yes, thank you. You've been very kind.
3 *A* You're covered with mud.　　3 *covered with.*
  B Yes, I've been in the garden.　　That's why I'm covered with mud.
4 *A* Where's Tom?　　　　　　4
  B He's not here. He's gone.　　*He's gone* = he has gone.
  A Where's he gone (to)?　　　Q-*Where* + he has gone.
  B He's gone to the shops.
  A (*later*) Oh, there you are, Tom.　*there you are :* see I.11.1.
    Where have you been?　　　 = where did you go to and come back from?
  B I've been to the shops.　　　cp *been in the garden*, II.9.3.
5 *A* Where's Jack?　　　　　　5
  B He's been here, but he's gone out again.　 = He has come here and has gone away.
6 *A* Have you ever [been][1] to Paris?　6 *ever* = at any time before now.
  B I've been there [once][2].　　　*once* = at one unspecified time.
  C Not yet. I've never been there yet.　*not yet*, in short answers.
    I haven't ever been there.　　*never* = not ever.
  A How often have *you* been there?
  D I've been there [several times][2].
7 *A* How long have you been here?　7 Q-*How long.*
  B We've been here since /ten o'clock/　*since ten o'clock* = from that point of past
    /Tuesday//last month/.　　　time until now.
  A So you've been here (for) /(three) hours/　*for three hours* = from beginning to end
    /(two) days//(three) weeks//a long time/　of that period: *for* can be omitted in
    /(the last few) months/.　　　such an example.
  B We got here at ten o'clock, and have　*We got here* = we arrived (here).
    been here since then.

8   *A* What has happened?
   B There has been a fire.
   A How long ago did it happen?

   B Two hours ago.
   A How long did it last?
   B Only half an hour.

8

PRESENT PERF of *there is . . .*
Asking for length of period from a PAST
EVENT until now.

Asking for length of duration of the
event.

Lexicon
1 *been, gone*
2 *once, twice, three times, four times,* etc
3 *not yet, already, just*
4 *for* a period of time, *since* a point in time

II.10 Past tense and past participle of regular and irregular verbs

Models
I slept outdoors last summer.
I have often slept in a tent.
I drove a car yesterday.
I have often driven a car.

Notes

1   Travellers stay at hotels.

   A We stayed at an hotel last week.

   B What hotel did you stay at?

   C We stayed at the Grand (Hotel).
   D I've often stayed at the Grand.

2   Scissors cut paper.

   A I cut my finger this morning.
   B Did you cut it with a knife?
   C No, I didn't (cut it with a knife).
   D I've cut my finger. It hurts.

3   I usually sleep indoors[1].
   A I slept outdoors last summer.
      Did you sleep outdoors[1] last summer?
   B No, I didn't (sleep outdoors).
      Tom has often slept in a tent.

4   Many people drive cars.

   A I drove a car yesterday.
   B Whose car did you drive?
   C I didn't drive *yours*.
   D You've often driven mine.
      Have you driven Tom's?

5   Many people learn a foreign language.
   A Have you learnt your lesson?
   B Yes, I learnt it this morning.

1 *-ll*-in *traveller, travelling, travelled* in
British Eng, *-l*-in American.
stayed, SIMPLE PAST, with ADV-T, PAST
I've stayed, PRESENT PERF, no time specified.
stay, REGULAR; PAST, *stayed*; PAST PART.,
stayed.

ADV-F, eg *often*, used as in I.29.

2 *Scissors*, like *trousers* and *clothes*, used
only as PLURAL. Cp *cars*, I.13.7.
cut : PAST and PAST PARTICIPLE, also *cut*.
For similar VERBS see Appendix B.

3 *indoors* = inside the house.
outdoors = outside the house.
sleep, slept, slept. For other IRREGULAR
VERBS with PAST and PAST PARTICIPLE the
same, see Appendix B.

4 *drive, drove, driven*—the three
principal parts all different. For other
VERBS with three different principal
parts, see Appendix B.

5 *learn, learnt, learnt*, can also be REGULAR.
For similar VERBS, see Appendix B.

6   I haven't driven a car for two years.   6   Do not omit *for* after a NEGATIVE.
                                                    Cp II.9.7.

I stayed/slept/drove/learnt
Did you stay/sleep/drive/learn? I didn't stay, etc
I have stayed. Have you stayed? I haven't stayed

Lexicon
1   *indoors, outdoors;* cp *upstairs, downstairs* (I.19.8)

II.11   Past tense and present perfect with SP 5a, SP 6a, SP 6b, SP 7 and SP 8

Models   **Notes**
We looked at the picture.
They came in quietly.
I put the books back.
Which shelf have you put it on?
What did you talk about?

1 *A* Mr Turner isn't [in]¹. He's [gone out]².   1 = *He has gone out.* PRESENT PERF, SP 5a.
   B When did he [go out]?   Q-*When*, asking for ADV-T, PAST TENSE.
   A He went out [half an hour ago].   PAST, SP 5a.
   B Why did he go out?   Q-*Why*.
   A He wanted to [buy] [some stamps].   SP 6b PAST; *want to*, see I.22.2. NB
                                                        INFINITIVE (*to buy*) is unchanged.
   B He went out (very) [quietly].   ADV-MANNER at the end of SP 5a.
2 *A* I've put your book [on]³ [one of those   2 PRESENT PERF in SP 6a. Listen to the
        shelves].   difference between *I've put* and *I put.*
   B Which shelf have you put it [on]³?   Q-*Which* applied to SP 6a.
   A I put it on the [top]⁴ [shelf].   *A* switches from PRES PERF to PAST.
3   We [looked at]⁵ [the picture] [carefully]. 3 PAST TENSE, SP 7; ADV-MANNER after
                                                        OBJECT.
        We looked at it carefully.
4   What did you [talk about]⁵?   4 Q-*What* applied to SP 7.
5 *A* I can't find my book.   5
   B Have you looked for it properly?   PRES PERF in SP 7, with ADV-MANNER.
6 *A* I borrowed three books from this library   6
        last week.
   B Have you [put]⁶ [the books] [back]⁶ yet?   PRES PERF in SP 8.
   A I've put one back.   *one*, stressed = one of the three books.
        I put it back this morning.   PAST in SP 8.
   A (*later*): I've [put back]⁶ the other two.   Alternative position for ADV-PARTICLE in
                                                        SP 8 when NP OBJ is not PERSONAL
                                                        PRONOUN.
        I put back the others this morning.   *the others* = the other [books].
        I put them back this morning.   No alternative position for ADV PARTICLE.
   B Did you put them back properly?   SP 8 with ADV-MANNER, at the end.
   A Of course. I always put things back   *Of course:* the question was unnecessary;
        properly.   *put*, PRESENT; ADV-MANNER at end.
   B You didn't put them back on the [wrong]   Statement-form, with rising intonation at
        shelf?   end, to indicate question.
   A Of course not. I put them back on the   *Of course not* = of course I didn't (do that).
        [right]⁴ shelf.

Lexicon
1 *in, out, up, down*
2 *come |in||down||up| ; get up ; go |away||back|* etc, *sit down ; stand up ; wake up*
3 *on, in*
4 *top, bottom, middle, right, wrong, first, second,* etc
5 *ask for ; laugh at ; listen to ; look at ; look for ; talk about ; wait for*
6 *bring in ; give away ; give back ; put back ; put on ; take back ; take off ; turn on (a light) ; turn off*

II.12 Future reference. Adverbials of future time

Models

I'm going to post your letter.
It's going to rain.
I'll see you later.
Will there be a holiday on Monday?

Notes

1 *A* Where [are] [you] going (to)?
   B [I'm] going to [the post office].

1 *be* [*go*]*ing* used as in I.18.
   ie I am on my way there.

2 *A* Have you [posted my letter]?
   B I'm going to [post it] [later]¹.
        I'm going to post it [in five minutes]².

2

   My intention now is to post it later. *Later* could be replaced by any ADV-T, FUTURE.

3 *A* That letter's [urgent]³. Post it now.
   B Don't worry. [I'm] just going to [post it].

3

   just going to indicates intention to do something in the immediate future.

4 *A* [Are you] going to [post that letter]?
   B Yes, [I am]. [I'm] going to.
        or No, [I'm] not. [I'm] not going to.
        I'm not going to post it.

4 Q-*Yes/No.*
   Short AFFIRMATIVE answers.
   Short NEGATIVE answers.
   Full NEGATIVE answer.

5   What is going to happen?
      What are you going to do?
      Who is going to [help you]?

5 Q-*What.*

   Q-*Who.*

6 *A* Take an umbrella with you.
      It's going to rain.

6

   There are present signs of future rain.

7   There's going to be [a storm].
   B Is there going to be [a storm]?
        or There isn't going to be a storm.

7 *going to* in SP 3c.
   Q-*Yes/No* applied to previous model.
   NEG applied to the same model.

8a *A* There's someone at the door.
   B All right. I'll go.

8

   'll go, simple reference to future.

 b   Good-bye. I'll see you later.
      I'll see you then.
      I'll see you in [two months] (time).
      I'll see you next.

 b Without emphasis on present intention.

   time, optional addition if the meaning is [two months] from now. *Next* as ADV-T.

9   It'll be [Tuesday] [tomorrow].
      There'll be a /holiday/ on /Monday/.
      We'll be away for two weeks.

9 *'ll be*, simple reference to future.
   'll be in SP 3c.
   (*for*) [*two weeks*] : cp note II.9.7.

Lexicon
1 ADVERBS of future time, cp II.3 Lexicon 1: *this afternoon, this evening, tonight ; tomorrow, tomorrow |morning||afternoon||evening||night| ; the day after tomorrow ; on Friday (next) ; next |week||Monday|* etc, *next |month||January||spring||summer|* etc ; *on December 31st (next) ; in 1999 ; then, next*
2 *in |five||a few|* etc, *minutes ; in half an hour ; in |a few||several| months'||years' time*
3 *urgent, important*

II.13 *Will* and *shall* with future reference; choice between *will* and *be going to*

Models

The 12.15 train will leave from Platform Four.
We shall arrive at the North Station at 6.45.

Notes

1 *A* Will there be a holiday on Monday?
  B Yes, there will. There will be.
    There *will* be a holiday on Monday.
2 The 12.15 train for Liverpool will leave from Platform Four.
  It'll leave from this platform.

3 There will not be a holiday next Monday.
  There'll not be a holiday.
  There won't be a holiday.
  There won't be. There won't.
4 *A* When will the train arrive?
  B It'll arrive soon.
  A What will the passengers do?
  B They'll go to a hotel.
  A Who'll meet them?
  B /I/you/he/she/we/ will.
    /I/you/he/she/we/'ll meet them.
5 /I/We/ shall arrive by air.
  /I/We/ shall not be late.
  /I/We/ shan't be late.

6 *A* Will George be home for dinner?
  B George won't, but /I/we/ shall (be).
    John and I will be.
7 *A* Are you going to get up?
  B Yes, I think I /will//shall/.

1 See II.12.9: '*ll* replaced by *will* when initial or final, or when *will be* is final, or for emphasis or in formal style.
2 *will*+ INFINITIVE, referring to the future, in formal style.
  will frequently contracted to '*ll* in informal style.

3 *will not*, formal or emphatic.
  Contraction, '*ll*+ not.
  Contraction, NEGATIVE informal.
  Can occur initially and finally.
4 *will* frequently reduces to the sound /l/ after *Wh*-question-words, especially *Who*, after PERSONAL PRONOUNS and *there*.

  will permissible after all PRONOUNS.
  '*ll* permissible after all PRONOUNS.
5 *shall* reduces to /ʃəl/ in fluent speech except when final, optional replacement for *will* after *I* and *we* in plain FUTURE.
  shall not = *shan't* informal typical of British English.
6 *Will*, *won't* for 2ND or 3RD PERSON;
  will or *shall* after *I* and *we*;
  but only *will* after [*somebody*] *and I*.
7 As in II.12.4.
  /*will*//*shall*/ normal here: intentions not highlighted.

Notes on choice between *be going to* and '*ll*, *will*, *shall*:

i Throughout II.13 /*will*/*shall*/ is grammatically replaceable by *be going to*, except in 7B. However—
ii prefer *be going to* in informal style when emphasis is on present intentions, or indication of what the future will bring;
iii use '*ll*, *will* or *shall* when there is no such emphasis, though exclude '*ll* when initial, final or before final *be*;
iv use *will* in any case in formal written style, but—
v treat *shall* as optional replacement for *will* after *I* or *we*.

II.14 *Can*, *may* and *let* making and answering requests; also SP 6d

Models

Can I have some sugar?
May I go with you?
Let me go with you.

Notes

1 *A* Ask (me) for some tea.
  B I [want]¹ some tea, please.

1 *Ask (somebody) for :* cp *look for,* I.25.3.
  All the models in II.14 are variations on
  the theme *I want.*

2 *A* [Can]² [I]³ have [some sugar], please ?
     Please can [I] have [some sugar] ?
  B Yes, you can.
     No, you cannot. You can't.

2 Cp I.23. Here the speaker's wants are
  expressed in a question forming a request.
  = you have permission, are free to have it.
  Permission withheld.

3 *A* I [want]¹ to go with you.
     May [I]³ [go with you] ? May I ?
  B You may. You may not.

3

  can/may inter-replaceable in this sense,
  may = have permission. Avoid *mayn't.*

4 Which one $\left\{ \begin{array}{c} can \\ may \end{array} \right\}$ [I] [take] ?

  When $\left\{ \begin{array}{c} can \\ may \end{array} \right\}$ [I] [go home] ?

5 *A* [Let]⁴ [me]⁵ go with you. [Let]⁴ me.
  B All right. You can come with me.
     I'll let you come with me.

5 SP 6d : *let* + NP + INFINITIVE without *to.*

  Here *let* indicates permission : cp 7 below.

6 *A* Open the door. I want to come [in].
     [Let]⁴ me [in]⁶, please.

6

  Let + NP + ADV PARTICLE, SP 8.

7 I want to [go and swim].
  Let's [go and swim].
  Don't let's stay indoors.
  Let's not stay indoors.

7 = I want to go and want to swim.
  Let's (go) makes a suggestion. Distinguish
  let's from *let us go, let us in,* 5 and 6 above,
  where *let us* is not contracted.

8 *A* Can $\left. \begin{array}{c} he \\ she \\ they \end{array} \right\}$ $\left\{ \begin{array}{c} have \\ go \end{array} \right\}$ $\left\{ \begin{array}{c} some\ sugar ? \\ home ? \end{array} \right.$
     May

  B /He//she//they/ $\left\{ \begin{array}{l} can, can't. \\ may, may\ not. \end{array} \right.$

8 The speaker makes a request on behalf of
  a third person.

  Permission granted or withheld.

Lexicon
1 *want, need*
2 *can, may.* These two verbs are MODALS, which pattern like *can* in I.23.2–4
3 *I, we*
4 *help* and *make* also fit into the pattern *let me go* ; and *ask, help* fit into the pattern *let me in*
5 *me, us, him, her, them*
6 *in, out, up, down*

II.15 *Will, shall, can* and *may* in questions containing offers, invitations, requests, instructions; SP 6c

Models
Will you have a cup of tea ?
Will you open the door, please ?
Shall I open it for you ?
Won't you sit down ?
Shall we sit here ?

Notes

1 *A* Do you want [a cup of tea] ?
     Will you have a cup of tea ?
     Won't you sit down ?
  B Yes, please, I will.
     or No thank you, not now.

1 Cp II.14.1.
  Will you have : the speaker makes an
  offer ;
  B accepts the offer, repeating *A*'s *will* :
  I won't would be a firm refusal.

2 *A* Will you [open the door], please?

   B Certainly².

3 *A* Will you [open the door], (please).

   I [want]¹ you to open this door.
   B *quiet obedience,* or No, I won't.
4   When will you have your tea?
5 *A* Do you want me to open the door?
   Do you want me to?
   Shall I open the door (for you)?

   B Yes please. Please do.
   or That's all right. I can manage.
6 *A* Shall we sit here?

   B Yes, let's sit here.
7 *A* Can you open the door?

   B Yes, certainly./I'm sorry, I can't.

8 *A* $\begin{Bmatrix} \text{Can} \\ \text{May} \end{Bmatrix}$ I open the door for you?

9 *A* Who will have some chocolate?
   B I will. Tom will.

2 With rising intonation = Please open the door.
Or *B* could quietly comply with *A*'s request.

3 With intonation falling on *door*: this is an order.
I want—you will open: SP 6c.
I won't—rebellious refusal.

4

5 Do *you* want it? If so, *I* will open it. SP 6c.

   Shall not replaceable by *will* in this question, which contains an offer to do something for *B*.

ie I can do it myself.

6 Here *Shall we* ... makes a suggestion, as in II.14.7.
B's *Yes + let's* indicates agreement with *A*.

7 *Will* replaceable by *Can* in the form of request made in 2 above.

8 This could be a request as in II.14.2 and 3 or an offer as in II.15.5.

9 = Who wants some chocolate?

Lexicon
1 *ask, tell, want*
2 *certainly*

II.16 *Be able to ; may* expressing probability; *must, have (got) to,* obligation or prescription

Models
Baby is able to walk.
That chair may be unsafe.
We have (got) to go now.

Notes

1 [Baby]¹ can walk. He is already [able]² to walk.
   A Can he walk yet? Is he able to (walk)?
   B Yes, he can. He's able to already.
   or No, he can't. He's not able to.
   He isn't able to. He's unable to.
2   What are you able to do?
   Are you able to answer the telephone in English?
3 *A* Can you come out with me?
   Can you see Mr Evans?
   B Yes, I can. No, I can't.

1 *can,* as in I.23, replaceable by *be able to.*

   able to, cp *want to,* I.24.11.

   unable = not able, prefix *un-* = not.

2 *be able to,* replaceable here by *can* emphasising the idea of ability.
in (a language).

3 Are you free and willing to come?
Are you free and willing to?
I'm not free or willing.

4 *A* Be careful of that chair. It may be unsafe.
It may not be very strong. Perhaps it's
broken.

4 *may* = perhaps (it) is, present probability;
unsafe, unable. Exclude Q-*Yes/No* with
may, in this sense.

5 *A* It's late. I must go now.
  B Oh, must you go? Must you really?
  A Yes, I must. I really must.

I $\left\{ \begin{array}{l} \text{have (got)} \\ \text{'ve got} \end{array} \right\}$ an appointment.

I have to see my dentist.
I've got to see him today.

5 *must* as in I.23.8.

Defer NEGATIVE of *must*. Use instead the
NEG forms in 6 below.

must replaced by *have to*, or by *have got to*,
especially when action is prescribed.

6 *B* Do you have to see him?
  A Yes, I do. I have to. I've got to.
  or No, I don't (have to). I haven't got to.

6

This form of the NEGATIVE, rather than
NEG of *must*, can be safely used at this
stage.

7 *A* Why must we leave?
Why do we have to leave?
Why have we got to leave?
  B Because I tell you (to).

7

See I.28.3.

Lexicon
1 *Baby* (without ARTICLE) *serves as a* PROPER NOUN, *like Father, Mother, Grandfather, Grandmother, Uncle, Doctor, Captain*
2 *able, unable*
3 (*have*) *an appointment ; dentist*

II.17 *Can, must* and *have to* in future and past

Models

Can we go home tomorrow?
I'll be able to drive soon.
My father could climb high mountains
twenty years ago.

He $\left\{ \begin{array}{l} \text{was able} \\ \text{managed} \end{array} \right\}$ to climb Mount
                        Snowdon once.

Notes

1 *A* Can we go home tomorrow?
  B Yes, you can.

1 II.14.2 with ADV-T future.
Permission granted for future action.

2 *A* May we go home early?

  B Yes, you $\left\{ \begin{array}{l} \text{may.} \\ \text{can.} \end{array} \right.$

2 *can* replaceable by *may*.
Permission granted for future action.

3   Be careful of that chair.
It may collapse.
  A Will it collapse?
  B I don't know. It may. It may not.

3 II.16.4.
Probability of future action.
Asking for definite prediction.
Future uncertain.

4 *A* Can you see Mr Evans next Tuesday?

  B Yes, I can see him then.

4 Will you be free and willing to see him
then?
I shall be free and willing.

5   I can't drive very well yet.
I'll be able to drive well soon.

5 I haven't that ability now.
I shall have the ability later: exclude *can*
in this sense with future reference.

6 My father can't climb mountains. He could climb very high mountains ten years ago. I { could not. / couldn't.	6 He hasn't that ability now. *could* as past equivalent of *can*, ability. He had that ability then; I didn't.
7 He { was able / managed } to climb Mount Snowdon twenty years ago.	7 He succeeded in that achievement. Do not use *could* for past achievement.
8 *A* Could you go home early yesterday? *B* Yes, we could.	8 Cp 2 above. Exclude *may* or *might* in this situation.
9 *A* Must you / Have you got to / Do you have to / Will you have to } go tomorrow? *B* Yes, I { must. / have (got) to. / 'll have to.	9 *Must* can be used with ADV-T, future; *Have (got) to* to indicate prescription for the future; *Will have to* stresses future. Do not use * *will have got to.*
10 *A* Will you have to go? *B* Yes, I'll have to.	10 With no ADV-T stated or implied, *will have to* is obligatory to indicate future prescription.
11 *A* I must stay in bed today. *B* You had to stay in bed yesterday. Did you have to stay in bed? You didn't (really) have to.	11 Use *had to* for past of *must*. Q-*Yes/No* applied to previous model. NEG applied to the same model.
12 I've been able to mend my typewriter. I've had to buy a new ribbon.	12 PRESENT PERF of II.16.1 and II.17.7. PRESENT PERF of II.16.5.

II.18 Gradable adjectives. Adjectives and adverbs modified by adverbs of degree

Models

It's quite hot today.
This table is too heavy.
It's too heavy to lift.
I'm not strong enough to lift it.

Notes

1 *A* How [hot][1] is it?
  B It's (not) (quite) hot enough.

  It's [quite][2] hot.
  It's very hot (indeed).
  It's a [very][3] hot day.
  It's [quite][4] a hot day.

1 *How* + GRADABLE ADJECTIVE.
  not quite = not 100%: cp II.5.4; *hot enough*: cp *enough* + NOUN, II.5.1.
  Here *quite* = rather.
  hot is a GRADABLE ADJECTIVE.
  a very hot day, but *quite a hot day*.

2 *A* How is your wife?
  B She's /quite//very/ well, thank you.

2
  well, ADJ as in I.8.1.

3 *A* How [well][5] did Tom play?
  B He played /well enough//quite well/ /very well (indeed)/.
  A How often does he play?
  B /Quite//very/ often; often enough.

3 *How* + ADV; *well*: ADV as in I.30.1.
  ADVERBS OF DEGREE. *Enough* follows an ADJ or ADV: cp II.5.
  Also, *often* and *frequently* can be modified as in 1 above.

4   This [chair] is quite [heavy][1].
      [I] can (only) just [lift] it.
      This table is too heavy: I can't lift it
      (at all).
      The table is too heavy to lift.
      It's too heavy for her to lift.
      She's too weak to lift it.
      She's not strong enough to lift it.

4   *Heavy* is GRADABLE.
      (*only*) *just* = (I can) do that and no more.
      The degree of heaviness is greater than
      I can manage; *at all*, see II.5.1.
      I, and others, can't lift it.
      She can't lift it.

5   [You] [are] (not) quite [right][6].
      The [pot] is (not) quite [full].
      Your answer is quite perfect.
      You answered quite perfectly.

5   See I.8.6 and II.5.4. When ADJ or ADV
      (eg *right* and Lex 6) represents an
      'absolute', it can be modified by *quite*
      in the sense of 100%, not normally by *very*,
      enough. *Not quite* = nearly, almost.

6   I [quite][7] [enjoyed][8] the [party].
      There were [quite][7] a lot of people.

6   There are degrees of enjoyment, so *quite*
      here = adequately.

7   I /quite understand//quite believe it/.

7   'Absolute': *quite* = 100%.

8   How hot it is today!
      How [nice][9]!

8   Exclamation.

Lexicon
1 *good, bad ; hot, cold ; strong, weak ; heavy, light ; fat, thin*, etc
2 *quite, rather, too, very ;* also *fairly*, but not with ADJECTIVES or ADVERBS like *bad, badly* expressing
     lack of desirable qualities
3 *fairly, rather, very* (exclude *quite*)
4 *quite, rather* (not *fairly, very*)
5 *well, badly, carefully, sensibly*
6 *right, wrong ; full, empty ; perfect, complete, unique*
7 *quite, rather*
8 *believe, enjoy, like, understand*
9 *beautiful, funny, nice, silly*

II.19 *How* + adjective in questions

Models

How old are you?
How much are those pens?
How heavy is this parcel?
How much does it weigh?

Notes

1 *A* How old is John? What is his age?
      What age is he?
   B He's twelve (years old).
      He's twelve years of age.

1 *How* + ADJ, as in II.18.1. *How old are you?*
      could be introduced earlier, as a formula.
      '*years old*' may be omitted with animates.
      Use this form for humans only.

2 *A* Look at that tree! How old is it?
   B It's two hundred years old.

2
      '*years old*' obligatory with inanimates.

3

3

a *A* How much are those pens?
      How much (money) do they cost?
      What do they cost? What price are they?

a

   B They $\left\{\begin{array}{l}\text{are}\\\text{cost}\end{array}\right\}$ ten pence (each).

each : see II.27.8.

b *A* How much are they worth?
   B They are (not) worth ten pence.
      I /gave//paid/ ten pence for them.

b = What is their real value?

pay, paid for.

4 *A* How heavy is this parcel?
       /What//How much/ does it weigh?
       How many kilos does it weigh?
       What weight is it? What's its weight?
   B /It's//It weighs/ 2 kilos 250 grams.

5 *A* How tall is that /boy//tree/
       /building/?
   B What height is [he]? What's his height?
       [He]'s 1 metre 99 centimetres (tall).

6 *A* How high is that mountain?
   B It's 2000 metres (above sea level).

7 *A* How [long]¹ is that [river]³?
       What [length]² is it? What's its length?
       It's a thousand miles long.

8 *A* Is it far (from here) (to London)?
       How far (away) is London?
       How far is it (from here) to London?
       What is the distance from here to
       London?
   B It's not far (away). It's far away.
       It's (quite) a long way. It's very far.
       It's 600 miles away.

9 *A* How big are those shoes?
       What size are they?

10 *A* What shape is this swimming pool?
   B It's [square]⁴.

11 *A* Is the water hot? How hot is it?
       What temperature is it?
       What is the temperature?
   B It's 30 degrees Centigrade.

4 The inclusion of this item implies pre-
   senting weights and measures.
   kilos: see I.14, Lex 5.
   its, POSSESSIVE of *it:* contrast *it's,* I.1.4.

5 *tall,* used for measurement of humans
   and objects: focus on vertical dimension.

6 = How far is it above a certain level?

7 See Lex 1 and 3 below.
   See Lex 2 below.

8 Note the use of *far* in questions and
   NEGATIVES: cp 8*B.*

   A PREPOSITION, eg *from,* can precede an
   ADV-P like *here* or *there.*
   not far; far away.
   a long way: avoid *far,* except with *very* or
   away, in an AFFIRMATIVE sentence.

10 = pool for swimming in: stress *swimming.*

Lexicon
1 *long, wide, deep*
2 *length, width, depth*
3 *river, lake, valley*
4 *square, round, circular, oval,* ADJECTIVES; *a square, a circle, an oval,* NOUNS.

II.20 Comparison of adjectives with *-er* and *-est*

Models
Jim is as tall as Ron.
Jim is not [as/so] tall as Ron.
Tom is taller than Jim.
Tom is the tallest (boy) in/of ...

Notes

1   [Jim] is as [tall] as [Ron] (is).
    He is as [tall] as I (am).
    He's as [tall] as [me].

2   Jim is not [as/so] tall (as Tom).
    Jim is not so tall.

3 *A* What's the [water] like?
   B It's [as cold as ice]¹.

1 GRADABLE ADJ (II.18.1). In the models
   opposite, the quality is equal in Jim, Ron
   etc; *tall as me,* informal.

2 *as* or *so* acceptable after *not.*
   This may also mean *Jim is not very tall.*

3

   Established simile: see Lex 1.

4 *A* Compare this with that.
  B *a* This is [clean]²er than that (is).
     b This is [bigg]³er than that (is).

     c This is [nice]⁴r than that (is).

     d This is [tid]⁵ier than this (is).

     e This is [narrow]⁶er than that (is).

     f This is stronger than that.

4 Rules for spelling of COMPARATIVE:
  a add *-er* to form COMPARATIVE.
  b spelling rule as in II.7.2d, cp *muddy* (II.1.6).
  c spelling rule as for *arrived*, II.7.4; cp *noisy*.
  d spelling rule as for II.7.2b: *tidy*, *tidier*, see Lex 5.
  e for other words of two syllables compared in this way, see Lex 6.
     In *narrower*, pronounce the /w/.
  f In *longer*, *stronger*, *younger*, pronounce a /g/ after /ŋ/. Contrast *longing*, *singing*, *singer* where /g/ is not added after /ŋ/.

5 *A* Compare Tom and Jim.
  B Tom is (the) taller. He's much taller.

  A Now compare Tom, Ron and Jim.
  B Tom is the tallest.
     Tom is the tallest of the three.
     He is the tallest in the class.

5
  taller, of two; *much* modifying a COMPARATIVE.

  tallest of more than two.

6 *A* Compare this thing with those things.

  B This is the cleanest/biggest/nicest/ tidiest/narrowest/strongest.

6 Rules as in 4 above. Again, pronounce /g/ in *longest*, *strongest*, *youngest*.

7   Where is the nearest [bus-stop], please?

7 *near*, *nearer*, *nearest*.

8   Everest is the highest mountain in the world.
      The first was the strongest of them all.

8 the [highest] in a place.

  the [strongest] of a group of people or things.

9   Which (of those two) is the stronger?
      Which /thing//person/ is the stronger?
      Which (of the three) is the strongest?

9 Which person or thing of a specified pair.

Lexicon
1 Similar expressions: *as white as snow, as light as a feather, as heavy as lead, as sharp as a razor, as clear as crystal, as hard as iron, as dry as dust, as quiet as a mouse, as good as gold, as old as the hills*
2 *clean, clear, great, high, low, small, quick, quiet, slow, thick, weak*
3 *big, fat, sad, thin, wet*
4 *brave, fine, nice, safe, strange, true, wise*
5 *busy, dirty, dry, early, easy, happy, healthy, noisy, pretty, tidy, ugly ;* also *unhappy, unhealthy, untidy*
6 *common, clever, feeble, gentle, narrow, simple*

II.21 Irregular comparison of adjectives; *more, most* as determiners

Models
Your writing is better than mine.
Yours is the best in the class.
I've got more money than you.
Tom has the most.

Notes

1 *A* Your writing is very good.
     It's (much) better than mine.
     Yours is the best in the class.
  B Yours is bad. It's worse than mine.
     It's the worst in the class.

1 *good*
  better
  best.
  bad, worse, worst.

2 *A* Is June well? Is she better?
  B She's a little better.
  A Jim is still ill. He was worse yesterday.

2 *well* (ADJ), *better* (= recovered).
  = Her condition is a little better.
  ill (ADJ PREDIC), COMPARATIVE *worse*; no
  SUPERLATIVE for *well* or *ill*.

3 John is a little boy. He's smaller than
  Jack.

3 *little, smaller, smallest.*

4 Tom is older than Jim. He's older.
  Who is the oldest man in this town?
  Tom is Jim's elder brother.
  Tom is the elder (brother).
  Who is the eldest (person) in the family?

4 *old, older, oldest* is regular.

  Use *elder, eldest* attributively only, and
  only when comparing members of a human
  family; *elder* of two, *eldest* of more than
  two.

5 *A* I've a little money.
     How much have you?
  B I've got more (money) than you.
     Tom has much more than I have.

     So he has the most (money).
  A I have less (money) than you.
     So I have the least.

5

  much (as in II.5.1), COMPARATIVE *more*.
  much modifying a COMPARATIVE, as in
  II.20.
  much, more, most

  little (as in II.4.3), *less, least.*

6 *A* I've got a few stamps.
     How many have you?
  B I've got more (stamps) than you.
  A Tom has the most (stamps).
     I have fewer stamps than you.
     I have the fewest.

6

  many, more, most.
  few, fewer, fewest, though *less* [units] and
  the least [units] are often heard.

7 This cost less than five pounds.

7 Use *less* in any case in expressions like
  less than two weeks or *This cost less than
  five pounds.*

8 *A* Do you need any more /money//stamps/?
  B No thanks. I've already got too /much/
     /many/.

8 *More* can be preceded by *any, some, much,
  many, a lot, plenty, a little, a few, no.
  Too much, too many* = more than one
  needs.

9 Most people want too much.

9 *Most people* = the majority.

II.22 Comparison of longer adjectives, comparison and similarity

Models
This car is more expensive than that one.
That one is not so comfortable.
This is the most comfortable.

Notes

1 *A* How do these two [cars] compare?

1   *The one* = the thing mentioned (+ POST-
MODIFIER). /*more*//*less*/ *expensive*: regular
COMPARATIVE for ADJECTIVES of more than
two syllables.

   B The one on the left is more [expensive][1]
than the one on the right.
That is less [expensive] than this.

2 *A* How does this [car] compare with
the others?

2   *the others* = the other cars.

   B It's /more//less/ [comfortable][1] than
the others.
It's the /most//least/ comfortable.

Regular SUPERLATIVE for longer ADJEC-
TIVES.

   It's the most comfortable car in the shop.
That one is not so/as comfortable as
the next one.

the next one = the one after.

3 *A* Which do you prefer, the town or
the country?

3 Note the DEFINITE ARTICLE in *the town*
as distinct from *the country; the land,
the sea.*

   B Life is (pleasant/more pleasant) in the
country, I think.

Some two-syllable ADJECTIVES may form
comparison with -*er*, -*est*, or with *more,
most.* See Lex 2. Teachers may prefer to
present only one form for *pleasant* etc at
this stage.

4 *A* What's Jane like?

4

   B She's very careful—(much) more
[careful][3] than Elizabeth.
She's the most [helpful] girl I've ever
met.

Other two-syllable ADJECTIVES form
comparison with *more, most.*
See Lex 3.

   A Then she's more like John.

Note *more like:* only this form acceptable.

5 *A* $\begin{Bmatrix} \text{What} \\ \text{Which} \end{Bmatrix}$ is the most [interesting][1]
[book] you've ever [read]?
I prefer this book; the story in it is
more real.

5 *Which* and *What*, referring to something
inanimate, are interchangeable when
choice has to be made from an INDEFINITE
SET: cp II.20.9.
Note *more real:* only this form is acceptable.

6 *A* Is my book [the same as][4] yours?

6 *the same* (+ NOUN) *as.*

   B No, mine is not the same book (as yours).
Mine is different.
It's [different from][4] yours.
It's a different book.

*different from;
a different* + NOUN.

7 $\begin{Bmatrix} \text{What} \\ \text{Which} \end{Bmatrix}$ is the most beautiful [city][5]
in the world?

Lexicon
1 *beautiful, comfortable, dangerous, expensive, important, interesting, natural, necessary, reliable, sensible,
serious, unimportant.* But *unhealthy, untidy,* etc may follow the same pattern as *healthy,* etc
2 *clever, common, pleasant, polite*
3 *careful, careless, certain, equal, famous, foolish, frequent, helpful, modern, normal, private, public,
sudden, useful, violent*
4 *the same as, different from*
5 *city, country, place, town, village*

II.23 Comparison of adverbs; and adverbs with the same form as adjectives

Models

John drives more carefully than Dick.
He drives better than Dick.
Dick drives too fast.
He drives faster than John.

Notes

1 A Does [John] [drive] as [carefully]¹ as [Dick]?

    1 *as*+ ADV-M+ *as*: cp II.20.1.

  B He drives more carefully than Dick.

    Dick doesn't drive $\begin{Bmatrix} as \\ so \end{Bmatrix}$ carefully as John.

    as or *so*+ ADV-M+ *as*.

    He drives (much) less carefully.

    less+ ADV-M+ *than*.

    Tom drives (far) too slowly.

    too+ ADV-M modified by *much, very much* or *far*.

    John drives the most skilfully.

    the most ADV-M, SUPERLATIVE, with *the*.

    John drives most carefully.

    most+ ADV-M (without *the*)= *very*+ ADV-M.

2 Sue dances as gaily as Jane.

    2 *gay, gaily;* cp *day, daily.*

3 Can you explain that more simply?

    3 *simple, simply; gentle, gently; noble,* etc.

4 John drives /well//better than Dick/.
   Dick drives /badly//worse than John/.

    4 *well,* ADV; COMPARATIVE, *better.*
    badly, ADV; COMPARATIVE, *worse.*

5 A How far did you walk yesterday?

    5

  B I walked $\begin{Bmatrix} \text{very far.} \\ \text{a long way.} \end{Bmatrix}$

    Cp II.19.8.

  C I walked $\begin{Bmatrix} \text{farther} \\ \text{further} \end{Bmatrix}$ than you.

    far, farther or *further,* COMPARATIVE.

  D I walked the $\begin{Bmatrix} \text{farthest.} \\ \text{furthest.} \end{Bmatrix}$

    farthest or *furthest,* SUPERLATIVE.

6 Dick drives quickly. He drives [fast]².
   He drives /too fast//faster than John/.
   He drives the fastest.

    6 *fast* and other ADVS in Lex 2 below have the same form as the corresponding ADJ and take *-er, -est* in comparison.

  A How fast does he drive?
  B He drives at 100 kilometres an hour.

7 A You're working too hard.

    7 *hard* (ADJ) *work; work hard* (ADV).

  B Yes, I can [hardly]³ keep awake.

    hardly, as in II.5.1.

8 A I swim several times a week.

    8

  B I swim $\begin{Bmatrix} \text{oftener} \\ \text{more often} \end{Bmatrix}$ than that.

    often: oftener or *more often.*

9 A We'll meet next Friday, I think.

    9

  B We'll meet sooner than that.

    soon, sooner, soonest.

10 Her room is (very) much tidier than his.

    10 ADJS and ADVS in the COMPARATIVE can be modified by *much, very much, far.*

    This is /(very) much//far/ more difficult.
    You don't write clearly enough.
    Please write (very) much more clearly.

Lexicon

1 *carefully, carelessly, dangerously, easily, gaily, gently, happily, patiently, quickly, quietly, skilfully* (NB *skill, skilful, skilfully*), *slowly*

2 *fast, hard; early, late; high* (as in *aim high*: distinguish from *highly* as in VI.16.3); *low* (as in *lie low*)
3 *barely, hardly, scarcely*
4 *farther, further*

II.24 The auxiliary used as a pro-form for a whole VP; question tags

Models

Tom's faster than I am.
He runs faster than I do.
You wear a hat, but I don't.
You're tired, aren't you?
Let's go, shall we?

Notes

1   Tom's faster than I am.
I'm slower than he is.
You were better than I was.
I was worse than you were.
John has more money than we have.
I've more stamps than he has.
Tom can run faster than I can.
You could climb higher than I could.
Tom runs faster than I do.
You write better than John does.
You wrote better than John did.

1 *be, have,* the AUXILIARY or the MODAL, at the end of each of these sentences could be omitted, in which case the PERSONAL PRONOUN could, in informal style, take the form *me, him, us,* etc.

The AUXILIARY *do, does, did* as a PRO-FORM for the VERB in the SIMPLE PRESENT or SIMPLE PAST.

2   George can swim, but I can't.
He could drive, but I couldn't.
He'll be home late, but I shan't.
I'll be home early, but he won't.

I have a camera, but John $\begin{cases} \text{hasn't.} \\ \text{doesn't.} \end{cases}$

I had a film, but John $\begin{cases} \text{hadn't.} \\ \text{didn't.} \end{cases}$

You wear a hat, but I don't.
You wore a coat, but I didn't.
John drives a car, but Jack doesn't.

2 In these sentences, *be, have,* the AUXILIARY or the MODAL cannot be omitted at the end.

John hasn't: I.15.4.
John doesn't: I.24.10.
John hadn't: II.6.4c.
John didn't: II.6.4b.

3   a [You're] [tired], [are]n't [you]?
He plays the piano, doesn't he?
There's a man at the door, isn't there?
I can go now, can't I?
b You aren't angry, are you?
He doesn't smoke, does he?
There isn't a letter for me, is there?
You can't see him, can you?
c I'm right, aren't I?

3 Question tags, AFFIRMATIVE STATEMENT + NEGATIVE tag, and b, *vice versa,* with rising intonation on the tag, converting the statement into a *Yes/No* question.

The NP in a question tag is a PERSONAL PRONOUN or *there.*

NB I am, *aren't I?* I'm not, *am I?*

4   *A* Let's go, shall we?
B Yes, let's (go).

4 See II.15.6.

5   *A* You're tired, aren't you?
B Yes, I am.
A You're not angry, are you?
B No, of course not.

5 Falling intonation on the tag, indicating that the speaker expects confirmation of the statement.

6 *A* He wants to go home.	6 AFFIRMATIVE statement.
B He does, does he?	AFFIRMATIVE tag with rising intonation, asking a *Yes/No* question, expressing sarcasm.

II.25 Repeat patterns. Emphasis. The auxiliary as a pro-form for the whole of the predicate, or used for emphasis

Models	**Notes**
Tom is ready. So am I.	
He's not writing. I'm not either.	
Nor am I. Neither am I.	
You go. Do go. Don't you wait.	

1 *A* Tom is ready.
  B I am also. I'm ready as well.
  C I am too.
  D So [am] [I]. So is the other boy.
  A You can go now. So can Tom.
  B I'm going to swim.
  C So am I. So is John.
  B I've brought my swimsuit.
  C So have I. So has John.
  D I like football.
  B So do I. So does Dick.
  C So did my father $\left\{ \begin{array}{l} \text{at one time} \\ \text{once} \end{array} \right\}$.

1

as well = also; no contraction in *I am also*.
too = as well; no contraction in *I am too*.
So am I = I am too. Stress *so* and the NP which may be PERSONAL PRONOUN or otherwise. The VERB in the *so am I* pattern is usually pronounced weak, and the vowel in *am*, *is*, *have*, *has* often disappears in fluent speech. As in II.24.1, *do*, *does*, *did*, replace full VERBS (except *be*) in SIMPLE TENSES. *Must*, *will*, *shall*, *could*, *may* can also be used in this pattern.

2 *A* [I'm] not [tired].
  B [I'm] not either. Neither [am] [I].
  C Nor am I. $\left\{ \begin{array}{l} \text{Neither} \\ \text{Nor} \end{array} \right\}$ is John.

2

Contraction is common before *not either*.
Similar comments as for *So am I* above.

3 *A* Who's coming with me?
  B *I* am. *We* are. *John* is.
  A Who's finished?
  B *I* have. *We* have. *John* has.
  A Who wants to go home?
  B *I* do. *We* do. *John* does.
  A Who broke the window?
  B *I* did. *I* didn't.

3 *Who's* = who is.
Stress the PRONOUN.
Who's = who has.
Stress the PRONOUN.

Stress the PRONOUN.

Stress the PRONOUN.

4 *A* [You're] not [ready].
  B I beg your pardon. I [*am*] ([ready]).
  A You haven't finished your work.
  B But I *have* finished.
  A You won't be ready.
  B I $\left\{ \begin{array}{l} \text{shall} \\ \text{will} \end{array} \right\}$ be (ready).
  A [It]'[s] [late].
  B I'm sorry, [it] [is]n't. It's *not* (late).
  A You don't understand.
  B I *do* (understand).

4

Stress uncontracted *be*, *have* AUXILIARY or MODAL to make emphatic AFFIRMATION. Here, *but* is an exclamation of protest.

Stress the [*is*] of [*is*]n't, or stress *not* to make emphatic denial: I'm sorry (*to contradict you*). Supply stressed *do*, *does*, *did* with SIMPLE TENSES of full VERBS, except *be*.

5	Go. Don't wait.	5 Normal IMPERATIVE.
	You go. Don't you wait.	Stressing person addressed: cp I.18.1.
	Do go, (*please*).	Stressing VERB.

II.26 *Such a* + NP and *so* + adjective; *what a* or *an* + unit etc

Models
I can't afford an expensive car.
Why is it so expensive?
What a nice day!

Notes

1
This car is much too expensive.
I don't want a car as expensive as this (one).
I can't afford such an expensive car.
Why is it so expensive?

1
as + ADJ + *as*.

such a or *an* + ADJ + COUNT NOUN.
so + ADJ used PREDICATIVELY.

2
This coffee is far too sweet.
I can't drink coffee as sweet as this.
I can't drink such sweet stuff.
Why is it so sweet?

2

such + ADJ + MASS NOUN: *stuff*, often used of something one doesn't like.

3
These parcels are as heavy as lead.
I can't carry parcels as heavy as these.
I can't even lift such heavy parcels.
Why are they so heavy?

3 See II.20.3.

such + ADJ + COUNT NOUN PLURAL.

4
You've been so kind.
How kind you are!
How clearly you speak!
You speak so clearly.

4 Here, *so* = very.
Exclamation: contrast *How old are you?*
How can modify ADJ or ADV.
so can modify ADJ or ADV.

5
I can't do /so many exercises//so much work/.
I can't do such a lot (of /exercises/ /work/).

5 See II.21.7. *do an exercise*.

such a lot = so /much//many/.

6 *A* What a [nice day]!
  B Yes, it's such a [nice day].
  A What [bad luck]²!
  B Yes, it's such [bad luck]².

6 *What* + *a* + (ADJ) + COUNT NOUN, SINGULAR.
What + (ADJ) + MASS NOUN.
such + (ADJ) + MASS NOUN.

7 *A* What interesting people!
  B Yes, they're such interesting people.
    They're so interesting.

7 *What* + (ADJ) + COUNT NOUN, PLURAL.
such + (ADJ) + COUNT NOUN, PLURAL.
so + ADJ alone.

8 *A* Let's go to the cinema.
  B What a good idea!

8 As in II.14.7.
Agreeing to the suggestion.

9 What wonderful [weather]³!
  What strange music!

9 NB *weather* and the other words in Lex 3 below are MASS NOUNS.

10 It's [quite]⁴ a fine day.
   It's a rather fine day.

10 Use only with COUNT NOUNS, SINGULAR.

Lexicon
1 *crowd, idea, lot, noise, nuisance, pity, pleasure, shame*
2 *bad luck, good luck, fun, rubbish*
3 *furniture, music, weather*
4 *quite, rather*

II.27 Predeterminers. Various positions for *all, both, each*

Models

Some of these cups are broken.

/Both//All/ (of) these cups are white.

Every⎱
Each ⎰ house has a white door.

Every one ⎱
Each (one)⎰ has a bathroom.

Notes

1 [Some]¹ of[these]³ cups are broken.
   [Some]² of[this] bread is stale.
   Some of them are broken. Some of it . . .
   Some of /you//us/ know this already.

1 All the determiners in Lex 1 and 2
   (see II.4 and II.5) can be used in the
   pattern *some of*+ DEFINITE DETERMINER+
   NP. Choice of PREDETERMINER depends
   on whether NP is COUNT NOUN, SING or
   PLUR, or MASS NOUN.

2 None of them ⎰is ⎱ broken.
              ⎱are⎰
   None of it is stale.
   One of these cups is broken.

2 *None*: see II.5.1–2. Accept *none is* or *are*.

   Only *none is* with a MASS NOUN.
   One determines concord with VERB *is*.

3 a All (of) the cups are white.
      All of them are white. They are all
      white.
      You've broken /all the cups//
      ⎰all of them⎱/.
      ⎱them all ⎰

3 a *All* referring to more than two units.
      All of them⎱
      They all ⎰—SUBJECT.

      all of them⎱
      them all ⎰—OBJECT.

   b All (of) the bread is stale.
      All of it is⎱ stale.
      It is all ⎰

   b *All* referring to mass.

   c We waited all day, all night, all
      /the morning//the week/.

      We waited a whole day, the whole day.

   c Use *all* without article before a COUNT
      NOUN, SINGULAR, only in fixed expres-
      sions like this.
      whole+ COUNT NOUN.

4 a Half (of) this bread is stale.
      Half (of) these cups are broken.
   b [Double]⁴ this /amount//number/ . . .
   c A quarter of this /amount//number/ . . .

4 a *Half (of)* a mass or a number.

   c Sim. *a third, a fifth, a sixth*, etc.

5 /Both (of) the cups//Both (the) cups//
   ⎰Both of them⎱/ belong to me. I bought
   ⎱They both ⎰
   them both.
   Both cups are broken.

5 *Both*, referring to two units only, can
   replace *all* in every pattern in 3a above.

   Both cups= both (of) the cups.

6 They /are all hungry//are all waiting/
   /have all sat down//all want some food/.

6 *all* and *both* can occupy the same position as ADV-F: see I.29.

7 All (of) the [houses] [have white doors].
   Every⎱ house has a white door.
   Each ⎰
   Every one ⎱ has a bathroom.
   Each (one)⎰
   Every⎱ single one has a garden.
   Each ⎰

7 *All* referring to *the* [*houses*] collectively.

   Every and *Each*, inter-replaceable here.

   PRONOUNS: *every one, each one* or *each*.

   Every, Each= all the houses indivi-
   dually.

8   They both passed the examination.
/Each boy//Each (one)/ will get a prize.

8 Use *every* and *each* for more than two;
but only *each*, not *every*, for only two.

9   a They /will each get//each got/ a prize.
b They all got two pounds each.

9 *each*, not *every*, patterns as in 6 above.
Only *each* occurs in this pattern.

10 *A* I like all of them.

10

B I don't like any of them.

A I like /both//the pair/ of them.

any = a single one of more than two.

the pair = both, of the same kind.

B I {don't like /either (of them)//either (boy)/
like neither (of them)// neither
(boy)/.

neither = not . . . either.

Lexicon

1 *all, both ; some, several ; a lot, lots, plenty ; most, many ; none ; hardly any ; (a) few ; each (one), every one ; enough ; more*
2 *all ; some ; a lot, lots, plenty ; most ; much ; none, hardly any ; (a) little = enough, more*
3 *the, this, that ; my, your, his, our*, etc; *Tom's*, etc; *these* or *those* units
4 *double, half, twice, three times, four times*

II.28 Indefinite pronouns. Also *everywhere, nowhere*

Models
Everybody's business is nobody's business.

Notes

1   All men must eat.
Every man must eat.
Everyone }
Everybody } must eat.

1 *All men* = all the people in the world.

Everyone }
Everybody } stress on 1st syllable = every person; contrast *every one*, II.27.7.

2   Listen. They're all singing.
Everyone }
Everybody } is singing.

2 They are all . . . ; everyone is . . . .

ie all the people in a certain context.

3   Everyone }
Everybody } knows his job, doesn't he ?
(Everyone knows their job, don't they ?)

3 CONCORD: *Everybody* }
Everyone } knows his . . . etc.
This kind of CONCORD, common in informal style, need not be presented deliberately.

4 *A* Hallo. Is { anyone
anybody } in ?

There isn't { anyone
anybody } in.

There's { no one
nobody } in.
Who's that ?

4 The use of *any* (or *some*) in questions, *any* in NEGATIVE statements and *some* in AFFIRMATIVE, as in I.17.1, applies also to all the compounds of *any* and *some* treated in II.28.

C There's { someone
somebody } at the door.
I don't know who.

some—definite but unspecified, unstated.

5 *A* The room's neat and tidy.
B Yes. Everything is in its place.
A Is there anything in that box ?

5

Everything = all the things [in the room].

B No. There isn't anything in it.
   There's nothing in it at all.
C There *is* something in it, but I don't
   know what.

not anything = nothing.
is—emphatic AFFIRMATIVE, as in II.25.4.

6 *A* Where's your pen?
  B I can't find it anywhere.
    I've looked for it everywhere.
    It's somewhere, I don't know where.
  A Where did you go yesterday?
  B Nowhere. I didn't go anywhere.
7 *A* Does this knife belong to anybody?
  B It's someone's—I don't know whose.
8   This isn't my hat. It belongs to someone
    else. It's someone else's.
9   Go away. Go somewhere else.

7

Similarly, *somebody's, anybody's*, etc.

8

someone else = some other person.
9 *else* can be added to all the compounds
  in II.28.

10 *A* I don't want any tea, thank you.
   B Have something else. What else will
    you have?

10

What else = what other thing.

Lexicon
1 *everyone, everybody, everything, everywhere ; no one, nobody, nothing, nowhere ; anyone, anybody,*
  anything, anywhere ; someone, somebody, something, somewhere
2 *else*

II.29 Combining simple sentences with *and, so, but, or* to form compound sentences

Models

He speaks and writes English.
He speaks English, but he doesn't write it.
Come and open the door.
No one heard me, so I went away.

Notes

1 We speak English. We write it too.
  We speak and write English.
  Jack speaks English but (he) doesn't write it.

1 Two simple sentences.
  Two sentences combined into one with
  and and *but*; the subject need not be
  repeated if it refers to the same person or
  thing.

  Mary speaks English. Tom doesn't.
  Mary speaks English but Tom doesn't.

  Different SUBJECTS, both stated.

2 I was ill. I couldn't go out.
  I was ill and (I) couldn't go out.
  I was ill, so I couldn't go out.
  I was ill, and so I couldn't go out.

2

  Same SUBJECT, need not be repeated.
  Same SUBJECT, usually repeated with *so*.
  Same SUBJECT, usually repeated with
  and so.

3 Tom is waiting. Jim is waiting, too.
  Tom and Jim are both waiting.
4 We met Mary. We met Jane as well.
  We met Jane as well as Mary.
  We met Jane but not Elizabeth.

3 Different NP SUBJECTS.
  NP SUBJECTS joined by *and*, PLURAL VERB.
4 Different OBJECTS; *as well*: II.25.1.
  OBJECTS transposed with *as well as*.
  Same VERB, need not be repeated with
  and, but, or.

5 You will go. I $\left\{ \begin{array}{l} \text{will} \\ \text{shall} \end{array} \right\}$ go.   5

You and I will go together.   *You and I* forming one NP SUBJECT.
He gave it to you. He gave it to me.
He gave it to you and me.   *you and me*, forming one NP OBJECT.
6 He developed the film. He printed it.   6 OBJECTS the same, VERBS different.
He developed the film and printed it.
He developed and printed the film.
7 Come here. Open the door.   7
Come and open the door.
That's no good. Try and do better.   Double IMPERATIVE, common with *go*,
8 He went into the library, chose a book and   *come* and *try*.
sat down.   8 When more than two words or structures
He went into the shop, looked at several   are combined, the CONJUNCTION usually
books but didn't buy any one of them.   occurs between the last two; elsewhere
9 He chose a book (and then sat down).   the CONJUNCTION is replaced by a comma.
                                                    9 *then* = after that.

II.30 Combining simple sentences by using *both . . . and, either . . . or,*
       neither . . . nor, not only . . . but also, not only . . . but . . . as well. Simple
       examples of subordinate clauses

Models   Notes
Both John and Jack are away today.
Either Tom or Jim has your pen.
Neither Tom nor Jim has it.
You may speak either English or [your
own language].

1   Both John and Jack are away today.   1 *Both . . . and . . .*; PLURAL VERB; *away* =
                                                       absent.
     Either Tom or Jim has your pen.   *Either . . . or*; SINGULAR VERB.
     Neither Tom nor Jim has it.   *Neither . . . nor*; SINGULAR VERB.
     Either Tom has your pen or Jim has (it).
2   You can speak English and you can   2 *speak English*, no article.
     speak French.
     You can speak both English and French.   You have the ability to speak both.
     You may speak either English or French.   You have the choice of speaking either;
                                                       either . . . or, referring to the OBJECT.
3   Tom speaks not only English but also   3 *not only . . . but also.*
     German.
     Jim speaks not only Spanish but
     Russian $\left\{ \begin{array}{l} \text{too.} \\ \text{as well.} \end{array} \right.$ *not only . . . but . . .* $\left\{ \begin{array}{l} \text{too.} \\ \text{as well.} \end{array} \right.$
     I speak neither Chinese nor Japanese.   *neither . . . nor*, referring to the OBJECT.
4   He not only developed the film but   4 See II.29.6.
     also printed it.
     He not only developed the film but
     printed it $\left\{ \begin{array}{l} \text{too} \\ \text{as well} \end{array} \right\}$.
     He either bought it or borrowed it.   *either . . . or*, referring to the VERB.

He neither spoke nor even wrote to us again.

neither . . . nor, referring to the VERB.

5   He'll either write to us (or) telephone us or send us a telegram.

5   If the optional *or* is omitted, put a comma instead of it.

6   I have never seen such a pretty girl before.
She's the prettiest girl I've ever seen.

6   *such a*, II.26.

Simple occurrence of RELATIVE CLAUSE for practice with SUPERLATIVES, II.20.

7 *A*   I can't do my work. I'm too hungry.
I can't do my work when I'm hungry.

7   Two simple sentences, joined by a sub-ordinating CONJUNCTION (*when*), in which case the SUBJECT must be stated in both CLAUSES.
As in II.17.6.

B   My father could climb mountains once.
He was much younger then.
He could climb mountains when he was a young man.

C   Tom is tall. I am not so tall.

I am not $\left\{\begin{matrix} as \\ so \end{matrix}\right\}$ tall as he is.

He is taller than I am.

when he was . . ., ADV–TIME CLAUSE for practice with PAST TENSE, II.7 and II.17.6.
Two simple sentences combined as in II.20.1.

Summary of Stages I and II

Stage I, plus the following:

SENTENCE PATTERNS
additional ones listed on page 3. Simple and compound sentences, and simple examples of SUBORDINATE CLAUSES as in II.30.

NOUN PHRASE
DETERMINERS: used either with COUNT NOUNS or with MASS NOUNS, or with both, eg *many, much, (a) little, (a) few, every, each*
PREDETERMINERS: eg /*Some*//*Both*//*All*/ *of the books*. Also *all* and *both* in other positions
INDEFINITE PRONOUNS: eg *everyone (else), everyone's, everyone else's*

VERB PHRASE
VERBS
seem, feel, etc replacing *be* in SP 2 and SP 1
have as an ACTION VERB
PAST TENSE of *be* and other VERBS
PRESENT PERFECT
IRREGULAR VERBS, an arrangement and selection
be going to with future reference
will and *shall* with future reference
can, may and *let* making and answering requests
be able to : may, probability; *have (got) to*
can, must, have to, future and past

AUXILIARIES and MODALS as PRO-FORMS and in tags, as in II.24 and 25
ADJECTIVES
GRADABLE ADJECTIVES modified by ADVERBS of degree, eg *quite, (much) too, so*
How old . . . ? How long . . . ? etc

Comparison of ADJECTIVES, *-er, -est*. *The biggest in the world. The biggest I've ever seen*
IRREGULAR comparison
comparison of longer ADJECTIVES, *more . . . than, less . . . than*

as tall as, not $\left\{ \begin{matrix} so \\ as \end{matrix} \right\}$ *tall as*

ADVERBS
with the same form as ADJECTIVES, eg *hard, fast*
comparison of ADVERBS

OTHER ELEMENTS
CONJUNCTIONS
(either) or ; (neither) nor ; (both) ; and *when* introducing a temporal CLAUSE

Stage III

Contents

13 RELATIVE CLAUSES in which the RELATIVE PRONOUN is the SUBJECT: *He's the man who lives next door; there's the plane that crashed; that's the plane which flew over our house.*

14 RELATIVE CLAUSES in which the SUBJECT does not refer to the same person or thing as the antecedent: *That's the coat I want; is this the magazine she asked for?; this is the watch he gave me; is that the policeman he told?; was that the robbery he told the policeman about?* Also *That's /what I want/ /where I live/ /when/* etc.

15 Simple examples of ADVERBIAL CLAUSES: *I want to speak English as Tom does; I want to sit nearer because I can hardly see; because I couldn't see clearly, I had to sit nearer; I'm staying at home today, although I feel much better; when I get home, I have tea; I telephoned you as soon as I got home; Tom cleans his teeth before he goes to bed; I have lived here since I was a boy.*

16 *If*-sentences with the same tense in both CLAUSES; and sentences with *'ll, will, shall* in the MAIN CLAUSE and the PRESENT TENSE in the *if*-CLAUSE: *We stay in school if it rains; you'll get very wet if it rains; there'll be a picnic tomorrow, unless it rains; don't go away, in case I need you.*

17 TEMPORAL CLAUSES with the PRESENT TENSE, when *'ll, will, shall* occur in the MAIN CLAUSE: *I'll give him these letters when I see him; I'll see you as soon as I'm free;* use of *until* and *by* a certain time: *We'll wait until seven o'clock, until you get back; we'll leave by eight; we won't leave till eight.*

18 PAST PROGRESSIVE: *When I got up this morning, it was raining; the accident happened while I was working in the garden.* And *There were some children playing in the garden when I came in.*

19 PRESENT PERFECT PROGRESSIVE: *I have been waiting for three hours; it has been raining, but it has stopped now.*

20 *Would, could* and *might* in more hesitant requests, etc, than those dealt with in II.14 and II.15: *Would you have a cup of tea?; I would like some tea, please; I'd like to see the manager; would you like me to carry that?; could I see you /now/ /tomorrow/?; could you open that door for me?; might I borrow your typewriter?; be careful of that chair—it might collapse.*

21 Prohibition and absence of obligation: *must not*; and *need* as MODAL and as full VERB: *You must not do that; you need not do it; you don't need to do it.*

22 *Should* and *ought to* indicating duty or (escapable) obligation: *You* $\left\{ {ought\ to \atop should} \right\}$ *take more exercise; there* $\left\{ {ought\ to \atop should} \right\}$ *be a light here.* Also *I should like to see the manager.*

23 Four main types of PHRASAL VERB: (1) *He came across a very old man;* (2) *he had to give up;* (3) *bring up children;* (4) *stand up for your friends.* Also *He broke open the safe; he broke it open.*

24 *-ing,* as GERUND: *I enjoy listening to music; would you mind closing the window?; I'm tired of waiting; we use it for cutting bread.*

25 Questions ending with a PREPOSITION or ADVERB PARTICLE: *What is it about?; who is it by?; what did you do that for?; who are they talking to?; who is she ringing up now?; which table are they sitting at?*

26 *Very much, too much, so much, a lot, a little,* etc, as ADVERBS modifying VERBS: *I don't like sugar in my tea very much; I walked a lot; you ought to eat more.* Also *He has hardly moved; I've never heard that word before.*

27 PAST PERFECT: *The black car wasn't there: it had gone.*

28 The PASSIVE, SIMPLE PRESENT and SIMPLE PAST: *These cars are made in Coventry; our house was built in 1969.*

29 PHRASAL VERBS of the type *break down* in the PASSIVE; and PASSIVE PERFECT: *A big tree was blown down last night; my car has been repaired; it had not been stolen; it had been towed away.*

30 PASSIVE with MODALS, and with *have to, used to* and *be going to*: *It's going to be opened next month; this must be done as soon as possible; shoes used to be made by hand.*

III.1 Indirect commands, indirect statements, with the original tense retained in the subordinate clause, then with the past tense in both clauses

Models
Tell him to wait.
Tell him not to wait any longer.
He says he can't hear you.
He said he was hungry.

Notes

1 *A* Harry [wants]¹ to see you.
   B [Tell]² him to wait a minute.
   A Wait a minute, Harry.
   A to B I've told him to (wait).

1 SP 6b, as in I.22.2.
   SP 6c, as in II.15.5: indirect command.
   IMPERATIVE, as in I.18.1.
   Reporting a command.

2 *A* Ask Mr Johnson to sit down.
   B Will ⎫ you sit down?
        Won't ⎭
   A What did you say to Mr Johnson?
   B I asked him to sit down.
   A Don't ask him to come in yet.
   B *says nothing or* Please wait there.

2
   Request, as in II.15.
   For NEG-INTERROG, see III.5.

   Reporting a request.
   The first VERB is NEGATIVE.

3 *A* Tell him not to wait any longer.
   B Don't wait any longer, Mr Johnson.

3 Now the second VERB is NEGATIVE.

4 *A* I'm hungry.
   B What does he say? I can't hear him.
   C He says he's hungry.
   A What does *B* say?
   C He says he can't hear you.

4
   C reports *A*'s statement, then *B*'s, keeping the original tense but changing the PRONOUN according to the person referred to.

5 *A* I left home at eight, I've just finished my work, I'm going to have lunch at two, I'll be back at three.
   C *A* says he left home at eight, he's just finished his work, he's going to have lunch at two, he'll be back at three.

5
   PRESENT TENSE in MAIN CLAUSE, keeping the PAST etc, in SUBORDINATE CLAUSE. Defer *He said he would* till IV.12; *back* see I.20.6.

6 *B* What did *A* say? What did *I* say?
   C He said he was hungry. You said you couldn't hear him.

6 These questions refer to 4 above; PAST TENSE in both CLAUSES.

7a *A* [said]³ to *B* 'There is some petrol in the tank'.
    'There are some maps in the car.'
    'I have (got) a bad cold.' 'I must go to bed.' 'I don't drink wine.'
    'I never wear an overcoat.'

7 Actual words spoken by *A*: see 7b below.

b *B* You /said/ /told me/[4] there was some
petrol in the tank, there were some
maps in the car, you had (got) a bad
cold, you had to go to bed, you didn't
drink wine, you never wore an
overcoat.

say+ statement; tell [somebody]+
statement.
[*You*] *had to*, see II.17.11; but[*you*]
must is also permissible in *reported
speech*, even when referring to the
past.

Lexicon
1, 2 See Appendix A1 and 2
3 *answer, call out, cry, exclaim, reply, shout*
4 *inform* [*me*] (*that*), *say* (*that*), *tell* [*me*] (*that*): see also IV.11 and accompanying Lexicon: and V.30

III.2 Indirect questions when the original question is Q-*Yes/No*, Q-*Who* or *What* asking for subject or for complement of *be*, or Q-*Wh* asking for object, adv-p, adv-t, adv-f

Models
Ask (him) if he is a doctor.
Ask (him) who telephoned.
Ask (him) where he went on Monday.

Notes

1 *A* I'll ask (you) a question.
Are you a doctor?
Now ask if *he* is a doctor.
   B Is he a doctor?
   A Now ask him if he is a doctor.
   B Are you a doctor?

1 *ask* in SP 10: contrast II.14.1.

= ask me or someone else if he is etc.
Note use of *if* in indirect Q-*Yes/No*.
= ask *him* if *he* is . . .

2 [Ask Mary][1] if she is happy.
[Ask Mary][1] if there is a doctor here.
[AskTom] if he has (got) a book.
[Ask John] if he can swim.
[Ask him] if he likes Chinese food.
[Ask Tom] if he had a haircut.
[Ask Mary][1] if they've arrived yet.
[Ask me] if I slept outdoors last
summer.

2 For original question, see I.8.2.
For original question, see I.12.1.
For original question, see I.15.4.
For original question, see I.23.4.
For original question, see I.24.1.
For original question, see II.6.4.
For original question, see II.8.2.
For original question, see II.10.3.

3 I asked Mary if she was happy.
I asked if there was a doctor here.

3 Past reported question: same tense in
both CLAUSES.

4 Ask who telephoned the doctor.
Ask the policeman what has happened.
Ask which book is yours.

4 Target, SUBJECT: see II.7.3.
Target, SUBJECT: see II.9.8.
Target, SUBJECT: see I.6.4.

5 Ask that boy what his name is.
Ask him what *that* is.
Ask whose book this is.
Ask /how/ /where/ he is.

Ask /how much soup/ /how many sweets/
there is/ /there are/ in the pot.

5 Target, COMPLEMENT of *be*: see I.1.5.
Target, COMPLEMENT of *be*: see I.2.4.
Target, COMPLEMENT of *be*: see I.4.3.
Target, COMPLEMENT of *be*: see I.8.1,
I.10.1.

Target, COMPLEMENT of *there is* etc,
II.5.1–2.

6	Ask what Mr Turner is reading.	6	Target, OBJECT: see I.21.1.
	Ask what newspaper he reads.		Target, OBJECT: see I.24.5.
	Ask Tom what he did last night.		Target, OBJECT: see II.6.3.
	Ask me what I am looking at.		Target, OBJECT of PREPOSITION: see I.26.1.
	Ask who this car belongs to.		Target, OBJECT of PREPOSITION: see I.26.5.
7	Ask Tom where he went on Monday.	7	Target, ADV-P: see II.7.4.
	Ask Tom when he arrived.		Target, ADV-T: see II.7.4.
	Ask Tom when we can go home.		Target, ADV-T: see II.14.4.
	Ask Tom how long they have been here.		Target, ADV-T: see II.9.7.
	Ask Tom how often he's been to Paris.		Target, ADV-F: see II.9.6.

Lexicon

1 *ask (someone), [I] want to know, let me know, may I ask, may I enquire, tell me, [I] wonder*

III.3 -*self* and -*selves* as (a) reflexive pronouns and (b) emphatic pronouns; *each other*, *one another* as reciprocal pronouns

Models

I asked myself a question.
I asked that question myself.
They love /each other/ /one another/.

Notes

1	I cut my finger with a knife.	1	As in II.10.2.
	I cut myself with a knife.		[*my*]*self*, unstressed, OBJECT of vt.
2a	I [enjoy][1]ed myself.	2	*enjoy (a party), enjoy (-self)*, always vt.
	You [enjoy][1]ed yourself.		*yourself*, second PERS SING.
	He [enjoy][1]ed himself.		*himself*.
	She [enjoy][1]ed herself.		*herself*.
	We [enjoy][1]ed ourselves.		*ourselves*, PLURAL form as in I.14.7.
	You [enjoy][1]ed yourselves.		*yourselves*, second PERS PLUR.
	They [enjoy][1]ed themselves.		*themselves*.
b	An automatic watch winds itself.		*itself*.
3	Self-service. In a self-service shop one serves oneself; people serve themselves. One fills one's (own) basket.	3	*one* = anyone, SINGULAR; *oneself. People do that* = one does that. Stress -*self* in these examples.
4	She looked at herself in the mirror. Some people talk to themselves. He showed us a picture of himself.	4	-*self* as NP[2] in SP 7. -*self* after PREPOSITIONS, -*self* stressed. Contrast: *He showed us his picture*, ie the picture that belonged to him.
5	A mother always likes to have her family {round/around} her.	5	After (*a*)*round*, and *about*, meaning *around*, ie place, avoid the reflexive form.
6	I asked myself a question. She [bought][2] a [dress] for herself. She bought herself a dress.	6	SP 10, with -*self* unstressed, as NP[3]. SP 9a, with -*self* as NP[3], -*self* stressed. SP 10a, with -*self* as NP[3], -*self* unstressed.
7	The old man lives (all) by himself. I'll go /by myself/ /without you/. I did this (all) by myself.	7	= alone, without company; -*self* stressed. = alone, without company; -*self* stressed. = alone, without help; -*self* stressed.
8 *A*	I wonder if he really loved her.	8	See III.2.2.
B	I asked that question myself.		Contrast with 1 and 6 above. Here, -*self*, stressed, emphasises the SUBJECT.

9   They both [love]³d each other.
     They fought against each other.
     They all loved one another.
     They fought /among/ /amongst/
     themselves.
     They gave each other presents.
     They told one another stories.
10   John met Mary. Mary met John.
     John and Mary met (each other).

9   In these examples, *each other* refers to
     two people, *one another* to more than two,
     though these reciprocal PRONOUNS are
     often used interchangeably. Similarly,
     between two, among *more than two*,
     though *between* is widely used for more
     than two.

Lexicon
1 *cut, enjoy, hurt, look at, respect, talk about, think /of/ /about/, worry about*
2 *build, buy, choose, find, get, make, order, pour, save*
3 *dislike, fight against, hate, like, love, play with, think /of/ /about/*

III.4 Use of prepositional phrases on the pattern *by bus, on the bus, in the car.*
SP 5b and 5c: *Here comes the bus. Here it comes*

Models

We $\begin{Bmatrix} \text{took} \\ \text{caught} \end{Bmatrix}$ a bus.

We went into town by bus.
We went there by the 4.30 train.
I came /on the bus/ /in my car/.

Notes

1   A Shall we take a [taxi]¹ into town?

     B No, let's $\begin{Bmatrix} \text{take} \\ \text{catch} \end{Bmatrix}$ this [bus]².

        Let's go there by [bus]³.

2   We travelled to London by train.

3   A A train goes to town every hour.
        A train leaves once an hour.
        A bus goes every half hour.
     B Then let's go by the [bus]⁴.
        Let's get on this [bus]⁴.

4   A I didn't see you on the bus.
     B No, I came in my car.

5   A Did you come /by/ /on/ the 3.30 train?
     B No, I missed it. I came /by/ /on/ the
        4.15 (train) instead.

6   A How did you get here? By car?
     B No, by bicycle. On my bicycle.
     C I walked. I came on foot.

7   A This letter came by (the) post.
        Shall we send the answer by [post]⁵?
     B No, we must send it /by hand/ /by
        telegram/.

1   *take a taxi; into town*, see I.29.3.

     take or *catch* a [*bus*]¹.

     go by bus.

2   *by* [*bus*] normally follows an ADV indi-
     cating direction.

3

     This re-states the previous model.

     the can occur when a contrast is made
     or when a particular bus is referred to.
     Get /on/ /off/ a [*bus*].

4   *the* occurs after a PREP other than *by*;
     on or *in the bus, coach, train; on the
     boat, ship; in the car, taxi.*

5   *the* obligatory in these examples.
     miss a train = fail to catch it.
     = *instead* (*of the 3.30*).

6   Here, *get* = arrive.
     the will not occur after *by* in this case.
     on foot; no ARTICLE in this case.

7   *the* can occur between *by* and *post*.

     the does not occur between *by* and
     hand or between *by* and *telegram*.

8   *A* I'm waiting for a bus.   8

     B { One is coming.
          { There is one coming.

     C I'm waiting for the bus, too.

     B It's coming now.   Contrast INDEF *one* above, with DEF

     A Here it comes. In you go.   *it* SP 5b; cp SP 3a. (Do not use the
                                                                PROGRESSIVE with these patterns.)
          Here comes the bus.   SP 5c; cp SP 3b.

9   Your book is on the bed.   9   See note on *by the bus* in 3 above.
          There's a spider in the bed.   See also I.15.6 (*at school*), I.19.1,
          There are workmen in the school: (*in bed*), I.19.8 (*to bed*). Note that *the*
          they are painting the walls.   occurs when the PREP is changed
                                                                (*on the bed*) or when the meaning
                                                                associated with the fixed expression is
                                                                not intended; see I.19, Lex 1.

10a   He lives across the road.   10a *across*, *through*, *over* can indicate
          We're safely over (the obstacle).   position at the end of the movement
                                                                in I.19.9–10.

  b   The lesson is over. The game is up.   b = The /lesson/ /game/ has finished.

Lexicon
1 *boat, bus, coach, plane, ship, taxi, train*
2 *boat, bus, plane, train*
3 as for Lex 1 + *bicycle*
4 *boat, bus, coach, plane, train*
5 *hand, post, telegram, telephone*
See also Appendix G

III.5 *Used to* as a modal indicating past habit or state. Adv-f with past tense. Negative-interrogative, eg *Don't you know?*

Models   **Notes**
He used to be a sailor.
I never used to go by car.
Don't you remember?

1   He used to be a sailor.   1   *used to*, in SP 1, to indicate a past state,
                                                                in contrast with a different present state;
     He never goes to sea now.   *go to sea*: fixed expression.

2   She has lost a lot of weight.   2   *lose (a lot of) weight*: opposite, *put on
     She used to be quite fat.   (a lot of) weight*. *Used to* in SP 2.

3 *A* Where did this vase come from?   3

   B Don't you remember?   NEGATIVE-INTERROGATIVE, expecting the
        It used to be in the hall.   answer *Yes, (I do)*. *Used to* in SP 3.

4 *A* There used to be a stand for it.   4   *used to* in SP 3c.
        What (has) happened to it?   Either SIMPLE PAST or PRES PERF accept-
                                                                able in such a situation.

5 *A* { Have you got } a television set?   5
        { Do you have }
                                                                a /radio/ /television/ set.
   B We used to have. We used to have one.   *used to* in SP 4.
        We haven't got one now.

A My address is 16, [North] Street.

B Didn't you live in [Penn] Road?

6 *A* a I used to live there.
  I lived there for five years.
  I used to walk in the park.
  I $\left\{\begin{array}{l}\text{walked}\\\text{used to walk}\end{array}\right\}$ two or three miles
  every day.
  I often $\left\{\begin{array}{l}\text{walked}\\\text{used to walk}\end{array}\right\}$ round the park
  before breakfast.
  b I never used to go by car.

7   What did they usually give you for
     lunch at school?
8 *A* I like classical music.
  B Really? You never used to (like it).
  A Oh yes, I'm very fond of it now.
  B Hm, you never used to be.

[*North*] *Street*, stress on [*North*], not on *Street*.

NEG INTERROG, expecting reply *Yes* (, *I did*); [*Penn*] *Road*, stress on both [*Penn*] and *Road*.

6 a *used to* in SP 5.
     Exclude *used to* when length of period is given.
     SIMPLE PAST, *lived*, is used for single past event, or past state, or repeated events in the past.
     ADV-F, eg *often*, before SIMPLE PAST TENSE, cp I.29.3, and before *used to*.
  b A 'safe' NEGATIVE for *used to*. Regard *didn't use to*, like *did you use to?* as widely used in conversation but not in formal style.

7 A 'safe' way of avoiding *did they use to* in formal style.

8
The utterance can end with . . . *used to*.

Retain *be* in this case.

III.6 SP 2a, with adj modified by a prepositional phrase

Models
I/'m/ /feel/ sorry for Mary.
Well done. We/'re/ /feel/ proud of you.
Mary/'s/ /feels/ very angry with John.

Notes

1 *A* Jane isn't at all well.
  B Yes, I/'m/ /feel/ [anxious][1] about her.
2   I/'m/ /feel/ [anxious][1] about my exam.
3 *A* I can come on Sunday, but Tom can't.
  B Oh, I'm sorry about Tom.
4   Tom is [good][2] at mathematics.
5 *A* No one ever asks Mary out.
  B Yes, I/'m/ /feel/ [sorry][3] for her.
6   I'm hungry. I'm ready for lunch.
     That book is $\left\{\begin{array}{l}\text{not suitable}\\\text{unsuitable}\end{array}\right\}$ for /you/
     /our library/.
7   [Chalk] is different from [cheese].
8 *A* Why don't you drive any more?

  B Why not? Because I'm afraid.

1
ADJ+ *about*.
2 *exam*= examination, informal style.
3
  = sorry to hear it: cp 5 below.
4 ADJ+ *at*.
5 = asks her to go, or come, out.
  = I sympathise with her, ADJ+ *for*.

7 See II.22.6; ADJ+ *from*.
8 NEG INTERROG: You don't drive. Why not?

A Of what? What of?

B Of the traffic. I'm [afraid]⁴ of it.

9   Well done. We/'re/ /feel/ /proud/ of you.

10   This box is full. It's full up.
     It's full of old clothes.

11 A John's rather [keen]⁵ on Mary.
   B I think he's keener on football.

12   I'm very [grateful]⁶ to you.

13 A Mary is very, very angry.

   B Who with? With whom?

A With John. She's [angry]⁷ with John.

14 A What's /the matter/ /wrong/?
   B With you—or with your car?

= You're afraid of something. What is it?
PREP PHRASE as short answer.

9 ADJ + of.

10 Completely full—full to the top.

11 keen on = fond of; ADJ + on.

12 ADJ + to.

13 very, very—common conversational intensifier.
whom is obligatory immediately after a PREPOSITION.
ADJ + with.

Lexicon
1 *anxious, concerned, worried*
2 *bad, brilliant, clever, good, quick, slow*
3 *responsible, sorry*
4 *afraid, sick, tired*
5 *keen*
6 *faithful, grateful, loyal, polite*
7 *angry, annoyed, pleased*
See also Appendix F

III.7 -*ing* forms and past participles used adjectivally

Models
His story amused us.
His story was very amusing.
He himself was very amusing.
We ourselves were very amused.

Notes

1 A Tom's story amused us.
     His story was very amusing.
     He himself was very amusing.

     We ourselves were very amused.

   B It was an amusing story, wasn't it?
     Tom's an amusing fellow, isn't he?

   C Sometimes he's too amusing.
     I think he's rather boring.
     I was quite bored myself.

1

amusing, as ADJ used PREDICATIVELY, applied both to the story and to the story-teller.
We, the hearers, were amused, ADJ PREDIC.
amusing, ADJ used ATTRIBUTIVELY, applied to both the story and the story-teller.
amusing, amused can be modified by *very, too, rather, quite*, cp the ADJ, eg *amusing*, with the VERB, as in *He is amusing the children.*

2   I thought /he/ /his story/ was extremely interesting, didn't you?

2 -*ing* forms and PAST PARTICIPLES, as well as ordinary ADJS, can be modified by INTENSIFIERS other than *very*, eg *extremely*, ie to a very high degree.

3 *A* I'm [worried]¹.
  B What about?
  A I'm worried about /you/ /money/.
    Our expenses are very worrying.
  B I'm more worried about Jane.

4   You've behaved very badly. I'm
    [surprised]² at /you/ /your behaviour/.
    Your behaviour was most surprising.
5   /You were/ /Your behaviour was/
    embarrassing.
    We were all very [embarrassed]³ by it.
6   /He/ /His story/ was very interesting.
    We were all very [interested]⁴ in it.
7   I'm rather [tired]⁵ of this subject.
8   We're /entirely/ /completely/ [satisfied]⁶
    with /Tom/ /his work/.

3 PAST PARTICIPLES used ADJECTIVALLY can
  be modified by PREP PHRASES, as in III.6.

All the PARTICIPLES in the Lexicon below
can be compared as in II.22.

5

For *by* + NP after PASSIVE, see IV.20.1.

8 *entirely, completely,* ie to the maximum.

Lexicon

a Only certain participles can be used adjectivally. All the words in b can be used in the patterns
  an interesting man, an interesting thing, /he/ /it/ is interesting, he is interested (+ PREPOSITION + NP).
  In this Lexicon, both the *-ing* and the *-ed* PARTICIPLE can be modified by *very, too, rather, quite, so*
  and *extremely*

b After the *-ed,* the PREP *by* can be always used if the PARTICIPLE is part of a PASSIVE construction. But
  if the PARTICIPLE is used ADJECTIVALLY, as in III.7, other PREPOSITIONS can occur, as indicated in
  parentheses in the following: *alarm, amaze, amuse, annoy (annoyed with him, about something), astonish*
  (astonished at him), bore, confuse, disappoint (disappointed with /him/ /it/), disturb, embarrass, excite,
  fascinate, frighten (frightened of /him/ /it/), interest (interested in /him/ /it/), satisfy (satisfied with
  /him/ /it/), shock, surprise (surprised at /him/ /it/), thrill, worry (worried about /him/ /it/)
  Defer PASSIVE constructions till IV.22

III.8 Adjectives used predicatively but not attributively; SP 2b, with adj + infinitive; and adj + clause

Models
That child is afraid.
It's a very frightened child.
It's afraid to speak.
I'm sorry I can't help you.

Notes

1   That child is [afraid]¹.
    It's a frightened child.
    It's [ill]¹. It's a sick child.
2a Mary's delighted (with her presents).
 b Mr Bull is busy. He's engaged.
 c Dick and Anne are married.
    Bob and Sue are engaged.
3   We've arrived home. We're glad.
    We're very [glad]² to be home again.

4   The child doesn't (want to) speak.
    It's afraid.
    The child is [afraid]³ to speak.
    It's afraid to.

1 A number of ADJS can be used PREDICA-
  TIVELY but not ATTRIBUTIVELY (see I.8
  Lex, and Lex 1 below).
2a *delighted:* no corresponding ADJ in *-ing.*
 b Defer *engaging* = attractive.

3 *We've arrived:* the action has taken place.
  = We're very [glad] because we have
  arrived. The arrival has occurred.

4

In this case, the speaking has not
occurred.

5 We're at home. We're very pleased.
We're very [pleased]⁴ to be at home.
6 We've heard your news.
We're absolutely astonished.
We're absolutely [astonished]⁴ to hear
your news.
7 You're right, I'm sure.
I'm [sure]⁵ you're right.
I'm [sure]⁵ you did your best.
I'm [sure]⁵ they've arrived by now.
I'm [sure]⁵ you'll be happy here.
I'm [sure]⁵ you are, you did, they have,
you will.
8 I can't help you. I'm sorry.
I'm sorry I can't help you.
I'm afraid I can't help you.
I'm sorry if I'm late.
9 You can come after all. We're so
delighted. We're so [delighted]⁶ you
can come after all.

5 Certain PARTICIPLES used ADJECTIVALLY
can be followed by an INFINITIVE: Lex 4.
6

absolutely as an INTENSIFIER.

7 A number of ADJS (Lex 5) can be followed by a CLAUSE in the same way that
think etc (I.23.9) and *say* (III.1.5) can be.
The CONJUNCTION *that* is optional after
[*sure*].

8

I'm afraid+ CLAUSE= I'm sorry to say ...

9 *after all*= despite the uncertainty, etc;
certain PARTICIPLES used ADJECTIVALLY
can also be followed by a CLAUSE: see
Lex 6.

Lexicon
1 ADJECTIVE used PREDICATIVELY, but not, normally, ATTRIBUTIVELY: *afraid, alive, alone, ashamed, asleep, aware, awake; well, ill; sorry, glad, pleased; all right*
2 *glad, happy, lucky, proud, sorry.* See also IV.28, Lex 1–2
3 *able, afraid, anxious, certain, curious, ready, (un)willing.* See also IV.28, Lex 3
4 *amused, annoyed, astonished, delighted, disgusted, embarrassed, fascinated, interested, pleased, satisfied, shocked, surprised, terrified*
5 *afraid, certain, glad, positive, sorry, sure*
6 *astonished, delighted, pleased, satisfied, surprised*

III.9 SP 2 and SP 1, with *be* replaced by *get* or *become*

Models   Notes
Get ready quickly.
He became very famous.
He became a famous inventor.

1 'Aren't you ready yet, Tom?
[Get]¹ ready quickly, will you?'
I'm getting ready.
Tom got ready at once.
2 A I've just had 'flu, so I soon get tired.
I'll go to bed soon.
B Don't [get]¹ too cold, will you?
3 You soon get [tired]² [of television].
4 Bob and Sue /are going to/ /will/ get
married next month. They'll soon get
used to /each other/ /married life/.
5 A Tom used to be quite thin.
He's got /fat/ /(much) fatter/.
B He's /getting fatter and fatter/
/putting on more and more weight/.

1 = You're not ready. You ought to be.
get not replaceable by *become* here.
will you? with rising intonation.
PAST of *get ready. At once*=immediately.
2 *I've had 'flu:* see II.1.4. 1st *soon*=
quickly; 2nd= in the near future.
will you? with falling intonation.
3 *You* meaning *one* as in III.3.3.
4 See III.8.2c.
/be/ /get/ *used to*= /be/ /get/ accustomed
to.
5 *used to* as in III.5.
PRESENT PERF of *get fat.*
All COMPARATIVES can be intensified in
this way.

6a   Most parents $\left\{\begin{array}{l}\text{get}\\\text{become}\end{array}\right\}$ anxious about their children.

Bob and Sue $\left\{\begin{array}{l}\text{got}\\\text{became}\end{array}\right\}$ engaged last month.

They've $\left\{\begin{array}{l}\text{got}\\\text{become}\end{array}\right\}$ engaged (to each other).

6a   When *get* and *become* are interchangeable, regard *become* as more formal.

b   Tom is $\left\{\begin{array}{l}\text{getting}\\\text{becoming}\end{array}\right\}$ interested in science.

b   *get* and *become*, progressive aspect.

7a   Edison $\left\{\begin{array}{l}\text{got}\\\text{became}\end{array}\right\}$ interested in electricity.

7a   Prefer *become* in formal narrative.

b   He invented the electric bulb and became very [famous][3].

b   *the electric bulb*, ie that class of thing. *become* not replaceable by *get* when followed by more 'dignified' ADJS (Lex 3).

We /are/ /'ve got/ /'ve become/ used to electricity now.

8   He became a very famous [inventor][4]. Lister became a doctor. His students became doctors.

8   *become* not replaceable by *get* in SP 1.

9   *A* What did you do when your wife became so ill?

B I ran out and got a doctor.

9

get + NP = obtain, fetch.

10   When water freezes it becomes ice.

10   *become* not replaceable by *get*.

11   Get $\left\{\begin{array}{l}\text{in}\\\text{into}\end{array}\right\}$ the car.

Don't get into trouble.

11   SP 3: *into* obligatory when used META-PHORICALLY, eg before *trouble*, *difficulties*.

Lexicon

1 Use *get*, not *become*, with IMPERATIVES, and with ADJS referring to personal physical condition, eg *cold, dry, hot, hungry, sleepy, thirsty, tired, warm, wet*
2 Use *get* informally, or *become* more formally with *angry, anxious, familiar, fat, fit, fond of . . ., hard, ill, jealous, keen on . . ., sick, soft, strong, tall, thin, weak; annoyed, bored, engaged (to . . .), interested (in . . .), tired of . . ., worried*
3 Use *become* with *aware (of . . .), embarrassed, famous, proud*
4 As in I.5, Lex 1

III.10 Simple constructions beginning with *it*, when *it* does not refer to an NP already mentioned

Models
It /seems/ /feels/ colder today.
It gets dark early in winter.
It's a pity.
It doesn't matter.

Notes

1 *A* It /seems/ /feels/ [colder][1] than it was yesterday.

B Yes, winter's coming.

1 See I.9.3, II.1.5 and II.20.3.

2 *A* When does it get [dark]?
  B About five o'clock. It gets dark early
    in winter.
  C It gets dark suddenly in the tropics.
3   It suddenly got very dark.

4 *A* Hurry (up). It's getting late.
  B It's all right. It's early yet.
5 *A* Is it raining?
  B It is indeed. It's raining hard.
6 *A* Will you go on the excursion tomorrow?
  B It depends.

  A On what?
  B (It depends) on [the weather].
7 *A* How do you open this safe?
    It's [impossible]³ (to open it).
  B It's very [easy]⁴ (to open it).
  A It may be easy for *you*.
    It seems easy when *you* do it.
8 *A* John can't come this evening.
  B What a [pity]⁵. It's (such) a [pity].
  A Yes, it's a [pity] he can't come.
  C It doesn't matter.
9 *A* Thanks very much. I'm most grateful.
  B Not at all. It's a pleasure.
    I'm so glad I could help you.
    It's been a pleasure to meet you.
  A You're very kind. That is very [kind]⁶
    of you.
  B Don't thank me. It's [not necessary]⁷.
10   Don't say that; it's [unkind]⁸.

2 Cp III.9.2.

suddenly as ADV-M = quickly.
3 *suddenly* in a very short time after the
  event previously mentioned.

5 I.20.4.
  hard, see II.23.6, note.
6

  ie my decision depends on circumstances.

  depend on.
7

  = To open it is easy.
  = Perhaps it is easy for you.

8

  See II.26.6.
  It's a pity + CLAUSE.

9 *most grateful*: cp *most carefully*, II.23.1.
  Not at all or *Don't mention it.*
  As in III.8.8.
  = Meeting you has been a pleasure.
  See also IV.29.9.

  ie thanking me is not necessary.
10 ie what you said is unkind.

Lexicon
1 *cold, cool, warm, hot*
2 Lex 1 + *dark, light*
3 *essential, important, (im)possible*
4 *easy, difficult, hard*
5 *nuisance, pity, shame*
6 *generous, good, helpful, kind, sweet, wrong*
7 *important, necessary, unimportant, unnecessary*
8 *impolite, unkind, rude*

Lexical Supplement to III.9 and III.10. Inchoative verbs, or 'resulting'
copulas: *become, come, fall, get, go, grow, run, turn*

Models
He grew older and wiser.
The leaves turned yellow.
The child fell fast asleep.

Notes

1a Be quiet. Be silent. Be still.
    Be prepared. Be ready by six.
 b Get ready. Get washed.
    Get (un)dressed. Get up. Get out.

2a They got very tired.
    It suddenly got dark.
    We're getting used to the noise.
 b He's getting to be a good player.
    I got to know him (well).

3a He became /angry/ /used to it/.
 b He became proud and ambitious.
 c He became a distinguished writer.

4a He grew /old/ /older/ and /wise/ /wiser/.

    She grew thin and pale.

 b He grew to be more like his father.

5a Her dreams came true.
    The handle came loose.
    A button has come off (my coat).
    The envelope came unstuck.
    The parcel came /undone/ /untied/.
 b I came to realise the truth.

6a She went pale when she heard the news.
 b He went bald. She went mad.
    All our knives went rusty.
    The food went bad, the milk went sour.

7a The milk turned sour.

    The weather turned /cold/ /colder/.
    The leaves on the trees turned yellow.
 b He turned traitor.
 c Water turned /to/ /into/ ice.
 d She turned into a princess.
    The fairy turned him into a frog.

8a The child fell /ill/ /(fast) asleep/.
 b The post /became/ /fell/ vacant.

9   The stream ran dry. Supplies ran low.
    We ran /out of/ /short of/ flour.

10 The damp atmosphere /made the knives
    go/ /caused the knives to go/ rusty.
    The thundery weather /made the milk/
    /caused the milk to/ /go/ /turn/ sour.

1a In these IMPERATIVES, the emphasis is
    on the final state, eg *Be ready by six*.
 b Here, the emphasis is on a *change* of
    state: you're not ready now, so *get
    ready*.

2a *get* as in III.9.2 and accompanying Lex.
    As in III.10.2 and accompanying Lex.
    As in III.9.7.
 b = He's beginning to be one.
    = state of 'not knowing' changed to
    that of 'knowing (well)'.

3a *become* replacing *get*, as in III.9.3.
 b *become*, not *get*, as in III.9.7b.
 c *become* only, as in III.9.8.

4a *grow, fat, old, strong, tall, tired* (= no
    longer interested), *thin, weak, wise*.
    This suggests a long process: cp *went
    pale*, 6a below.

 b *He got to be* (2b above) replaceable by
    He grew to be.

5a *come*.

    See V.3.8.

 b *Got to know* replaceable by *came to
    know*.

6a This suggests a sudden change: cp 4a.
 b This suggests a change for the worse.

7a *turn*: A chemical or physical deteriora-
    tion.
    Usable with COMPARATIVES.

 b Change of role, deterioration.
 c Change into a different substance.
 d Complete change of body and person-
    ality.

8a *fall*: usable with a few ADJECTIVES
    only, not with COMPARATIVES.

9   *run*.

10 *make* and *cause* stg *to* indicating how a
    change in state came about.

Note: All the verbs in this supplement, except *be*, can occur in the PROGRESSIVE aspect

III.11 Verbs occurring either in SP 5 or in SP 7 (see I.25) and prepositional verbs occurring only in SP 7

Models

They're talking about us.
She's smiling at you.
We're longing for the holidays.

Notes

1 You must obey (/me/ /the rules/).
  This box contains books.

1 *obey* as vi, in SP 5, or as vt in SP 6.
  contain only in SP 6: STATIVE VERB.

2 I can't afford a car.
  I can't afford to take a holiday.

2 *afford*, as vt in SP 6, or as vt with INFINITIVE as OBJECT, in SP 6b, as in III.1.1.

3 Those two girls are talking.
 a They're talking about us.

3 *talk*, as vi in SP 5.
 a *talk about* NP, SP 7: we are the subject of their talk.

 b *A* You look very untidy.
   B I don't care (about that).

 b
   As in II.1.2.
   care as vi in SP 5, or *care about* in SP 7.

 c She's smiling (at you).
 d We're arriving (at the station).

 c *smile* (*at*).
 d *arrive* (*at*): *arrive on* or *in* also occurs if the destination is a surface or a space.

 e I must apologise (for my mistake).
 f I'll call (for you) at six.

 e *apologise* (for a mistake).
 f *call* (*for*) = go to a house etc for someone or something.

 g Mother's suffering (from a headache).
 h Many people died (of hunger).
 i You must speak (to Mary) (about John).
 j I agree (with you) (about that).

 g *suffer* (from a pain or illness).
 h *die* (*of*).
 i *speak* (*to*) = *to* indicating direction of talk.
 j *agree* (*with someone*) (*about something*).

4 Point (to the man in the picture).
  Don't point (at people): it's rude.

4 *Point to*, in that direction.
  point at, as if aiming at a target.

5 Did you attend (the lecture)?
  Attention. Attend (to me) please.

5 *attend* a function. SP 6.
  attend to—give your attention to. SP 7.

6 I've been thinking (about the problem).
  Don't worry, I'm thinking of you.

6 *think* as vi in SP 5; or in SP 7.
  think of, only in SP 7; you're in my thoughts.

7a Mother cares for us all.
 b I don't care for that photograph.
 c We're longing for the holidays.
 d Water consists of oxygen and hydrogen.
 e Don't lean on that table; it'll break.
 f We'll deal with this subject tomorrow.

7a *care for*, only in SP 7 = take care of.
 b *care for*, SP 7 = like.
 c *long for*, SP 7.
 d *consist of*, SP 7, 'STATIVE'.
 e *lean on*, SP 7.
 f *deal with*, SP 7.

Lexicon
See Appendix A5

III.12 SP 7a with the preposition closely linked with the verb, and SP 7b, with the preposition associated with the object

Models

Thank you for your letter.
Please remind me of your name.
I'll take care of you.

Notes

1	Please remind me to post this letter.	1	SP 6c, as in III.1.1: *you* /remind/, *I'll* [post].
2	Promise me to post it today. Promise me not to drop it.	2	Exceptionally, when *promise* occurs in SP 6c, *you* [promise] and *you* must [post]. As in III.1.3: *you* [promise], *you* won't [drop it].
3	Ask (him) (to come in). Ask (him) (a question). Ask (him) (for his tickets). Ask (him) (about his mother).	3	SP 5, 6 or 6c. SP 5, 6 or 10. SP 5, 6 or 7a = May I have your ticket? SP 5, 6 or 7a, eg How is your mother?
4	You must pay. You must pay him. You must pay (him) (the money). You must pay (him) (for the ticket).	4	*pay* (vi) or *pay someone*, or *pay some money* or *pay someone some money*. *pay* in SP 5, 6, 7 or 7a.
5	I must charge (you) for the damage. Divide (this number) by two. Divide this cake between you (two), among you (all).	5	*charge* (= make you pay) in SP 7 or 7a. *divide* (a number) *by*. *divide* something *between* or *among*.
6a	Tell me (all) (about the party).	6a	*tell* someone *about* something or someone.
b	Thank you (for your letter).	b	*thank* someone *for* something.
c	I borrowed a book (from the library).	c	*borrow* something *from*.
d	Please remind me (of your name).	d	*remind* someone *of*.
e	I congratulate you (on your success).	e	*congratulate* someone *on*.
f	May I discuss this (with my husband)?	f	*discuss* something *with* someone.
7a *A*	Oh, I've hurt my leg.	7a	
B	Don't make such a fuss (about it).		*make* a fuss about something; SP 7b.
b	You'll be all right. I'll take care of you. I'll take care of your luggage.	b	*take care of* something. Contrast: *Take care! Take care not to bump your head.*
c	Don't make fun of me. I don't like it.	c	*make* fun of someone or something.
d	Don't take any notice (of that man).	d	*take* notice of someone or something.
e	Pay attention (to your work).	e	*pay* attention to someone or something: cp *attend to*, III.11.5.
f	Be careful. You'll set fire to the house.	f	*set fire to* something.

Lexicon
See Appendix A6

III.13 Relative clauses in which the relative pronoun is the subject

Models	**Notes**
He's the man who lives next door. There's the 'plane that crashed. That's the 'plane which flew over our house a moment ago.	

1	That's Mr Green. He lives next door. That's the man $\begin{Bmatrix} \text{who} \\ \text{that} \end{Bmatrix}$ lives next door. He's the man $\begin{Bmatrix} \text{who} \\ \text{that} \end{Bmatrix}$ lives next door.	1	*He lives* . . . He's the man *who lives* . . . Relative CLAUSE on SP 5; *who*, RELATIVE PRONOUN, SUBJECT, personal, replaceable by *that*.

2 Mr Green has a moustache.

He's the man $\left\{\begin{array}{l}\text{who}\\\text{that}\end{array}\right\}$ has a moustache.

He's the man with a moustache.
He's the man without a hat.

2

who has [a moustache] replaceable by

with [a moustache].
who hasn't replaceable by *without.*

3 They're the people $\left\{\begin{array}{l}\text{who}\\\text{that}\end{array}\right\}$ live next door.

3 *who* with PLURAL antecedent.

4 That man stole my purse.

That's the man $\left\{\begin{array}{l}\text{who}\\\text{that}\end{array}\right\}$ stole my purse.

4

RELATIVE CLAUSE on SP 6.

5 *A* That lady asked for soup.

  B Are you the lady $\left\{\begin{array}{l}\text{who}\\\text{that}\end{array}\right\}$ asked for soup?

5

RELATIVE CLAUSE on SP 7.

6 That's the boy $\left\{\begin{array}{l}\text{who}\\\text{that}\end{array}\right\}$ told a policeman about the robbery.

6 RELATIVE CLAUSE on SP 7a.

7 That's the kind gentleman $\left\{\begin{array}{l}\text{who}\\\text{that}\end{array}\right\}$ took care of us.

7 RELATIVE CLAUSE on SP 7b.

8 That's the man $\left\{\begin{array}{l}\text{who}\\\text{that}\end{array}\right\}$ gave

$\left\{\begin{array}{l}\text{this watch to me.}\\\text{me this watch.}\end{array}\right.$

8 RELATIVE CLAUSE on SP 9 and 10.

9 A song bird is a bird $\left\{\begin{array}{l}\text{that}\\\text{which}\end{array}\right\}$ sings.

Song birds are birds $\left\{\begin{array}{l}\text{that}\\\text{which}\end{array}\right\}$ sing.

9 RELATIVE PRONOUN with ANIMATE, non-personal ANTECEDENT. Notice CONCORD.

10 An elephant is an animal $\left\{\begin{array}{l}\text{that}\\\text{which}\end{array}\right\}$ has a trunk instead of a nose.
It's an animal with a trunk instead of a nose.

10 *that* replaceable by *which* when the ANTECEDENT is non-personal.

11 Look at that 'plane. It crashed yesterday.

There's the plane $\left\{\begin{array}{l}\text{that}\\\text{which}\end{array}\right\}$ crashed yesterday.

11

that replaceable by *which* when ANTECEDENT is INANIMATE.

12 An aeroplane is a machine $\left\{\begin{array}{l}\text{that}\\\text{which}\end{array}\right\}$ flies in the air.

A screwdriver is a tool $\left\{\begin{array}{l}\text{that}\\\text{which}\end{array}\right\}$ turns a screw and drives it into wood.

12 RELATIVE CLAUSE serving to build up a DEFINITION.

III.14 Relative clauses in which the subject does not refer to the same person or thing as the antecedent; preposition's at the end of relative clauses

Models

That's the coat I want.
Is this the magazine she asked for?
This is the watch he gave me.

Notes

1   That's Mr Green. We often see him.
    That's the man (   ) we often see.

    1 Contrast III.13.1.
    we is the SUBJECT of this RELATIVE CLAUSE,
    the zero relative pronoun referring to *man*
    is the OBJECT.

2   I want that coat, please.
    Yes, that's the coat (   ) I want.

    2
    I is the SUBJECT of this RELATIVE CLAUSE.

3 *A* Who are those people?
  B I met them last year. They're some
    people (   ) I met last year.

    3
    I met *them*—
    —people *I met*.

4   That man took my purse.
    That's the purse (   ) he took.

    4 See III.13.4.

5   That lady asked for a magazine.
    Is this the magazine (   ) she asked for?
  A I can't find one of my books.
  B Is this the one (   ) you're looking for?

    5 See III.13.5.

    the one = the book.

6 *A* John told a policeman something about
    a robbery.
  B Is that the policeman (   ) he told?
  C There was a robbery last night.
    Was that the robbery (   ) he told the
    policeman about?

    6 See III.13.6.

7   That kind man took care of us.
    We're the children (   ) he took care of.

    7 See III.13.7.

8 *A* That man gave me a watch.
    This is the watch (   ) he gave me.
  B So you're the boy (   ) he gave the
    watch to, are you?

    8 See III.13.8.

NB In all the above models, a RELATIVE PRONOUN (*who(m)* or *that* referring to humans,
otherwise *that* or *which*) could be inserted where the parentheses are, though the RELATIVE
PRONOUN is generally absent when the SUBJECT of the RELATIVE CLAUSE is a PERSONAL PRONOUN.

9   This is the house that Jack built.

    9 Here *that* is inserted for the sake of
    rhythm, as well as to separate the two
    NPS, *the house* and *Jack*.

10   Ah, that's just what I want.
    This is where I live.

    10 *just* = exactly; *what* = the thing which.
    where = the place where, the place in
    which.

  A It happened last week.
  B So that's when it happened.

    when = the time when, the time at which.

III.15 Simple examples of adverbial clauses, beginning with *as*, *because*, *although*, *when*, *as soon as*, *before*, *since*

Models
I want to speak English, like Tom.
I want to speak it as Tom does.
I'm staying at home, although I feel
much better today.

Notes

1   John is not clever, like Tom.
    He's not as clever as Tom is.

    1 *like*, PREPOSITION, followed by NP.
    See II.20.1: *as*, CONJUNCTION + CLAUSE.

2   I want to speak English, like Tom.
     I want to speak it as Tom does.
     I wanted to speak it as Tom did.

3   I can hardly see the blackboard, (and)
     so I have to sit nearer the front.
     I want to sit nearer the front because
     I can hardly see the board.

     Because I can't see very well, I have to
     sit nearer the front.
     Because I couldn't see very well, I had to
     sit nearer the front.

4   I feel much better, but I'm staying at
     home today.

     I'm staying at home {though / although} I feel
     much better.

     {Though / Although} I feel much better, I'm
     staying at home today.

     I went out yesterday {though / although} I still
     had a little fever.
     I still had a little fever, (and) yet I
     put on my coat and went out.

5   I have tea when I get home.
     When I get home, I have tea.
     I have tea as soon as I get home.
     As soon as I get home, I have tea.
     I telephoned you as soon as I got home,
     but you weren't in.

6   Tom cleans his teeth before he goes
     to bed.
     Before he goes to bed, Tom cleans etc.
     Before he went to bed, Tom cleaned etc.

7 A How long have you lived here?
   B I've lived here since I was a boy.
8 A Why are you sitting near the front?
   B Because I can't see very well.
   A When do you have tea?
   B As soon as I get home.
   A How long have you lived here?
   B Since I was a boy.

2   PRESENT TENSE in both CLAUSES.
     PAST TENSE in both CLAUSES.

3   MAIN CLAUSE followed by *so*-CLAUSE which
     cannot precede the MAIN CLAUSE.
     Previous model re-phrased, with CLAUSE
     beginning with *because*: I repeated,
     II.30.7. *Near, nearer, nearest.*
     A *because*-CLAUSE can come before, as
     well as after, the MAIN CLAUSE.
     PAST TENSE in both CLAUSES. Note the
     comma, obligatory when SUBORDINATE
     CLAUSE precedes.

4   ie I am at home now.
     Previous model re-phrased, with CLAUSE
     beginning *though*, replaceable by
     although.

     PAST TENSE in both CLAUSES.

     A *yet*-CLAUSE, like a *so*-CLAUSE (3 above)
     can only follow the MAIN CLAUSE.

5

     as soon as: I have tea immediately
     after my arrival.
     PAST TENSE in three CLAUSES.

7 See II.9.7.
   PRESENT PERF + *since* + PAST TENSE.

8

   An ADVERBIAL CLAUSE can be used as a
   'short answer' or as a 'minor sentence'
   in conversation, but it does not constitute a 'complete sentence' in formal
   composition.

III.16 *If*-sentences with the same tense in both clauses; and sentences with
       'll, *will*, *shall* in main clause, and present tense in the *if*-clause

Models   **Notes**
We stay in school if it rains.
We stayed in school if it rained.

You'll get very wet if it rains.
If it rains, you'll get very wet.

1	We stay in school if it rains. If it rains, we don't go outside. If it was too cold, we stayed indoors.	1 PRESENT TENSE in both CLAUSES; *if* replaceable by *when* in this case. PAST TENSE in both CLAUSES.
2	*A* Aren't you going to take an umbrella? *B* No, it doesn't matter. I won't bother. *A* I think it {'ll / 's going to} rain. You'll get very wet if it rains. You'll get very wet if it does. You'll be sorry if you don't take an umbrella.	2 It will probably rain. *'ll* in main CLAUSE. PRESENT in *if*-CLAUSE: an example of Type 1 *if*-SENTENCE.
3	If it's wet, there won't be a picnic. There will be one, unless it rains.	3 *If*-CLAUSE can come before or after the main CLAUSE; *unless*=if . . . not.
4	*A* Will there be a picnic tomorrow? *B* Yes, if it /'s fine/ /doesn't rain/ /isn't raining/. *A* Is there going to be a picnic tomorrow? *B* Not if /it rains/ /it's raining/. Yes, unless /it rains/ /it's raining/.	4 *if*-CLAUSE as 'short answer'. *will* replaceable by *going to*: see II.13. PROGRESSIVE possible here, but not in 2 above.
5	I'll sit near the door, in case there's a fire. {If there's a / In case of} fire, ring the alarm bell immediately.	5 FUTURE in MAIN CLAUSE, PRESENT after *in case*+ CLAUSE; *in case of*+ NP= if there is+ NP.
6	*A* Will you be in London again soon? *B* I'm not really sure. *A* Well, 'phone me if you are.	6 IMPERATIVE+ *if*-CLAUSE, PRESENT.
7	Don't go away yet. I may need you. Don't go away yet, in case I need you.	7 Re-phrasing of the previous model.
8	*A* I'm sure it's going to rain. *B* If it *is* going to rain, I'll take an umbrella.	8 *be going to*, but not *'ll*, *will*, *shall*, when they refer to the future, may occur in the *if*-CLAUSE.

Lexicon
1 *look, seem, sound*

III.17 Temporal clauses with the present tense, when *'ll, will, shall* occur in the main clause. Use of *until* and *by* (a certain time)

Models	Notes
I'll give him these letters when I see him. I'll see you as soon as I'm free. We'll wait until seven o'clock. We'll leave by eight o'clock.	
1 We go to bed when we're tired or when we're ill.	1 PRESENT TENSE in both CLAUSES: *when* not replaceable by *if* in this context.

2   Mr Green will be here at three.
    I'll see him then.
    I'll give him these letters when
    I see him.

2   *I'll see him* in an independent CLAUSE.
    I'll give in MAIN CLAUSE, *I see* in temporal
    CLAUSE.

3 *A on bus:* I want to get off at Penn Street.
    Will you tell me when we get there,
    please?
  B I'll tell you just *before* we get there.

3   Temporal CLAUSE introduced by CON-
    JUNCTION *before*: *just* = a very short time.

4   He'll get up when the bell rings.
    He'll wake up if that dog barks.

4   The bell will ring. Then he'll get up.
    That dog may bark. If it does, he'll
    wake up.

5 *A* When will you arrive?
    Let me know when you'll arrive.
  B I'll arrive at three on Monday.
    I'll 'phone you when I arrive.

5   Indirect question, as in III.2.7.

    Temporal CLAUSE as in 2 and 3 above.

6 *A* Come and see me before you go.
  B I'll see you as soon as I'm free.

6   IMPERATIVE in main CLAUSE, then
    present.

7 *A* Don't go before I get back.

7   *get back* = return.

  B I'll wait $\left\{\begin{array}{l}\text{till}\\\text{until}\end{array}\right\}$ you get back.

    until and *till* interchangeable.

8a We'll [wait][1] until seven o'clock.
    We'll wait until then.

8a The act of *waiting* occupies a *period* of
    time which will extend until seven
    o'clock.

    We'll [leave][2] /before/ /by/ eight.
    We'll leave /before/ /by/ then.

    The act of *leaving* takes place at a *point*
    of time and will occur *by* (= not later than
    and perhaps before) eight o'clock.

    We won't leave until eight o'clock.

    Our *not leaving* will continue till eight.

  b We'll be ready by the time you get back.

  b *by the time* + CLAUSE.

9   We'll /be/ /get/ here by nine.
    We'll /be/ /stay/ here till ten.

9   *be* meaning *get* or *arrive*.
    be meaning *stay* or *remain*.

10 We waited until seven o'clock.
    We left /before/ /by/ eight.
    We didn't leave till eight.
    We /were/ /got/ there by nine.
    We /were/ /stayed/ there till ten.

10 *by* and *until* with the PAST TENSE.

Lexicon

1 VERBS referring to actions occupying a period of time: *play, read, sleep, study, wait, work; not beginning, not finishing,* etc
2 VERBS referring to actions taking place at a point of time: *begin, finish, get up, go to sleep, leave, start,
  stop, wake up*

III.18 Past progressive, progressive aspect as in I.18

Models

When I got up this morning, it was
raining.
It happened while I was working in
the garden.

Notes

1 *A* Look out of the window. What's the
weather like?
 B It's raining /hard/ /slightly/.
2 *C* He looked out five minutes ago.
It was raining.
 D Was it raining very hard?
 C Yes, it was *or* No, it wasn't.

3 *A* What was Tom doing when you went to
his house last night?

 B Watching television.
 A Were his parents watching too?
 B Yes, they were. No, they weren't.
4 *A* What did Tom do when you banged on
the door?

 B He jumped up (out of his chair).
5   Mr Turner usually reads the newspaper
while he is having his breakfast.
He never says a word during /the meal/
/that time/.
6   I'll do this while you're doing that.
7 *A* Did you see the accident?
 B No, I didn't. I was working in the
garden when it happened.

It happened while I was working in the
garden.
8a   There's someone outside. He's waiting.
There's someone waiting outside.
 b   There he is. He's standing by the gate.

There he is, standing by the gate.
9a   There were some children in the garden
when I came in. They were playing.
There were some children playing in the
garden when I came in.
 b   There he was, standing by the gate.
 c   He ran towards me, waving a piece of
paper.

III.19 Present perfect progressive

Models
I have been waiting for three hours.
It has been raining; but it's stopped.

1 *A* You haven't done any work at all.
 B How do you know (I haven't)?

1
PRESENT PROGRESSIVE, as in I.18.
2 *looked out* (of the window).

Q-*Yes/No*.
Short AFFIRMATIVE and NEGATIVE
answers.
3 Q-*What*, asking for VP. Here *doing*
suggests action in progress; *went*, an
event occurring at a point of time when
that action was in progress.
Short answer, as in I.18.3.
Use *was* and *were* as in II.3.

4 Cp this question with first question
in 3. What happened at that point
in time?
up, ADV PARTICLE, + PREPOSITION, *out of*.

5
while = during the time that, + CLAUSE.
during as in II.3.5; cp *while* + CLAUSE.

6 Tense sequence as in III.17.4.
7

when-CLAUSE could also precede MAIN
CLAUSE.

8a SP 3c and 5.
SP 3c, with NP + PARTICIPLE CLAUSE.
 b SP 3a and SP 5, with PREP PHRASE
adjunct.
SP 3a, with PARTICIPLE CLAUSE.
9

 b as in 8b above.
 c ie he ran towards me. He was waving a
piece of paper.

Notes

1 PRESENT PERFECT, as in II.8.

A Because I have been watching you ever since the class started.

PRESENT PERFECT with PROGRESSIVE aspect, emphasising action in progress during a period ending now. In this model, the action is continuing.

2 A I'm sorry $\left\{ \begin{array}{l} \text{I'm} \\ \text{to be} \end{array} \right\}$ late.
   Have you been waiting long?
  B No, I haven't (been).
   I haven't been waiting long.
     or Yes, I have (been).
   I've been waiting (for) a long time, (for) the last three hours.
  A Really? Do you mean you've been waiting since ten o'clock?
  B I've been waiting since the 'plane landed, of course.

2 As in III.8.8 and III.8.3.

Q–*Yes/No; long* = for a long time.
Short NEGATIVE answer.
Full NEGATIVE.
Short AFFIRMATIVE answers.
for (as in II.9.7) introducing length of the period extending till now.

since + point of time when period began; *since* + CLAUSE with SIMPLE PAST TENSE, as in III.15.7 and III.19.1. See also II.9.7.

  A What have you been doing all that time?
  B Waiting for you. Walking about.
   I've been reading a detective story for the last few hours.

Q–*What*, asking for VP.
Short answers, as in III.18.3.

last obligatory in this structure with *few*.

3 A Is it raining?
  B It *has* been.
   It's been raining quite hard.

   But it has stopped now. It's stopped.

3

been obligatory in this short answer.
It has been raining during the period ending now: it is not raining now.
Contrast the progressive with *it has stopped* which refers to action completed.

4 A Someone has been sitting in my chair.
  B How do you know?
  A It's still warm.

4 The PRESENT PERFECT, whether PROGRESSIVE or non-PROGRESSIVE, is often used with reference to evidence of activity during the period ending now.

5 Something is wrong with my typewriter.
   Who has been using it?

5

ie doing something I disapprove of.

6 A Where have you been?
  B Upstairs. I've been packing your suitcase.
   I've been upstairs packing your suitcase.

6

Cp III.18.9.

III.20 *Would, could* and *might* in more hesitant requests, etc, than those dealt with in II.14 and II.15

Models
Would you open the door, please?
Would you like some more coffee?
Could I see you for a moment?

Notes

1 Would you have a cup of tea?
   Would you open that door, please?
   Would you open that door!

1 *Will*, as in II.15.1–3, replaceable by the more hesitant *Would*.

2 *A* I want some tea, please.
       I would like some tea, please.
       I'd like some tea, please.
   B So would I.

3 *A* Would you like some more coffee?
   B Thank you⎱,I would.
       Yes please ⎰
       or {Thank you, no more⎱.
            {No more, thank you⎰

4   I would [like]¹ to [see the manager].
       Would you be so kind as to tell him?

5 *A* Would you like to see a film?
   B Yes, I'd like to.
       or No, I don't think {I would.
                               {so.
   A What would you like to do then?
   B (I'd prefer) to go for a walk.

6 *A* Would you like me to carry that?
   B Thank you⎱.
       Yes please ⎰
       or It's all right. I can manage.
       I wouldn't like to bother you.

7 *A* I'd like to have a word with you.
       Could I see you now?
   B No, I'm afraid not. I'm busy.
   A Could I see you tomorrow, then?

   B Yes, (I think) you could.

8 *A* Could you open that door for me?
   B Yes, certainly.

9 *A* Might I borrow your typewriter for
       a moment, do you think?
   B Perhaps you might, if you're very
       careful with it.
       or I'm sorry, you can't. I'm using it
       myself.

10 *A* Be careful of that chair. It might be
       unsafe. It might collapse.
   B *Will* it collapse?
   A It might or it might not.
       It mightn't: you might be lucky.
   B Might it?

2a As in II.14.1.
    Not so demanding as previous model.
    I would contracted to *I'd*.
  b See II.25.1.

3   Q-*Yes/No*. More hesitant than II.15.1.
    Thank you = *Yes please* in reply to an
    offer.
    Thank you alone might indicate accept-
    ance.

4   See Lexicon. *I would* [*like*] etc referring
    to wishes and preferences for the
    future.

5

    No I wouldn't would be a rude rebuff.

6   *Would like* in SP 6c; cp II.15.5.

    As in 3 above.

    wouldn't like to.

7

    Can (II.14.2) replaceable by more
    hesitant *could*.
    Can (II.17.1) replaceable by more
    hesitant *could*.
    Less definite, less committal, than
    you can.

8   *Can* (II.15.8) replaceable by more
    hesitant *could*.

9   *May* (II.14.3) replaceable by very
    hesitant *Might*; the *do you think* tag
    stresses the hesitancy.

    Avoid *you might not* in this situation.

10 See II.16.4. *May* replaceable by *might*,
    which expresses even less certainty.
    Is that a certainty?
    Both possibilities are open.

    Do not use *May it?* in this sense.

Lexicon
1 *hate, like, love, prefer*

III.21 Prohibition, and absence of obligation. *Must not ;* and *need* as modal and as full verb. See also V.12

Models
You must not do that.
You need not (do it).
You don't need to (do it).

Notes

1 DANGER. No smoking within 50 yards of this sign.
Put out that cigarette.

Didn't you see the sign?
You must not smoke here.
You're not allowed to (smoke).

1 Smoking forbidden.

or *Put that cigarette out :* structure II.11.6.

ie smoking prohibited.

2 Do not lean out of the window.
Passengers must not lean out of the window.

2 Typical notice in railway trains.

3 *A* Can $\Big\}$ I /smoke/ /lean out/?
    May

   B No, you $\Big\{$ cannot, can't.
                   may not.
   /In fact/ /On the contrary/, you mustn't.

   I want you *not* to smoke.

3 Permission asked for, as in II.14.2 and 3.

Permission not granted.

You must do the opposite of what you asked.
Cp *tell him not to,* in III.1.3.

4 *A* Must I wait?
   B Yes, you must.
       or No, you need not. You needn't.

   You don't have to (wait).
   I don't want you to, but you can wait if you like.

4 Have I that inescapable obligation?
Yes, you have that obligation.
No obligation. *Need* as MODAL in NEG sentence.
As in II.16.6.
In other words, you needn't.

5 *A* Need I wait? Do I have to wait?
   B Yes, you must. You have to.
       or No, you /needn't/ /don't have to/.

5 *need* as MODAL in INTERROGATIVE.

Absence of obligation.

6 You're driving very dangerously.
You're exceeding the speed limit.
You mustn't drive so fast.

6

Contrast *you needn't* in 7 below.

7 We're early. We've plenty of time.
You don't have to go now.
You $\Big\{$ needn't $\Big\}$ go now.
          don't need to

7

= You're not obliged to.

= It isn't necessary.

8 *A* You need a haircut. You need to have a haircut. Do *I* need to?
   B No, *you* don't need to.

8 Use *need* as a full VERB in the AFFIRMATIVE, *need* as full VERB in INTERROGATIVE. NEGATIVE of full VERB *need*: it isn't necessary.

9 *A* Could you smoke when you were a boy?
   B No, we weren't allowed to (smoke).
   A Did you have to work very hard?

9 = Were you allowed to?
As in III.28.7.
PAST of *Must you . . .?*

B Yes, we had to.
   or No, we didn't (have to). We didn't
   need to.

PAST NEG of *needn't*, absence of obligation.

10   B needed to have a haircut.
      A didn't need to.

10 PAST of 8 above.
    It wasn't necessary.

III.22 *Should* and *ought to* indicating duty or (escapable) obligation, or expressing advice. *Would* replaceable by *should* after *I* or *we*

Models

We $\left\{ \begin{array}{l} \text{should} \\ \text{ought to} \end{array} \right\}$ apologise.

You $\left\{ \begin{array}{l} \text{should} \\ \text{ought to} \end{array} \right\}$ take more exercise.

I $\left\{ \begin{array}{l} \text{should} \\ \text{would} \end{array} \right\}$ like to see the manager.

Notes

1 A Have we said the wrong thing?

   B Yes. We $\left\{ \begin{array}{l} \text{should} \\ \text{ought to} \end{array} \right\}$ go and apologise.

   A Should we (apologise)?
   B Yes, and so should Jim.
   A Ought we to take some flowers?
   B I ought to, and so should Jim.

1

should, replaceable by the stronger
ought to, indicating duty or (escapable)
obligation.
Q-*Yes/No*.
See II.25.1.
Probably less frequent than *Should we*.
The strongly marked *ought* is not likely
to be repeated in the second part of the
sentence, though *so ought Jim* is possible.

2 A You $\left\{ \begin{array}{l} \text{should not} \\ \text{ought not to} \end{array} \right\}$ do that.

   You $\left\{ \begin{array}{l} \text{shouldn't} \\ \text{oughtn't to} \end{array} \right\}$ do that.

   B Why shouldn't we?

2 You have a duty *not* to do it.

Avoid *oughtn't we to*, which is possible
but awkward.

3 A $\left. \begin{array}{l} \text{Shouldn't we} \\ \text{Should we not} \end{array} \right\}$ wait?

3 See III.5.3. Regard *Should we not* as
(very) formal. Similarly,

$\left. \begin{array}{l} Are \\ Have \\ Do \\ Can \end{array} \right\}$ we not ...

   $\left. \begin{array}{l} \text{Oughtn't we to} \\ \text{Ought we not to} \end{array} \right\}$ wait?

4 A You're getting much too fat.

   You $\left\{ \begin{array}{l} \text{should} \\ \text{ought to} \end{array} \right\}$ take more exercise.

5   I like my job but it's too far away.
      What should I do? Should I look for
      something else?

Ought we not to (very) formal.

4

$\left. \begin{array}{l} should \\ ought to \end{array} \right\}$ expressing advice.

5

Request for advice. *Should* replaceable
by *ought to*, but *should* is more likely to
occur.

6 *A* Mind the step. You can hardly see it.

  B Yes, there $\begin{Bmatrix}\text{should}\\\text{ought to}\end{Bmatrix}$ be a light here.

  C Why should there be $\begin{Bmatrix}\text{a light?}\\\text{one?}\end{Bmatrix}$

  B Because somebody might fall.

7   /I/ /We/ $\begin{Bmatrix}\text{should}\\\text{would}\end{Bmatrix}$ like to see the manager.

8 *A* Would you like to fly to the moon?

  B Yes, /I/ /We/ $\begin{Bmatrix}\text{would.}\\\text{should.}\end{Bmatrix}$

  or No, /I/ /We/ $\begin{Bmatrix}\text{wouldn't.}\\\text{shouldn't.}\end{Bmatrix}$

6 *Mind* = be careful of.

  should, ought to in SP 3c.

7 See III.20.4. *Would* replaceable by *should* after *I* or *we*: cp II.13.5.

8 *Would* not replaceable by *should* here. *Would* in these examples avoids possible confusion with the *should* of obligation.

III.23 Four main types of phrasal verb. The term 'phrasal verb' is here restricted to the examples in 1c, 2c, 3c and 4c below

Models

He came across a very old man.
He had to give up.
Bring up children. Bring them up.
Stand up for your friends.

Notes

1a He came across the room.
   He went up the stairs.
 b He asked for some more soup.
   I think of you all the time.
 c He came across a very old man.

   He looked after us very well.
   We can't do without sleep.

2a Come in. Go out. Stay away.
   Keep down. Get on (eg the bus).
   Turn /over/ /round/.
 b /Go/ /Come/ /Get/ /Keep/ /Carry/ on.
   Plants grow. Children grow (up).
   /Eat/ /Drink/ /Save/ up.

   Hurry up. Don't hurry.
   He /walked/ /ran/ /set/ off.
   The fire broke out, died out.
   The machine broke down.
   The factory closed down.
 c George was last in the race.
   He tried to catch up, then to keep up;
   but he had to give up, so he dropped out
   (of the race).

   Mind your head. Look out.

1a VERB expressing simple physical action + PREPOSITIONAL PHRASE (I.19).
 b PREPOSITIONAL VERB as in I.25 and III.11.

 c *come across*, PHRASAL VERB of Type 1, meaning 'meet or find by chance'. Similarly, *look after, do without*.

2a VERB, of motion or position, + ADV PARTICLE, as in I.20. *Get on* (a surface). Stress the PARTICLE.
 b *on*, meaning 'forward': *get on* = continue. *up*, suggesting 'upwards' or completion. *up*, suggesting completion; *save up* [*money*].
   up, intensifying the AFFIRMATIVE only.
   off the starting line, ie away.
   break out = begin; *die out* = end.
   break down = cease to function.
   close down = close finally.
 c

   catch up, PHRASAL VERB, Type 2, meaning 'go faster so as to be with the rest'; *keep up* = maintain his position; *give up* = abandon (the race); *drop out* = stop being in the race or a member of the team.

   Look out = Attention. Danger.

3a Bring the box up. Bring it up.
    Bring up that box of books.
  b Keep an employee on.
    /Find/ /Point/ out /the truth/ /a mistake/.
    /Ring/ /Call/ up one's friends.
    Lock up /valuables/ /a prisoner/.
    Close down a factory.
  c Bring children up. Bring them up.
    Bring up one's children.

3a As in II.11.6. Similarly, *give* /*back*/
    /*away*/, *send* /*back*/ /*away*/, *let in*, etc.
  b Expressions that follow the same pattern
    as *bring up* in 3a, with PARTICLES used
    as in 2b.

  c *bring up*, PHRASAL VERB of Type 3,
    meaning 'educate'. The PARTICLE is
    stressed in all the constructions in 3a, b
    and c.

4a Go up to the top floor.
    Come down to the basement.
  b Get on with your work.
  c Catch up with the leaders.
    Stand up for your friends.
    Look out for the signal.
    Get rid of that rubbish.
5   He broke the safe open; broke it open;
    broke open the safe.
6   He just ran past our house.
    He was running about the room.
    Don't stop—let's walk past.
    Stand still—don't run about.

4a VERB + PARTICLE + PREPOSITION;
    PARTICLE stressed, PREP unstressed.
  b *Get on*, as in 2a above + PREP *with*.
  c *Catch up*, as in 2c, + *with*;
    Stand up for = support;
    Look out, as in 2c, + *for*;
    Get rid of, PHRASAL VERB, Type 4.
5   VERB + ADJ, following same patterns as
    in PHRASAL VERB, Type 3.
6   Regard [*run*] *past* and [*run*] *about*, + NP,
    as similar examples to those in 1a above.
    Regard [*walk*] *past* and [*run*] *about*, not
    followed by NP, as similar to examples
    in 2a.

Lexicon
For further examples of PHRASAL VERBS, see Appendix C

III.24 -*ing* as gerund; SP 6e, with -*ing* as object of vt; SP 2, with adj modified by preposition + -*ing*

Models
I enjoy listening to music.
I'm tired of waiting.

1 *A* Do you [like][1] swimming?
  B Oh yes, I often go swimming.
     What do you like doing?
  A I enjoy listening to music.
     I really enjoy it.
2 *A* It's cold in here. Would you mind
     closing the window?
  B Not at all.
3 *A* I don't mind sitting here, but do
     you mind not making so much noise?
     Do you mind keeping quiet?
4   These things are not worth buying.
     They're not worth looking at.
     It's no /good/ /use/ wasting our time.

Notes

1 SP 6e, with -*ing*, GERUND, as OBJECT of vt.
   SP 5, with -*ing* as ADJUNCT after vi.

   SP 6e, with -*ing* + PREP PHRASE as OBJECT.
   I enjoy it: contrast *I want to.*
2 *Would you mind* + -*ing* in INTERROGATIVE
   sentence making a request. *I wouldn't
   mind a cup of coffee* (= I'd like one).
3 I don't object to it.
   do you . . . (not) doing something: this is
   more of an order than a request.

5 *A* I'm not going to wait any longer. I'm tired of waiting for that man.	5 SP 2, with ADJ modified by PREP PHRASE + *-ing*.
B I'm used to it. I'm used to waiting.	*used to* as in III.9.4: contrast *used to* in III.5.
6 Dick is only interested in sport. Phil is only interested in making a lot of money.	6 As in III.7.6. SP 2, with PARTICIPIAL ADJ + PREP PHRASE + *-ing*.
7 *A* Good-bye. We'll meet again on Monday. *B* Indeed, we look forward to it. We look forward to seeing you then.	7 *look forward* + PREPOSITION + NP. *to* here is a PREPOSITION, followed by GERUND; it is not an INFINITIVE marker as in *I want to go*; *seeing* has an OBJECT here.
8 Thank you for helping me. Excuse me for interrupting.	8 *Thank you for* + NP, as in III.12.6, or + *-ing*.
9 He didn't say a word. He left us. He left us without saying a word.	9 *without* + *-ing*; *saying* has an OBJECT here.
10 Can't you help, instead of just sitting there and criticising?	10 *instead of* + *-ing*. *criticising* here is a PARTICIPLE, as in III.18.9c.
11 *A* What is a bread knife? What do we use it for? *B* It's a knife for cutting bread. We use it for cutting bread.	11 Compare this form of definition with that in III.13.12.

Lexicon
carry on (as in III.23.2b), *dislike, enjoy, go on, can't help, keep on, like, stop, suggest ; I don't mind,
I wouldn't mind, would you mind . . .? ; it's no good, it's no use, it's not worth ; thank you for . . ., excuse
me for . . . ; look forward to ; tired of, interested in.* See also Appendix A7

III.25 Questions ending with a preposition, or with an adverb particle

Models   **Notes**
What did you do that for?
Who are they talking to?
Which table are they sitting at?
Who is she ringing up now?

1 *A* I'm reading a very good book. *B* What is it about? *A* (It's) about skin-diving. *B* Who is it by? *A* (It's) by a famous skin-diver.	1 = What is the subject? Stress *about*. The PREP PHRASE can be a short answer. = Who is the author? Stress *by*.
2 *A* I have a present here. *B* Who is it for? (Is it) for me?	2 Stress *for* in 1st question, not in the 2nd.
3 *A* I've given my winter coat away. *B* What did you do that for?	3 = Why did you do that? Stress *that*, not *for*.
A It was too /short/ /tight/ for me.	

4 *A* I'm going to buy some flowers.	4
B Who are you going to buy flowers for?	Contrast *What . . . for?* in 3 above.
	Stress *flowers*, not *for*.
A (For) my wife. It's her birthday.	
5 *A* There are two film stars at a table behind you.	5
B Which table are they sitting at?	Stress *sitting*, not *at*.
6 Which country are we flying over?	6 Stress *flying*, not *over*.
7 *A* Those two girls are talking.	7 As in III.11.3a.
B Who are they talking to?	Stress *talking*, not *to*. As in III.23.1.
/Who/ /What/ are they talking about?	Stress *talking*, not *about*. As in III.23.1.
8 *A* Turn ⎫ on the radio, will you? Switch ⎭	8 *Switch on*, as in III.23.3.
B Which programme do you want to listen to?	Stress *listen*, not *to*. As in III.23.1.
9 *A* I've borrowed some money.	9
B Who did you borrow it from?	Stress *borrow*, not *it* or *from*.
10 *A* Which programme do you want me to switch on?	10 See 8 above. Stress the PARTICLE, *on*, as in III.23.3.
11 *A* Sue is speaking on the telephone.	11
B Again? Who is she ringing up now?	*ring up*, as in III.23.3b. Stress *up* and *now*.
12 *A* Look out for the signal.	12 See III.23.4c.
B Which signal do I have to look out for?	Stress the PARTICLE, *out*, not the PREP *for*.

III.26 /Very/ /Too/ /So/ *much; a lot, a little, more, less* etc, which appeared as determiners in II.5, now used as adverbs modifying verbs. Also *afterwards, before* and *since* as adverbs

Models	**Notes**
I don't like tea very much.	
I walked a lot.	
You should smoke less.	
I've never seen him since.	
1 You took too much (bread).	1 *too much* as DETERMINER + NP as in II.5.3.
You smoke too many cigarettes.	*too many*, as DETERMINER, as in II.5.3.
You smoke too much.	*too much*, as ADVERB modifying VERB *smoke*.
You shouldn't smoke so many cigarettes.	*so many*, DETERMINER, as in II.26.5.
You shouldn't smoke so much.	*so much*, ADVERB modifying VERB.
Why not buy fewer cigarettes?	*fewer*, DETERMINER, as in II.21.6.
Why not smoke less in future?	*less*, ADVERB modifying VERB.
2 *A* I don't like tea very much.	2 ADVERB follows OBJECT in SP 6.
B I like it, but I don't like sugar in my tea very much.	ADVERB follows OBJECT even when OBJECT is fairly long NP, eg *sugar in my tea*.
C I like sugar, but I don't like too much sugar in my tea.	Here *too much* is DETERMINER before NP *sugar*.

3 *A* What did you do in the holidays?
    Did you get very much exercise?

  B Yes, I walked a lot, quite a lot.
    I ate a good deal, too.
  A I only took a little exercise.
    But I walked a little every day.
4 *A* You're getting too thin.
    Are you sure you eat enough?
    You ought to eat more, you know.
  B I eat more than I used to.
5   Bob hardly takes any exercise.
    He just sits. He only watches football.
    He has hardly moved all day.
    He tried to climb a hill the other day
    and nearly collapsed.
6   I'll see you again before Thursday,
    before we go.
    I've never heard that word before.
    I met him after /six/ /he left school/.
    I spoke to him afterwards.
    I haven't seen him since /Sunday/ /he
    left school/.
    I've never seen him since.

3

very much as DETERMINER before NP,
exercise.
(quite) a lot, as ADVERB modifying *walked.*
a good deal, as ADVERB modifying *ate.*
a little, DETERMINER.
a little, ADVERB.

4

enough as ADVERB modifying *eat.*
more as ADVERB modifying *eat.*

5 *hardly, nearly, just, only,* as ADVERBS of
degree, occupy a similar position to that
of ADVERBS of frequency; see I.29.
the other day = a few days ago.

6 *before* as PREPOSITION.
before as CONJUNCTION + CLAUSE: III.17.6.
before as ADVERB.
after as PREP and CONJUNCTION.
afterwards, ADVERB.
since as PREP and CONJUNCTION.

since as ADVERB.

III.27 Past perfect

Models
The black car wasn't there.
It had already gone.
Mary had been waiting.

1 *A* Look and see if that black car is
    still outside the house.
  B It isn't there (any longer).
    It has (already) gone.

  C It left five minutes ago.

2 *A* *(half an hour later)* Was the car still
    there when you looked?
  B No, it wasn't there (any longer).
    It had (already) gone.

  C It had left five minutes before.

3 *A* Was it raining when you came in?
  B No, it had just stopped.

Notes

1 *Look and see:* II.29.7 and III.2.2.

PRESENT PERF: no time specified, as in
II.8 note 1; *already* = by now.
SIMPLE PAST, time specified, as in II.3.1;
ago = back from *now.*

2

PAST PERFECT (*had,* as in II.6.4 + PAST
PARTICIPLE, as in II.9.4) with no time
specified: cp *it has gone* in 1 above.
PAST PERF, with time specified; cp *It left*
in 1 above; *before* = back from *then.*

3

just = a very short time before: cp. II.8.3.

4 *A* Mr Green wasn't in his office when   4
     I called this morning.
  B Oh? Had he already left?   q-*Yes/No.*
  A Yes, he had. He'd left.   Short answer, and contraction. Distin-
                                  guish between '*d* = *had*, and '*d* = *would* as
                                  in III.20.2.

  B Where had he gone, I wonder.   q-*Where.*
     Had Mr Black arrived yet?   *yet*, used as in II.8.2.
  A /No, he hadn't/ /Not yet/.   Alternative short answers.
     He hadn't arrived yet.   Full NEGATIVE.

5 *A* When I got home last night, there were   5
     two policemen in the house.
  B Why? What had happened?   q-*What :* what had happened before my
                                  return?

  A We had had ⎱   PAST PERF of *have. We'd had* = *We had had.*
     We'd had   ⎰ burglars.
  B How long had the police been there?
  A (They'd been there) for twenty minutes,   *for* and *since* used as in II.9.7 and III.19.2.
     since nine o'clock.

6 *A* I'm sorry we're late. We missed the train.   6
     When we got to the station the train had
     left.   PAST PERF obligatory in this MAIN CLAUSE.
  B The train went before we even left our   PAST PERF optional in *this* MAIN CLAUSE,
     house, in fact.   since the order of events is clear without
                         it.

7   I saw John last week. He'd been ill.   7 PAST PERF necessary to express the idea
     He'd been away a fortnight. He hadn't   that John's illness and absence preceded
     gone back to work yet.   my seeing him.
8   John was very late. Mary had been   8 See III.19.2a. PAST PERF progressive.
     waiting for him impatiently.

III.28 The passive, simple present and simple past

Models   **Notes**
These cars are made in Coventry.
Our house was built in 1969.

1   I posted that letter last night.   1 SP 6: *posted*, SIMPLE PAST, ACTIVE VOICE;
     I put it in the letter-box.   *that letter*, OBJECT of *posted*.
     That letter was posted last night.   Previous model 'transformed' to PASSIVE,
     It was put in the letter-box.   with AUXILIARY *be* + PAST PARTICIPLE.
2   They make these cars in Coventry.   2 *They* = people, unspecified.
     These cars are made in Coventry.   PASSIVE transform of previous model.
3   They make this steel in Sheffield.   3 *They*, SUBJECT; PLURAL VERB, *are.*
     This steel is made in Sheffield.   *This steel*, SUBJECT; SINGULAR VERB, *is.*
4 *A* When was your house built?   4 PASSIVE in a question.
  B Our house was built in 1969.
5 *A* When did they build the house opposite   5 OBJECT, *the house opposite you.*
     you?
  B The house opposite us was built two   SUBJECT, *The house opposite us.*
     years ago.

We made all the furniture in this house
by hand. It was made by hand.
All the furniture in this house was made
by hand.

OBJECT, *all the furniture in this house*;
by hand: cp *by bus*, III.4.1.
SUBJECT, *All the furniture in this house.*

6a   There was a very serious accident
yesterday. Six people were killed and
twenty people were badly hurt.

  b *A* When were you born?

    B I was born in 1959.

  c *A* When was this book published?

    B It was published in 1973.

    C Wasn't it published in 1974?

6   Transforms from the ACTIVE are given
above only to lead up to the PASSIVE. This
does not imply that exercises in ACTIVE-
PASSIVE transforms are considered essential or even desirable. Typical examples
of sentences without corresponding
ACTIVE structure are given in 6.

7 *A* My parents don't allow me to stay out
late at night.
In other words, I am not [allowed][1]
to stay out late at night.

7   Example of SP 6c.

  B Why don't you come with us tonight?

  A I'm not allowed to.
Mary isn't allowed to, either.

= I can't, permission withheld, as in
II.14.2.

  B Why aren't you allowed to?

Lexicon
1 *allowed, asked, expected, invited, obliged, permitted*

III.29 Phrasal verbs of the type *break . . . down* in the passive; and passive perfect aspect

Models

A big tree was blown down.
My car has been repaired.
It had not been stolen.
It had been towed away.

Notes

1 *A* There was a strong wind last night.
It blew down a big tree near us.
A big tree near us was blown down.

1
blow down, as in III.23.3.
Previous model now in the PASSIVE: stress
down.
Note CONCORD.

  B Several trees were blown down in our
road, too.

2 *A* Can I give you a lift?

2 = Can I take you in my car?

  B I thought your car had broken down.

PAST PERFECT of *break down*, as in III.27.

  A They've repaired it already.

PRESENT PERFECT; *already* = *by now*.

    It $\left\{ \begin{array}{l} \text{has} \\ \text{'s} \end{array} \right\}$ been repaired already.

PRESENT PERFECT PASSIVE.

  B I can't believe it.

  A It *has* (been). Come and see.

It has (been): short answers, emphatic.

3 *A* Has my watch been mended yet?

3 Q-*Yes/No*: *Has* + NP SUBJECT + *been* +
mended.

  B Yes, it has (been).
    or (I'm afraid) it hasn't (been) (yet).
    It hasn't been mended.

Stress *has*, even when not emphatic.
Short NEGATIVE answers: stress *hasn't*.
Full NEGATIVE.

  A Hasn't it been mended *yet*?

NEGATIVE-INTERROGATIVE.

4 *A* There's been an accident.
   B Has anyone been /hurt/ /injured/?
   A Yes, someone's been hurt badly.

4 PRESENT PERFECT of *there is*, as in II.9.8.
PRESENT PERFECT PASSIVE.
Cp *badly hurt*, III.28.7a. In *hurt badly*,
ADV-M is emphasised and repetition of
hurt at the end of a sentence is avoided.

5 *A* Yesterday I parked my car outside the
      school. When I came out, it wasn't there.
      Why wasn't it?
   B Perhaps it had been stolen.
   A No, it hadn't $\begin{cases} \text{(been).} \\ \text{(been stolen).} \end{cases}$
   B What had happened to it, then?
   A It had been towed away by the police.

   B Why had your car been towed away?

   A Because it /was/ /had been/ parked in
      the wrong place.
   B Why /didn't you park/ /hadn't you
      parked/ it in your usual place?
   A Because I couldn't. A big tree had been
      blown down where I usually park.

5

PAST PERFECT PASSIVE.

hadn't, or *hadn't been* or *hadn't been stolen*.

This question invites the PASSIVE.
PASSIVE of *tow . . . away*, III.23.3, ie the
police had towed it away.
Why had + NP SUBJECT + *been* + *towed
away*?
SIMPLE PAST or PAST PERFECT can be used
in these examples. It is not necessary to
keep on stressing PAST PERFECT ASPECT.
ie where you usually park it.
Cp 1 above.

III.30 Passive with modals, and with *have to, used to* and *be going to*

Models

It's going to be opened next month.
This must be done as soon as possible.
Shoes used to be made by hand.

Notes

1 There's going to be a new supermarket
   over there.
   It $\begin{cases} \text{will} \\ \text{is going to} \end{cases}$ be opened next month.

2 When $\begin{cases} \text{will it} \\ \text{is it going to} \end{cases}$ be opened?

   It $\begin{cases} \text{won't} \\ \text{isn't going to} \end{cases}$ be opened yet.

3 *A* Can you mend this /watch/ for me?
   B Let me /see/ /have a look/.
      Yes, I think /I can/ /it can be done/.
      It can (be).
       or I'm sorry, I can't. It can't be done.
      It can't (be).

4 Hurry up and finish that work.
   It must be done as soon as possible.
   But it will have to be done carefully.
   It mustn't be done *too* quickly.

5 My homework wasn't good enough.
   I had to do it again.
   It had to be done again.

1 As in II.12.7.

will or *be going to* (see II.13) + *be* + *opened*:
PASSIVE with future reference.

3

can + *be* + *done*.

4

must + *be* + *done*.
will have to, as in II.17.9, + PASSIVE.

5

had to, as in II.17.10, + PASSIVE.

6   Cross the road very carefully.   6
     Look both ways, or you might be knocked   *might*, as in III.20.10; *knock down*, as in
     down. You might be killed.   III.23.3 and III.29.1.
     You might (be).

7 *A* These stairs are very dangerous.   7

     They $\left\{\begin{array}{l}\text{should}\\\text{ought to}\end{array}\right\}$ be repaired.

   B I think the whole house $\left\{\begin{array}{l}\text{should}\\\text{ought to}\end{array}\right\}$ be
        pulled down.

   A I agree. It $\left\{\begin{array}{l}\text{should}\\\text{ought to}\end{array}\right\}$ (be).

   C Why should it be pulled down?
        Why should such a nice house be   *should*+ NP SUBJECT + *be*+ PAST PART.
        /pulled down/ /destroyed/?

   D Because it's too dangerous.

8   Shoes, and many other things, used to be   8 *used to* as in III.5 + PASSIVE;
     made by hand. Now they're made by   *by hand*, as in III.28.6.
     machinery.

9   Bob and Sue will be married next month.   9 Either PASSIVE or *be*+ PARTICIPIAL ADJ.
     They're engaged to be married.   See III.8.2c.

Summary of Stages I, II and III

Stages I and II, plus the following:

SENTENCE PATTERNS, additional ones listed on page 3. Sentences containing the following
SUBORDINATE CLAUSES:

   that-CLAUSES in reported statements, as in III.1, and after ADJECTIVES, eg *I'm delighted* (*that*)
   you can come
   CLAUSES beginning with *if* or *whether* in indirect questions
   RELATIVE CLAUSES, defining only
   CONDITIONAL CLAUSES, as in III.16 only
   TEMPORAL CLAUSES with future reference
   other ADVERBIAL CLAUSES

   NOUN PHRASE
      PRONOUN *It* as 'dummy' subject, as in *It gets dark early*
      Reflexive pronouns, eg *myself*

   VERB PHRASE
      VERBS
      get and *become* in SP 2; and *become* in SP 1
      INCHOATIVE VERBS
      indirect commands and questions; and reported statements
      used to (*go*)
      PRESENT PERFECT PROGRESSIVE
      PAST PERFECT, and PAST PERFECT PROGRESSIVE
      would, *could* and *might*, as expressions of hesitation or deference
      should and *ought to* expressing obligation
      must not, *need not*
      the four types of PHRASAL VERB, as in III.23.
      the PASSIVE, as in III.28–30 only

ADJECTIVES

with PREPOSITIONAL PHRASE, INFINITIVE and *that*-CLAUSE as complement, eg *I'm sorry for him, afraid to speak, glad (that) you can come*

PARTICIPLES, eg *interesting, interested*, used ADJECTIVALLY, alone or followed by PREPOSITIONAL PHRASE, INFINITIVE or *that*-CLAUSE, eg *I'm delighted with it, to see you, (that) you can come*

PREPOSITIONS

PREP PHRASES of the type *by bus, on foot*

PREPOSITIONS at the end of questions, eg *What are you talking about?* and at the end of RELATIVE CLAUSES, eg *the boy he gave the watch to*

OTHER ELEMENTS

CONJUNCTIONS

after, (al)though, as, as soon as, because, before, if, since, that, till or *until, unless, while*

RELATIVE PRONOUNS

that, who, which

Part Two

A full range of sentence patterns recommended for presentation by the end of Stage VI, incorporating the patterns listed on page 3

Note : This list, based on Chapter 12 of *A Grammar of Contemporary English**, is divided into five main sections, as follows:

Ø Patterns in which the VERB has no COMPLEMENT
A Patterns in which the VERB is *be* or *become* etc, with COMPLEMENT
B Patterns in which the VERB is TRANSITIVE, with one OBJECT
C Patterns in which the VERB is TRANSITIVE, with two OBJECTS
D Patterns in which the VERB is TRANSITIVE, with COMPLEX COMPLEMENT

It is assumed that the normal order in which the basic elements of English sentence structure occur is

NP (SUBJECT) + VP, ie FINITE VERB + COMPLEMENT (if any)

NP (SUBJECT) will normally begin the sentence; it is not mentioned in the 'Structure' column below, except in the case of variations on the normal order, which are indicated by the sign VAR. The difference between one sentence pattern and another lies in the form taken by VP. This list is therefore largely one of VERB patterns. Certain VERBS will enter into one pattern or more, but not into others. For Lexicon, see Appendix A.

* By Randolph Quirk, Sidney Greenbaum, Geoffrey Leech, Jan Svartvik (Longman, 1972)

Pattern number	Structure	Examples	See	Passive see
Ø 1	vi	The sun is rising.	I.18.6	
a	vi + ADVERBIAL	George sat /beside me/ /on my hat/.	I.20.2	VI.11.1
b	vi + ADV PARTICLE	He came in.	I.20.1	
2 VAR	/Here/ /There/ /Up/ goes ...	There goes the bus.	III.4.8	
3	vt with OBJECT unstated	I'm reading.	I.18	
a	PREP VERB, OBJECT unstated	I'm listening.	I.18	
A 1 VAR	*There* + *be* + NP	There are four seasons.	VI.7	
2	*be* + NP	George is my friend.	I.1	
3	*be* + ADVERBIAL	He is in my class.	I.10	
a, VAR	/Here/ /There/ + *be* + NP	Here is an example.	I.11.3	
b, VAR	*There* + *be* + NP + ADVERBIAL	There is a dog in the garden.	I.11.4	
4	*be* + ADJECTIVE	He is young. They are alike.	I.6	
5	*be* + ADJ + PREP PHRASE	He was good at arithmetic.	III.6	
6a	*be* + ADJ + *that*-CLAUSE	I'm sure (that) he's here.	III.8	
b	*be* + ADJ + *that*-CLAUSE	It's true (that) he won.	IV.11.5	

108

Pattern number	Structure	Examples	See	Passive see
c	be + ADJ + *that*-CLAUSE	I'm sorry (that) you (should) feel that way.	VI.24.4	
d	be + ADJ + *that*-CLAUSE	It's right (that) you should feel that way.	VI.24.5	
7a	be + ADJ + INFINITIVE	We were happy to see you.	III.8.3	
b	be + ADJ + INFINITIVE	He must be happy to sing like that.	VI.9.1	
c	be + ADJ + INFINITIVE	We were ready to help you.	III.8.4	
d	be + ADJ + INFINITIVE	He was foolish to do that.	IV.28.6.	
e	be + ADJ + INFINITIVE	That is easy to remember.	IV.28.9	
f	be + ADJ + INFINITIVE	He is quick to see the point.	VI.9.4	

Pattern number	Structure	Examples	See	Passive see
B 1	vt + NP	They weighed the luggage.	I.21	III.28
a	vt + NP + ADVERBIAL	I put the car in the garage	I.21.4	III.28
b	vt + NP + ADV PART	I put the key in.	I.25.6	III.29
c	vt + *oneself*	We enjoyed ourselves.	III.3	
2	PREP VERB + NP	I'm listening to a record.	I.25.1	IV.21.10
3	vt + INFINITIVE	He wants to go home.	I.22.3	
4	vt + *-ing*	We enjoy swimming.	III.24	
5	vt + NP + INFINITIVE	I told him to go away.	II.15.3	IV.21.3
a		I asked for the doctor to come.	IV.30.11	
b		We want there to be no trouble.	IV.9.7	
6	vt + NP + bare INFIN	He made us wait. He saw him stop.	II.14.5	IV.21.12
7	vt + NP + *-ing*	We saw him running.	IV.10	IV.21.12
8	vt + /him/ /his/ + *-ing*	I dislike {him/his} doing that.	V.28	
9	vt + NP + PAST PART	We found our seats occupied.	IV.24	IV.24.12
10	vt + direct speech	They cried, "Stop that car!"	III.1.7	

Pattern number	Structure	Examples	See	Passive see
11a	vt + *that*-CLAUSE	He said (that) he was sorry.	III.1	VI.13
b	vt + *that*-CLAUSE (should)	I suggest (that) we (should) meet.	VI.24.3	VI.12.8
c	vt + *that*-CLAUSE (should)	We regret that this should have happened.	VI.24.4	VI.24.5
12	vt + *wh*-CLAUSE	I know what you said.	IV.13	VI.11.6
C 1	vt + NP + NP	He gave George a book.	I.28	IV.21.7–9
a	vt + NP + NP	He gave the car a wash.	II.2.8	IV.21.7
b	vt + INDIRECT OBJ	Show me.	I.28.3	IV.21.4
2	vt + NP + PREP PHRASE	He gave a book to George.	I.27	IV.21.9
3	vt + NP + PREP PHRASE	We thanked him for his help.	III.12.6	VI.11.8
4	vt + NP + PREP PHRASE	He paid attention to his work.	III.12.7	VI.12.4
5	vt + NP + *that*-CLAUSE	He told us (that) he was lost.	IV.11.2	VI.12.5
a	vt (+ NP) + *that*-CLAUSE	He showed (us) he was right.	IV.11.2	VI.12.6
6	vt + NP + *wh*-CLAUSE	He told us what he was doing.	IV.13.2	VI.12.7
a	vt (+ NP) + *wh*-CLAUSE	He asked (me) where I was going.	IV.13.2	VI.12.7
7	vt (+ *to* NP) + *that*-CLAUSE	He explained (to me) that there had been an accident.	IV.11.3	VI.12.8
8	vt (+ *to* NP) + *wh*-CLAUSE	He explained (to me) why he had said that.	IV.13.3	VI.12.8
D 1	vt + NP + NP	They appointed him Chairman.	IV.23.1	IV.23.1
a	vt + NP + NP	They made him Chairman.	IV.23.3	IV.23.3
2	vt + NP + *as* + NP	They regarded him as a genius.	IV.23.5	IV.23.5
3	vt + NP + *for* + NP	Others took him for a fool.	IV.23.7	IV.23.7
4	vt + NP + *to be* + ADJ	I like people to be punctual.	IV.24.2	
5	vt + NP (+ *to be*) + ADJ	I consider him (to be) stupid. We thought it right to tell her.	IV.23.8	IV.23.8
6	vt + NP + ADJ	We painted our house white.	IV.24.3	IV.24.3

Pattern number	Structure	Examples	See	Passive see
7	vt + NP + *as* + ADJ	They described him as hopeless.	VI.26.3	VI.26.3
8	vt + *it* + ADJ + *that*	We thought it wrong that she should be left in ignorance.	VI.5.10	

Stage IV

Contents

14 CONDITIONAL sentences with *provided, providing, supposing,* etc: *I'll tell you the secret provided that you keep it to yourself; I don't mind if it rains tomorrow—I'll go out even if it pours;* $\begin{Bmatrix} suppose \\ supposing \end{Bmatrix}$ *(that) you were left alone on a desert island . . . ; I should be grateful if you would.*

15 *Seem, appear, happen* + INFINITIVE: *He seems to be very intelligent; they seem to like their presents; we seem to be moving at last; he seems to have missed the train; it seems as if someone is following us.*

16 PROGRESSIVE and PERFECTIVE ASPECTS combined with future reference: *We'll be thinking of you tomorrow; I'll have read it by Tuesday; by next week, he'll have been working here for twenty years.*

17 PERFECTIVE with future reference in temporal and CONDITIONAL CLAUSES: *I'll tell you when I've read it; wait until I've put my shoes on; we waited until they'd finished.*

18 Unfulfilled past obligation etc: *You should have asked me; you shouldn't have promised; You /ought/ /oughtn't/ to have done that; I would like to have seen it.*

19 CONDITIONAL sentences of the type *He would have come if you had asked him; if you had dropped that vase, the owner would have been furious; if you had come earlier, you /could/ /might/ have met him.*

20 Further PASSIVE constructions: *'Hamlet' was written by Shakespeare; mind you don't get hurt; you must have your hair cut; I didn't hear my name called; women like to be admired; men dislike being criticized.*

21 Review of those SENTENCE PATTERNS so far presented that can be put into the PASSIVE: *We are supposed to leave now; our luggage is being weighed; the children were given sweets; we were made to wait; he has never been known to behave like that before.*

22 PAST PARTICIPLES followed by PREPOSITIONS other than *by: The lion was shot with a rifle; I'm surprised at you; not many people were interested in the subject; he is quite unknown to us; I can't be bothered with him; I'm worried about her.*

23 SENTENCE PATTERNS in which the OBJECT has a COMPLEMENT: *They made him captain; he regarded her as a friend; we considered him (to be) a good officer; they called him a taxi; they called him a coward.*

24 NP^1 + vt + NP^2 + ADJECTIVE or PARTICIPLE: *The jury found the prisoner guilty; I found him lying on the floor; we found all our seats occupied; the islanders paint their houses white; I can't imagine him flying to the moon.*

25 The *-ing* form as SUBJECT and in other constructions: *Swimming is good exercise; sailing a boat is good fun; I couldn't help laughing; those shoes* $\begin{Bmatrix} want \\ need \end{Bmatrix}$ *mending; what about having your tyres pumped up?*

26 RELATIVE CLAUSES involving the use of *whose, whom, which* and *that: That's the boy whose father is an astronaut; persons to whom this circular is addressed . . . ; the case to which you refer . . . ; all that remains of the ancient city . . . ; I'll give you all (that) I have.*

27 CLAUSES specifying the time when, the place where, etc: *I shall never forget the day we first met; I can't think of the reason why he came so early; that's just the way he spoke.*

28 The INFINITIVE as a COMPLEMENT to an ADJECTIVE: *I'm glad to have met him; he was foolish to do that; this tyre is likely to burst; that's an easy rule to remember.*

29 Further constructions beginning with *It: It's a pity to spoil your drawing; it was so kind of you to come; it took us five weeks to get there.*

30 Constructions where *for* marks the subject of a non-finite CLAUSE: *Here's a book for you to read; it's lucky for you (that) the other car wasn't going faster; shall we ask for Mary to come too?; I've arranged for our luggage to be sent to the station.*

IV.1 Words used as mass nouns, and structures in which they occur

Models
I would like some information.
We want peace with honour.
Honesty is the best policy.

Notes

1 We have a lot of [furniture]¹.
Luggage must not be left here.
Where can we find accommodation?
Take plenty of warm clothing.

1 See Lex 1 below for COMMON CONCRETE
NOUNS used as MASS NOUNS as in I.16. Do
not use these words in the plural.

2 A chair is a piece of furniture.
How many pieces of luggage do you have?
You'll find good accommodation in the town.

A garment is an article of clothing.

2 Devices for indicating one or more
separate examples of the things referred
to in 1 above. *Piece* replaceable by
article;
or *a piece* of clothing.

3 We won? That's very good news.
An interesting $\left\{\begin{matrix} \text{item} \\ \text{piece} \end{matrix}\right\}$ of news.

3 *news*: MASS NOUN, with SINGULAR VERB;
or *an interesting news-item*. Informally,
a bit of news.

4 Most children are fond of [play]¹.
We had a hard [game]¹, didn't we?
Work has to be done first.

4 *play* and *work* as MASS NOUNS, contrasted
with *game* and *job* as COUNT NOUNS. See
Lex 2. For *a play*, see IV.18.9, note.

5 We're making excellent progress.
I would like some information, please.
You've given me very sound advice.

5 *make progress*; *do good, do harm*; *have
fun*; good /behaviour/ /conduct/.
give, and *take*, *advice*.

6 In [physics]³, we study heat, light and
sound.

6 Contrast *light, sound*, the phenomenon
in general, with *a light, a sound*.

7 [Parking]⁴ is not allowed here.
Where can I find a [parking-place]⁴?

7 *-ing* forms used as NOUNS are generally
MASS NOUNS. See Lex 4.

8 Most people seek happiness.
We want peace with honour.

8 Many ABSTRACT NOUNS are used as MASS
NOUNS. *Happy*, ADJ; *happiness*, ABSTRACT
NOUN.

9 Honesty is the best policy.

9 *Honest*, ADJ; *honesty*, ABSTRACT NOUN.

10 May I have /the honour/ /the pleasure/ of
calling on you?

10 The DEF ARTICLE, *the*, before ABSTRACT
NOUNS to indicate a particular example.

11 The news is good. I want the truth.

11 *The* /news/ /truth/, a particular example.

12 That's a good idea. It's a nuisance.
Would you like to make a statement?
Europe has a temperate climate.

12 *idea, nuisance, proposal, scheme, sentence,
statement, climate*, as COUNT WORDS.
Contrast *weather*, MASS NOUN.

Lexicon
1 *accommodation, china, clothing, furniture, luggage, money, rubbish*
2 *bread, a loaf; clothing, a garment; laughter, a laugh; luggage, a suitcase; money, a coin* or *a currency;
pay, a payment; permission, a permit; play, a game; work, a job* or *a task*
3 *arithmetic, chemistry, English, French*, and other languages, *geography, history, mathematics, physics,
science*
4 *camping, a camping* /place/ /site/; *cooking, a kitchen; parking, a parking-place; shopping, a shopping
centre; training, a training-course*

IV.2 Structure NP^1 + verb + NP^2 when NP^2 is not a direct object or when the structure cannot be transformed into the passive

Models	Notes
It weighed twenty-one kilos.	
This watch cost ten pounds.	
The journey took five weeks.	

1   This car was made in Italy.

1 As in III.28. Transform of *They make these cars.*

2   I have a hat. I'm having tea.

2 No PASSIVE transform with *have*. Defer an exception like *A good time was had by all.*

3 *A*   What is he doing with our luggage?
What's happening to it?

B   He's [weigh]^{1}ing it.
It is being weighed.
The substance was weighed.

How much did it weigh?

It weighed twenty-one kilograms.

3

What is happening to it? as a lead up to the PASSIVE, eg *it's being weighed.*
PRESENT PROGRESSIVE, PASSIVE.
Structure widely used in scientific reports.
What happened to it? would be irrelevant here.
No PASSIVE transform in this case.

4   The thief stole ten pounds.

Ten pounds $\begin{cases} \text{was} \\ \text{were} \end{cases}$ stolen.

This watch cost (me) ten pounds.

4

That amount was stolen or *that number were.*
No PASSIVE transform in this case.

5   We [have come]^2 a very long way.

5 No PASSIVE transform.

6   We [walked]^3 [ten miles].

We [walked]^4 for ten miles.

6 = We completed a 10-mile walk.
Normally no PASSIVE.
Our walking continued throughout that distance.

7   We [slept]^5 all the time.
We [slept]^5 all (that) [morning]^6.
We worked all [night]^7.
We waited (for) two hours.
I swim every day.

7 No PASSIVE.
No PASSIVE.
No PASSIVE.
No PASSIVE.
No PASSIVE.

8   The [storm] [lasted]^8 (for) two days.

8 No PASSIVE.

9   This furniture has lasted (us) all our $\begin{cases} \text{life.} \\ \text{life-time.} \end{cases}$

9 No PASSIVE.

10   The journey took (us) five weeks.

10 No PASSIVE.

11   The temperature /rose/ /fell/ ten degrees during the /day/ /night/.

11 No PASSIVE. Note that *rise, rose, risen* is an INTRANSITIVE VERB. *Raise* is TRANSITIVE.

12   This flower looks like a lily.

It resembles a lily, but isn't.

12 See structure in II.1.10, which has no PASSIVE.
No PASSIVE. STATIVE.

13   Unfortunately, many clever people lack wisdom.

13

No PASSIVE. STATIVE.

14 This bottle contains poison.	14 No PASSIVE. STATIVE. Defer an example like *Much wisdom is contained in this little book.*

Lexicon
1 *measure, weigh*
2 |*have*| |*had*| *been, come, drive, drop, fall, go, jump, march, ride, run, swim, travel, walk*
3 as for 2 except |*have*| |*had*| *been*
4 *drive, march, ride, run, swim, walk*
5 *drive, march, play, ride, run, sleep, stay, stay awake, stay* |*away*| |*in*| |*out*| |*up*|, *travel, walk, work*
6 *afternoon, evening, week*
7 *day, night, Monday, Tuesday,* etc
8 *last, live*

IV.3 Order of adjectival and noun modifiers before the head-word in an NP

Models

A large, round iron cooking pot.
A charming little blue silk scarf.
A very beautiful Japanese brooch.

Notes

1 *A* This is a pot. What is it used for?

1 Leading up to GERUND which will come closest to the HEAD-WORD.
Stress: *cook*ing pot.

   B Cooking. It's a cooking pot.
   A What is it made of?
   B Iron. It's an iron pot.
      It's an iron cooking pot.

Stress: *iron pot*, as in II.1.8.
Stress: *iron cook*ing pot.

   A What shape is it?
   B Round. It's a round, iron cooking pot.

Stress: *round iron cook*ing pot.

   A What size is it?
   B It's a large, round iron cooking pot.

Stress: *large round iron cook*ing pot.

2 *A* What did you get for your birthday?

2 *get* = receive.
A silk scarf: stress as for *iron pot*.
Leading up to ADJ of colour, which will come closer to the HEAD-WORD than other descriptive ADJs.
charming, PARTICIPIAL ADJ as in III.7.
Contrast position of *charming* with that of *cooking* in 1 above. Note the stresses.

   B A scarf. A silk scarf.
   A What colour is it?
   B It's a little blue silk scarf.
      A pretty little blue silk scarf.
   A It's charming.
      A charming little blue silk scarf;
      a CHARMING little BLUE SILK SCARF.

3 *A* Where did that brooch come from?

3 ADJ indicating place of origin will come closer to the HEAD-WORD than ADJ of colour; but a NOUN MODIFIER (eg *silk*, *pearl*) will come still closer.

   B Japan. It's a Japanese brooch.
      It's a beautiful Japanese brooch;
      a BEAUTiful JAPanese PEARL BROOCH.
   A That's a BIG BLACK GERman CAR.

4 *A* What is that /box/ /pullover/ made of?

4

   B It's a /wooden box/ /woollen pullover/.

Exceptional ADJs: *wooden, woollen.*

   A What is that shed used for?
   B For storing wood. It's a wood shed.

wood shed: contrast *wooden box.*

5 *A* Gold comes from a gold mine.

5 *gold mine*; stress first element.
gold watch: stress both elements.
Use *golden* metaphorically only.

   B A gold watch is made of gold.
      The Princess had long golden hair.

6	Mary has very lovely large brown eyes. She has lovely, rather large, brown eyes.	6	*very* modifying *lovely*. *rather* modifying *large*.
7	She's a dear old lady. He's a wise old man. She's a pretty little child. He's a handsome young man.	7	Common combinations of ADJS. *Old*, *little*, *young* in such examples carry little meaning and are unstressed.
8	She's a pretty, intelligent child. She's a pretty intelligent child.	8	= She's both pretty and intelligent. Here *pretty* = rather, ADV modifying ADJ.
9	It was a long and tiring journey. It was a tiring but interesting journey.	9	Both long and tiring. Interesting, although it was tiring.
10	It was a long, tiring journey.	10	A comma in writing, or pause in speech, can replace the *and* in 9.

IV.4 Combinations and modifiers of determiners in a noun phrase

Models

He baked several thousand loaves a day.
Give me another two dozen eggs.
The first three boys will get a prize.
A friend of mine. That dog of Charles's.

Notes

1. Have /another biscuit/ /some more coffee/. Have some more biscuits.

   1. *another* = one more unit. Use *some more* with mass or units, PLURAL: see II.21.6.

2. Give me another /ten/ /two dozen/ eggs. He baked several thousand loaves a day. /A few/ /several/ /the first/ dozen.

   2. *another* + *ten* = ten more. Note that *some* /dozen/ /thousand/ = *about* /a dozen/ /a thousand/ . . .

3. /The/ /These/ /Those/ /My/ two boys are tall.
   The first three boys will get a prize.
   The last three will have to drop out.
   The three last boys finished together.

   3.

   ie the first, second and third.
   drop out: see III.23.2.
   There were three who were last.

4. The baker's (only) (other) (two) employees.
   The only other bread is stale.

   4. (*only*) (*other*) + (numeral) + units.

   (*only*) (*other*) + mass.

5. Some of the many people who came . . .

   5. *the* /many/ /few/ + units.

6. I have a good /few/ /many/ books.

   A great $\left\{ \begin{array}{l} \text{amount} \\ \text{deal} \end{array} \right\}$ of money.

   A great /number of/ /many/ people.

   6. *a good few* = more than a few.

   a great /amount/ /deal/ of + mass.

   a great /number of/ /many/ + units.

7a. That's about /all/ /enough/ /half/ /twenty/.
    That's almost /all/ /enough/ /half/ /twenty/.

   7a. Sim. *about* /a week/ /the only man/ /the first/ /the last/ ; and *almost* /a week/ /etc/.

   b. Almost /every egg/ /the whole lot/ was bad. There/'s/ /are/ almost none left.

   b. *almost every*, etc; *almost* replaceable by *nearly* in 7a and 7b.

   c. There's /not nearly/ /barely/ enough. I've hardly /any/ /enough/ for myself.

   c. Exclude *almost*, after *not*. *hardly* or *scarcely any*.

   d. That's more than /enough/ /half/ /ten/.

   d. *more than* . . . Also *less than*.

8. Over /a week/ /half/ /twenty/ . . .

   8. *over a* /week/ /month/ /year/ /etc/.

9   I've $\left\{\begin{array}{l}\textit{no}\\\textit{not}\end{array}\right\}$ more than twenty.

I've (no) fewer than twenty.

9   $\left.\begin{array}{l}\textit{no}\\\textit{not}\end{array}\right\}$ *more than.*

no fewer than.

10   Not $\left\{\begin{array}{l}\text{all books are}\\\text{every book is}\end{array}\right\}$ worth reading.

10   *Not all* = only some.

11   I've quite /a few/ /a lot/ /enough/.

11   *quite a few* = more than a few.

12   Very /few/ /little/ /much/; a very /few/ /little/.

12   *very few*, etc: see *few*: II.4.7. *a very few*: see *a few*: II.4.7.

13   Let's start at the very beginning.

13   = right at the beginning.

14   Tom is a friend. He's my friend.
He's one of my friends.
He's a friend of mine.
I don't like that dog. It's Charles's.
I don't like that dog of Charles's.

14   *a* and /*my*/ /*your*/ /*his*/ /etc/ cannot both occur as PREMODIFIERS in the same NP.

A similar comment applies to /*this*/ /*that*/ and a POSSESSIVE.

15a   A story that is too long is too long a story.

15a   Sim. *so long a story*. Avoid this structure with MASS NOUNS.

b   That is quite a story.

b   Sim. /*rather*/ /*such*/ *a story*.

IV.5   Modifiers occurring after the head-word in NP, and the effect this may have on (a) the article and (b) the passive

Models
/A/ /The/ book with torn covers . . .
/A/ /The/ man standing at the back . . .
/Something/ /Someone/ interesting . . .

Notes

1   Some books have torn covers.
One of those books has torn covers.

1
One is the HEAD-WORD determining CONCORD.
See I.15.8.

I don't want /a book/ /one/ with torn covers.
I don't want the /book/ /one/ with torn covers.

The PREP PHRASE identifies a particular example in this case.

2   The bomb wrecked a house near us.

2   *near us*—a POSTMODIFIER *or* ADV ADJUNCT.

A house was wrecked near us.
A house near us was wrecked.
The house next door to us was wrecked.

Here, *near us* is ADV ADJUNCT.
Here, *near us* is POSTMODIFIER in the NP.
Here, *next door to us* is POSTMOD in the NP.

3   We lost the key of the door.
The key of the door was lost.

3   A PREP PHRASE starting with *of* frequently helps to identify the particular example referred to by the HEAD-WORD, eg *key*.

4   This book is up to date.
It contains up-to-date ideas.

4   A PREP PHRASE seldom occurs before the HEAD-WORD. When it does, it is usually hyphenated.

5   He was in the house $\left\{\begin{array}{l}\text{that}\\\text{which}\end{array}\right\}$ was wrecked.

He lived in the house near us $\left\{\begin{array}{l}\text{that}\\\text{which}\end{array}\right\}$ was wrecked.

5   RELATIVE CLAUSE (III.13) as POSTMODIFIER.

PREP PHRASE + RELATIVE CLAUSE as POSTMODIFIER.

6 That's the book I want—the one (you've got) in your hand.
The book (you've got) in your hand was published last year.

6 *I want* and *you've got in your hand* as RELATIVE CLAUSE POSTMODIFIERS.
The book (you've got) in your hand is the whole NP, SUBJECT of *was published*.

7 A man $\begin{Bmatrix} who \\ that \end{Bmatrix}$ was standing at the back suddenly gave a shout.
The man $\begin{Bmatrix} who \\ that \end{Bmatrix}$ was standing at the back asked the first question.

7 There may have been more than one man standing at the back.
One particular man (*who was*) *standing at the back*.

8 Here is /something/ /someone/ interesting.
I want something (really) good.

8 ADJECTIVES follow the PRONOUNS dealt with in II.28.

9 Everyone $\begin{Bmatrix} except \\ but \end{Bmatrix}$ John was there.
or Everyone was there $\begin{Bmatrix} except \\ but \end{Bmatrix}$ John.

10 The above example. The example above. The example below. The upstairs room. The room upstairs. The man outside.

10 *above* can be PREMODIFIER or POSTMOD. *below* only POSTMODIFIER.
ADVERBIALS as POSTMODIFIERS in NP.

11 A book to read.
A book from the library.

11 See IV.7.8.
= A book that has come from the library.

IV.6 Infinitive with *to*, and *for* + NP or *for* + gerund, expressing purpose

Models
We took a taxi to get there in time.
I'm taking lessons (in order) to improve my English.
He went to the office for more details.

Notes

1 Why did you take a taxi?
What did you take a taxi for?
To get there in time.

We took a taxi to get there in time.
We arrived (right) on time.

1

Short answer: *in time* = without being late.
to + VERB: contrast *for* + NP, 9 below.
on time: exactly at the right time.

2 I am taking lessons $\begin{Bmatrix} so as \\ in order \end{Bmatrix}$ to improve my English.

2 Regard *in order* and *so as* as interchangeable, but *in order* as more formal.

3 He took a bus so as not to be late.
We must whisper in order not to wake the children.

3 Use *so as not to* or *in order not to*, but exclude *not to* alone, for the NEGATIVE. In both these models, the SUBJECT in each CLAUSE is the same.

4 We'll sit nearer the front $\begin{Bmatrix} in order \\ so as \end{Bmatrix}$ to hear better.
We'll sit nearer the front $\begin{Bmatrix} so \\ so that \end{Bmatrix}$ we can hear better.

4

so that is more formal

5 I'm going there (so as) to buy some stamps.   5 *I'll* buy the stamps.
 I'm going to send you to buy some stamps.   *You'll* buy the stamps.
 He left us to pay the bill.   Ambiguous: *he* would pay, or *we* should pay?

 He left us in order to pay the bill.   Unambiguous: *he* left us and *he* would pay.

 We were left to pay the bill.   Unambiguous: *we* had to pay it.

6 I write with a pen. I use a pen to write with.   6 *I* write with it.
 I've brought this stool to sit on.   *I* will sit on it.

7 Here is a pen to write with.   7 *You* can write with it.
 I'll bring you a cushion to sit on.   *You* can sit on it.

8 NB   8

 a I want you to give me that book.   a Example of SP 6c, as in II.15.3.
   I want it to stay on my desk.   Example of SP 6c, as in II.15.3.

 b I want it to keep on my desk.   b I want it /in order/ /so as/ to keep it on my desk.

9a I went to the travel agency   9a *for* + NP can indicate the purpose of my going to the travel agency.

$$\left.\begin{array}{l}\text{to get}\\\text{in order to get}\\\text{so as to get}\\\text{for}\end{array}\right\}\text{some information.}$$

 b This oil is only used for cooking.   b As in IV.3.1.

IV.7 Nouns and indefinite pronouns modified by infinitive with *to*, especially when the noun matches a verb which fits into SP 6b

Models

They made plans to live in Paris.
There is no need to say that.
I want a book to read.

Notes

1 They planned to live in Paris.   1 SP 6b, as in I.22.2.
 They made plans to live in Paris.   The VERB in SP 6b replaced by *make* + NOUN.

2 I have no [desire][1] to see him.   2 = *I don't wish* etc. *Desire, need, wish*
 There's no need to say that.   fit into SP 6b, as VERBS. The correspond-
 I've no [wish][1] to. There's no need to.   ing NOUNS have the same stem. *have no [desire][1]*.

3 We promised to be there.   3 VERBS *arrange, attempt, promise*, fit into
 We /promised/ /made a promise/ /not/ /never/ to do that again.   SP 6b and are replaceable by *make /an arrangement/ /an attempt/ /a promise/*.

4 They [decided][2] to leave.   4 *They /decided/ /failed/ /refused/ to*, in
 Their [decision][3] to leave was very [annoying].   SP 6b, matched by *Their /decision/ /failure/ /refusal/ to*. (NB not all VERBS that fit into SP 6b have corresponding NOUNS.)

5 Our [idea][4] is to [build a new] city.

6 Candidates must be able to speak well.

Ability to speak well is essential.

7 There'll be a chance $\left\{ \begin{array}{l} \text{to visit} \\ \text{of visiting} \end{array} \right\}$ Bath, I hope.

8 I want a book to read.
You need /something to eat/ /somewhere to sleep/ /someone to talk to/.
He has six children to educate.
Is that the way to do it?
What an awful thing to say!
The first boy to finish can go.

9 It's time to /stop/ /go to bed/.

10 Do you /hope/ /intend/ to go away?
I've no hope of going away yet. I've no intention of going yet.

6 *able to:* cp II.16.1, and *anxious to,* III.8.4.
able to, anxious to, curious to and *ability to, anxiety to, curiosity to.*

7 The NOUN *opportunity* could replace *chance* here. No VERB corresponding to *opportunity.*

8 = a book that I can read.
= some food, some place where you can sleep, someone that you can talk to.
= six children that he must educate.

The boy who finishes first.

10 Or *Do you intend going away?*
hope (VERB) *to; hope* (NOUN) *of+ -ing; intend to; intention to go* or *of going.*

Lexicon
1 NOUNS whose stem has the same form as the corresponding VERBS: *desire, need, wish*
2 *decided, failed, offered, promised, refused, threatened*
3 *decision, failure, offer, promise, refusal, threat*
4 *aim, hope, idea, intention, object, proposal, purpose, suggestion, wish*

IV.8 Conditional sentences of the type *He would come if you asked him*

Models
He would come if you asked him.
If he only tried, he could do well.
I shouldn't do that if I were you.

Notes

1   You'll get wet if it rains.

1 CONDITIONAL sentences Type 1. *If it rains* suggests a possible future fact. See III.16.

2 *A* Tom won't be at the party.
  B But have you asked him?
  A No, I didn't like to.
  B He would come if you asked him.
     If you asked him, he'd be thrilled.
  C Would Mary come if we asked her?
  B She certainly wouldn't come if you didn't invite her.
     She wouldn't come unless you /invited her/ /sent her an invitation/.

2

A non-fact: Tom has not been asked.
Type 2: *if you asked:* non-fact imagined as fact. *He would* reduced to *he'd.*

See III.16.3. Here, the meaning is *She would only come if invited.*

3 *A* What would you do if you were all alone on a desert island?

  B First, I'd look for something to eat.
     That's what I $\left\{ \begin{array}{l} \text{'d} \\ \text{would} \\ \text{should} \end{array} \right\}$ do.

3 Imagine that non-fact; then imagine the consequences of it. *all alone=* entirely by yourself, as in III.3.7.

would replaceable by *should* in conditional sentences after *I* or *we:* cp II.13.5.

4   If you have a problem, you should ask me to explain it.

4   *should* as in III.22.1, not contractable, replaceable by *ought to*. Cp the sequence of tenses here with that in 3*A* above.

5   *A* Shall we go out for dinner?
     B That would be very nice.

5   Suggestion, as in II.15.6.
     That = going out for dinner.

6a   George could do well /if/ /when/ he tried.

6a   PAST of *he can do well /if/ /when/ he tries*. He sometimes did try: then he could do well.

b   George makes no effort at all.
     If he only tried, he could do well.
     If he tried, he might do very well.

b   He doesn't try: non-fact.
     The CONDITIONAL CLAUSE can follow or precede the MAIN CLAUSE.

7   *A* Could you swim across the river?
     B Yes, it would be easy, it wouldn't be (very) difficult.

7   ie if you tried, wanted to, etc.
     it = swimming across the river.

8   If you bathe now, you /may/ /might/ catch cold.
     We can't bathe here. If we did, we might both be drowned.

8

     if we did = if we bathed here;
     might not replaceable by *may* here.

9   If I were you, I shouldn't do that.
     You wouldn't say that if he were still alive.

9   *were* often replaces *was*, after *I, he, she, it, there*, when the sense of non-fact is strong.

10a What would you do if there was a fire?

10a The sense of non-fact is not very strong.
     Contrast *What would you do* with *What should you do?* (obligation as in III.22.4).

b   There's no telephone here. If there *were* one, we could ring them up.

b   The non-fact is inescapable.

IV.9 VP with the infinitive without *to*

Models
He made us wait outside.
You'd better go now.
I'd rather not go yet.

Notes

1a   *A* Did he [ask][1] you in?
     B No, he made us wait outside.

1a   As in II.14.6.
     make + NP + BARE INFINITIVE.

b   *A* I'll make you pay for this.
     B You can't make me.

b
     = make me pay for it.

2   He made us feel welcome.
     He made us [feel][2] (that) he wanted us to stay longer.

2   *feel* + ADJ as in II.1.3.
     See IV.11.1.

3   *A* Can I help (you) carry that?
     Can I help (to) carry it for you?

3   *help* + (NP) + BARE INFINITIVE.
     Omit the PERSONAL OBJECT of *help* if *for* [*you*] is added.
     When the OBJECT of *help* is a long NP, the INFINITIVE with *to*, rather than the bare INFINITIVE, is normal.

     B Help the little boys at the back of the hall to carry the chairs out.

4a   *A* When shall we see you again?
     B I'll let you know.

4a
     = I'll inform you.

b   Don't let that glass slip.

5   Let go of my arm.

6   Let's go, shall we?
     Let us consider this matter from a
     different point of view.
     Please let us go, will you?

6   A suggestion, as in II.14.7. *Let's*
     normal in conversation; *let us* appro-
     priate in formal style.
     let us go, not contracted = may we go:
     a request.

7   Don't let there be any noise.
     Let there be no mistake about this.
     I [don't want]³ there to be any mistake.

7

     SP 6b combined with *there* [*is*].

8   I've never known him behave like this.

8   Use only with PERFECTIVE ASPECT.

9 *A* It's late. You'd better go now.

9   = I think you ought to go.

   B I'd rather not. I'd $\left\{ \begin{matrix} \text{rather} \\ \text{sooner} \end{matrix} \right\}$ stay.

     = I prefer to stay.

10   You'd $\left\{ \begin{matrix} \text{rather} \\ \text{sooner} \end{matrix} \right\}$ go, wouldn't you?
     You'd better go now, hadn't you?

11   Would you rather have tea?
     Hadn't you better do some work?
     What would you rather do, swim or go
     for a walk?
   A Let's climb in through the window.
   B No, we'd better not.

12   We'll have to make do with dry bread.

12   *make do* = manage, be content with.

13   You should have someone check these
     figures.

13   = You should arrange for someone to
     check them.

Lexicon
1 *allow, ask, help, let*
2 *believe, feel, think*
3 *would not like, would hate, don't want*

IV.10 Infinitive or *-ing* acceptable in the same structure, with either different emphasis or different meaning

Models

I saw him $\left\{ \begin{matrix} \text{cross} \\ \text{crossing} \end{matrix} \right\}$ the road.

I remembered to post your letter.
I remember dropping it in the box.

Notes

1   [Watch]¹ me climb that rope.
     Did you hear a dog bark?
     I saw him cross the road.
     Did you feel the floor shake?

1   See Lex 1 below. Prefer the INFINITIVE
     when emphasis is on the completed act.

2   [Look at]² him climbing the cliff.
     I saw him crossing the road.
     I heard that dog barking all night.

2   Prefer the *-ing* form when emphasis is
     on the action in progress. Notice the
     difference between *I heard the dog bark*
     and *I heard the dog barking all night.*

3a   I like $\left\{ \begin{matrix} \text{to lie} \\ \text{lying} \end{matrix} \right\}$ in the sun.

3a   *like, love, hate* + INFINITIVE or *-ing.*

 b   I like riding better than walking.

 b   *-ing* preferred in this case.

 c   I would like to lie in the sun.

 c   *would* /*like*/ /*love*/ /*hate*/ + INFINITIVE.

d I didn't like to disturb him.

e I didn't like disturbing him, but I felt I had to.

f I dislike having to disturb people.

4 I /propose/ /mean/ to start at once.
I propose starting at once.
I /advise/ /suggest/ starting . . .
The bus strike will mean walking to work.

5 They [started]³ { to sing.
{ singing.

They're [start]³ing to move.

6 They won't allow you to smoke here.
They won't allow smoking here.

7 I remembered to post your letter.
I remember dropping it in the box.

8 Try to do } better.
Try and do }

Try turning the handle the other way and see if that will work.

9 He stopped working a year ago.
He stopped to light a cigarette.

10 Never forget to thank your host.
I'll never forget seeing Mont Blanc.

11 We didn't stop. We went on walking.
We went on to visit the old castle.

12 I won't go out alone. I'm afraid to.
I'm afraid of waking the baby.

---

d This may imply that I didn't disturb him.

e This may imply that I did, or intended to, disturb him.

f *dislike*+*-ing*, not INFINITIVE: III.24.

4 *I* propose etc, and *I* will start.
I propose: I or we should start.
I advise, etc: you should start.
Because of the strike, I, you or we will have to walk.

5 When [*start*]³ is in the progressive, avoid *-ing* in the VERB that follows.

6 *You* won't be allowed to smoke.
You or others won't be allowed to: IV.25.2.

7 I remembered I had to, and I posted it.
I remember that action.

8 Make an attempt with the object of doing. Do not use *try and* [*do*] in PAST TENSE.
Make that experiment and see what will happen.

9 Then he didn't work any more.
As in IV.6.1. He stopped whatever he was doing, in order to light a cigarette.

10 = Always remember to thank him.
I /'ve seen/ /saw/ it, and shall not forget it.

11 *go on*, as in III.23.2, + *-ing*.
= We continued our tour and visited, etc.

12 ie afraid to go out alone in the future.
I'm afraid I might wake the baby.

Lexicon
1 *feel, hear, notice, see, watch*
2 *feel, hear, listen to, look at, notice, observe, see, watch*
3 *begin, cease, continue, intend, omit, prefer, start; also can't bear*

IV.11 *That*-clauses after verbs, nouns and adjectives

Models

Everyone can see (that) he's frightened.
It's true (that) he's frightened.
It's a pity (that) we can't go too.

Notes

1 Everyone can see him.
Everyone [can see]¹ (that) he's mad.

Everyone could see (that) he was mad.

1 *see* with NP as OBJECT.
see with *that*-CLAUSE, OBJECT; *that* optional.
PAST TENSE in both CLAUSES.

A What could everyone see?
B That he was frightened.

> *That* not omitted when the CLAUSE
> occurs as a short answer.

2   They told us the truth.
They [told]² us (that) the road was closed.
This shows (us) (that) he's right.

> 2   *tell* + INDIRECT OBJECT, personal + NP.
> *tell* + INDIRECT OBJECT, personal + *that-*
> CLAUSE. IND OBJ optional with *show.*

3   He [explained]³ (to us) that there were
four different roads to Rome.

> 3   *explain* (+ *to* + personal NP) + *that-*
> CLAUSE.

4a   I'm [sure]⁴ (that) it's all right.

> 4a   Personal SUBJECT + *be* + ADJ + *that-*
> CLAUSE.

  b   I'm not sure (that) I understand you.
I'm not sure if I understand.

> b   Restrict to *certain, sure.*

5   It's [certain]⁵ (that) you can go.

> 5   It + *be* + ADJ + *that-*CLAUSE.

6   It's a [pity]⁶ (that) we can't go too.

> 6   It + *be* + NOUN + *that-*CLAUSE.

7   The [fact]⁷ is (that) there are four
different roads to Rome.

> 7   NOUN + *be* + *that-*CLAUSE.

8   My [opinion]⁸ is (that) he really doesn't
understand you.

> 8   POSSESSIVE + NOUN + *be* + *that-*CLAUSE.

9   I've no doubt (that) you'll understand.

> 9   Exclude AFFIRMATIVE in MAIN CLAUSE.

10   We're [amused] to /see/ /hear/ (that)
you've met her at last.

> 10   Cp III.8.9.

11   I'll /see/ /make sure/ /make certain/
(that) you don't get lost.

Please /see/ /make sure/ /make certain/
that everything is in order.

> 11   The *that-*CLAUSE has future reference,
> but the sequence of tenses is as in
> IV.8.1.
> IMPERATIVE in MAIN CLAUSE, PRESENT
> TENSE in SUBORDINATE.

12   I agree (that) this is rather hard.
I [agree]⁹ (that) he should go.

> 12   ie I think that statement is true.
> I agree that he ought to go. See VI.24.

13a   I [hope]¹⁰ to see you there.

> 13a   = I hope (that) $\left\{\begin{array}{c} \text{I} \\ \text{I'll} \end{array}\right\}$ see you ...

  b   I hoped to see him.
  c   I hope you see him.

> b   = I wanted to see him (in the past).
> c   Exclude the INFINITIVE when the
> SUBJECTS are different, eg *I* and *you.*

  d   I hope I said the right thing.

> d   Exclude the INFINITIVE when the
> tenses are different, eg *I hope, said.*

Lexicon

1   *add, admit, agree, announce, answer, argue, assert, assume, believe, conclude, confirm, consider, declare,
doubt, dream, expect, feel, find, find out, forget, gather, guess, hear, hope, imagine, know, learn,
maintain, mention, note, notice, observe, pretend, realise, repeat, reply, report, say, show, state, think,
write*
2   *assure, convince, inform, persuade, remind, satisfy, show, teach, tell, warn*
3   *confess, explain, say, suggest, write*
4   *afraid, certain, delighted, disappointed, pleased, positive, satisfied, sure, surprised*
5   *certain, definite, likely, possible, true, unlikely*
6   *disgrace, nuisance, pity, shame*
7   *explanation, fact, position*
8   *explanation, feeling, opinion, view*
9   *agree, believe, feel, think; am afraid* (= sorry), *am certain, am sure*
10   *agree, hope*

IV.12 Use of tenses in indirect speech

Models	**Notes**

'I've never met her,' he said.
He said he'd never met her.

1	*A*	'I'm a stranger here.'	1
	B	What does he say?
	Ca	He says (that) he's a stranger here.	PRESENT TENSE in both CLAUSES.
	b	He says (that) he can't understand us.	PRESENT TENSE in both CLAUSES.
	c	He says (that) he may be late.	PRESENT TENSE in both CLAUSES.
2	*A*	'I'm going to get you some water.'	2
	C	He says (that) he's going to get us some water.	PRESENT in MAIN CLAUSE; then *be going to.*
3	*A*	'I'll get you some food.'	3
	C	He says (that) he'll get us some food.	PRESENT in MAIN CLAUSE; then *'ll.*
4	*A*	"I've never met her before," he says.	4
	C	He insists (that) he's never met her before.	PRESENT in MAIN CLAUSE; then PRESENT PERFECTIVE.
5	*A*	I've been trying to repair my car.	5
	C	He says (that) he's been trying to repair his car.	PRESENT in MAIN CLAUSE; then PRESENT PERFECTIVE-PROGRESSIVE.
6	*A*	'I fell down the stairs.'	6 Reporting PAST action.
	C	They say (that) he fell down the stairs.	PRESENT in MAIN CLAUSE, then PAST.
7a		You told us (that) you were a stranger here.	7a See 1 above. PAST reported speech.
b		You told us (that) you couldn't understand.	b *can* becomes *could* in PAST reported speech.
c		You told us (that) you might be late.	c *may* becomes *might* in PAST reported speech.

8   You said (that) you were going to get us some water. Where is it?

9   You promised that you $\left\{\begin{matrix}\text{'d}\\\text{would}\end{matrix}\right\}$ get us some food. What have you done about it?

8   See 2 above. /Am/ /is/ /are/ going becomes /was/ /were/ going.

9   See 3 above: $\left\{\begin{matrix}\text{'ll}\\\text{will}\end{matrix}\right\}$ becomes $\left\{\begin{matrix}\text{'d.}\\\text{would.}\end{matrix}\right\}$

10	He insisted (that) he had never met her before.	10 See 4 above. PRESENT PERFECTIVE becomes PAST PERFECTIVE.
11	He explained (that) he'd been trying to repair his car.	11 See 5 above. PRESENT PERF-PROGRESSIVE becomes PAST PERF-PROGRESSIVE.
12	They realised (that) he had fallen down the stairs.	12 See 6 above. SIMPLE PAST also becomes PAST PERFECTIVE if the falling preceded the realising.

13   'This road leads to Rome.'
He says (that) this road leads to Rome.
He said (that) this road led to Rome.
He said (that) this road leads to Rome.

13   Sequence of tenses as in 7a above.
This combination is possible, if the road *still* leads to Rome.

14   He said he would be here by seven.
He said he will be here by seven.

14   Sequence as in 9 above.
This sequence also possible if the statement is made before seven.

15   It was a pity we couldn't go too.

15   The sequence of tenses exemplified in IV.12 will also occur in the structures given in IV.11.2–10 inclusive.

IV.13 *Wh*-clause, as the object of a verb, or preposition; structures on the pattern *what to do*

Models
Let me know where he lives.
It depends (on) what you mean.
I'll tell him what to do.

Notes

1a   I [know]¹ the answer.

1a   [I know]¹ + NP.

b   I [know]
{
what you're doing.
where he lives.
who did it.
when it will take place.
why they won't help us.
how I can open it.
}

b   See III.2.6–7. [I know]¹ + *wh*-CLAUSE.

2a   I told you where he lived.

You asked (me) where he lived.

2a   I told you, at some time in the past, where he lived then.

b   I told you where he had gone.
You asked (me) where he'd gone.

b   I told you then where he had gone before then: *where he went* would also be acceptable, but the PAST PERFECT emphasises the idea of 'before then'.

3   [Explain]² (to me) ⎰what you /see/ /saw/.
Describe (to me) ⎱how you /do/ /did/ it.

3   Cp IV.11.3.

4a   What shall we do?

4

b   I don't know
{
what to do.
where to go.
who to ask.
when to stop.
how to get there.
}

b   *I* don't know what *I* can do, where *I* must go, etc.
Exclude *why*.

5

I don't know
{
what you can do.
where you must go.
who you can ask.
where you should stop.
how you can get there.
}

5   The structure in 4 above is normally used when the SUBJECTS and time references of both CLAUSES are the same: see IV.11.13.

6a   I'll tell him ⎰what to do.
⎱where to go, etc.

6a   = I tell *him* what *he* can do.

b   I'll explain (to him) what to do, etc.

7 *A* Do you know *who* to ask?
 B The *person* to ask is the secretary.
 A Do you know *what* to eat?
 B The best *thing* to eat is fruit.

7   Similarly, Do you know *when* to leave (the *time* to leave); *where* to buy it (the *place* to buy it); *how* to get it (the *way* to get it); *which* to choose (the /one/ /ones/ to choose).

8 *A* Are you going to answer this letter?   8

   B I don't know $\left\{ \begin{array}{l} \text{if} \\ \text{whether} \end{array} \right\}$ I'm going to

        answer it (or not).
        I don't know whether to answer it (or
        not).

Cp III.2.2: note *I don't know whether . . .
or not.*

Exclude *if* before the INFINITIVE.

Lexicon

1 *can find out, can guess, can imagine, know, remember, will tell you*
2 *asked, forget, can guess, can imagine, want to know, can't remember, will tell you, wonder*
3 *describe, explain*

IV.14 Conditional sentences, types 1 and 2, with *provided, providing, on con-dition that, even if, whether, supposing;* and sentences with *would* in both clauses

Models

I'll tell you the secret, on condition
(that) you don't tell anyone.
Supposing you were left alone on a
desert island, what would you do?

Notes

1a I'll tell you on one condition: you
    mustn't tell anyone else.

 b I'll tell you on condition (that)

    you $\left. \begin{array}{l} \text{don't} \\ \text{won't} \end{array} \right\}$ tell anyone else.

 c I'll tell you the secret, $\left\{ \begin{array}{l} \text{provided} \\ \text{providing} \end{array} \right\}$ (that)

    you keep it to yourself.

 d Promise $\left\{ \begin{array}{l} \text{you won't} \\ \text{not to} \end{array} \right\}$ tell anyone else.

2 You said $\left\{ \begin{array}{l} \text{you wouldn't} \\ \text{not to} \end{array} \right\}$ tell

   anyone else, remember?
   I told you on condition that you would
   keep it to yourself.

3 I don't mind if it rains tomorrow.
   I'll go out in any case.
   I'll go out even if it pours (with rain).
   Nothing will keep me here.
   Even if it rained in torrents,

   I $\left\{ \begin{array}{l} \text{wouldn't} \\ \text{shouldn't} \end{array} \right\}$ stay here all day long.

4 *A* The weather forecast says we'll have
       snow tomorrow.

   B I don't care. I'll climb the mountain
       whether it snows or not.
       I'd go whether you wanted me to or not.

1a *on a condition.*

 b *on condition (that).*

 c *provided, providing.*

 d *promise (that)* + CLAUSE; or *promise
    (not) to.*

2 Sequence of tenses as in IV.8.3*A*.

   Sequence of tenses as in IV.8.3*A*.

3 = if it rains or if it doesn't.
   I'll in the models replaceable by *I will*
   or *I shall.*

4

   whether or not.

5 *A* Suppose / Supposing } (that) all the doors are locked, how will you get in(to) the house?

5 *Suppose / Supposing* } *that* with sequence of tenses as in IV.8.1.

6 *A* Suppose / Supposing } (that) you were left alone on a desert island, what would you do first /what is the first thing you would do?

6 *Suppose / Supposing* } (*that*) with sequence as in IV.8.3*A*.

B First, I'd look for some /drinking water/ /water to drink/.

I'd replaceable by *I would* or *I should*.

The first thing I'd do would be to look for some water.

I'd replaceable by *I would* or *I should*.

IV.15 *Seem, appear, happen* + infinitive; *it /seems/ /looks/ as if* + clause

Models
We seem to be moving at last.
He seems to have missed the train.
It seems as if someone's coming.

Notes

1 *A* Tom is quite intelligent, I think.
B He [seems][1] (to be) very intelligent.
He seems to be.
He [happens][2] to be a friend of mine.
He happens to be.

1 Cp II.1. With *seem* and *appear, to be* is optional in the complete sentence. *to be* not optional with *happen*.

2 *A* They like their presents, I think.
B They [seem][2] to like them. They seem to.

2 *They like* becomes *They seem to like.*

3 *A* The ship's started. We're moving.
B Yes, we [seem][2] to be (moving at last).

3 *to be moving:* INFINITIVE, PROGRESSIVE.

4 *A* I think Dick has missed the train.
B He [seems][2] to have (missed it).

4 *has missed,* PERFECTIVE.
to have missed: INFINITIVE, PERFECTIVE.

5 *A* No, there he is, looking very hot.
B He [seems][2] to have been running.
A He [seems][2] to have been.

5 = I think he has been (running).

6 *A* Perhaps he missed the bus.
B He [seems][2] to have (missed it).

6 *missed,* SIMPLE PAST.
to have missed: same form as in 4 above.

7 *A* Mary was depressed at the party.
B She [seemed][2] to be (depressed).
A Jane [seemed][2] to be dancing all night.

7 *She was* becomes *She seemed to be.*
= I think she was (dancing). She seemed to be.

8 They [seemed][2] to have had (a quarrel).
They [seemed][2] to have been (fighting).

8 = I think they had (had one).
= I think they had been (fighting).

9 That old man [seems][2] to have been hurt.

9 = I think he has been hurt.

10 *A* Is anyone coming? /See/ /Look and see/ if anyone's following us.
*B*a Yes, it [looks][3] (to me) as { if / though } someone's following us.

10

a *It looks as if* or *looks as though.*

b It [seems]³ (to me) as $\begin{Bmatrix} \text{if} \\ \text{though} \end{Bmatrix}$ someone's coming.

c Someone [seems]² (to me) to be following us.

11 *A* A man with a stick is following us.

B It [seems]⁴ (from what *A* says) (that) a man with a stick is following us.

C It [seems]⁴ (to me) (that) he's limping.

D It [happens]⁵ that he *is* limping.

12 It [seemed]³ as if it was going to rain. It [seemed]⁴ (that) we had a lot of rain last night. It [seemed]⁴ (to me) (that we did).

b This can replace the previous model.

c This can replace the two previous models, but note Lexicon below.

11

This is a more certain statement than 10b above.

That is my view—I may be wrong.

Lexicon

1 *appear, seem*
2 *appear, happen, seem; chanced* (past only)
3 *appear, look, seem, sound*
4 *appear, seem*
5 *appear, happen, seem*

IV.16 Progressive and perfective aspects combined with future reference

Models

We'll be thinking of you tomorrow.
I'll have read it by Tuesday.
By next week, he'll have been working here for twenty years.

Notes

1 The procession is passing us now. It will be passing your flat in about ten minutes, I imagine.

1 PRESENT PROGRESSIVE as in I.18. PROGRESSIVE ASPECT, future reference.

2 We'll be thinking of you tomorrow, when you have your operation.

2

Sequence of tenses as in IV.8.1.

3 *A* $\begin{Bmatrix} \text{Will} \\ \text{Shall} \end{Bmatrix}$ we be using this book next term?

B No, you won't be (using this book).

4 *A* I haven't read your essay yet.

B Will you have read it by Friday?

A I $\begin{Bmatrix} \text{won't} \\ \text{shan't} \end{Bmatrix}$ start it till then.

I expect $\begin{Bmatrix} \text{I'll} \\ \text{to} \end{Bmatrix}$ finish it by Monday.

Anyway, I'll have read it all by Tuesday at the latest.

4

PERFECTIVE ASPECT, future reference.

For *by* and *till* with time, see III.17.10.

expect + *that*-CLAUSE, or *to* + INFINITIVE.

5 *A* Mr Turner has been working in this office for nearly twenty years. In fact, by next week he'll have been working here for twenty years exactly.

B Will he have been working here as long as you have?

5 As in III.19.

PERFECTIVE-PROGRESSIVE, future reference.

ie as long as you have been working here.

	A No, he won't have been (working here as long as that).		*he /will/ /won't/ have been:* short answer.
6	*A* I'll get the tickets tomorrow.	6	
	B That will be too late. They'll all have been sold by then.		PERFECTIVE, FUTURE, PASSIVE.
7	*A* I must go to the bank and stop that cheque, but I can't get there till half past ten.	7	
	B Will it have been cashed by then? It won't have been (cashed), (surely).		*It /will/ /won't/ have been:* short form.
8	They 'phoned to say (that) the procession would be passing our flat in about ten minutes.	8	1 above, in PAST REPORTED SPEECH.
9	You promised (me) (that) you would have read it by Tuesday.	9	4 above in PAST REPORTED SPEECH.
10	I got the tickets today. They would all have been sold by tomorrow.	10	PAST equivalent of 6*B* above.

IV.17 Perfective, with future reference, in temporal and conditional clauses

Models

I'll tell you when I've read it.
Wait until I've put my shoes on.
We waited until they'd finished.

Notes

1 *A* I haven't read your essay yet.
I'll have read it all by Tuesday.

  B What do you think of it?

  A I'll tell you [when][1] I've read it.

   I can't tell you / $\left\{ \begin{array}{l} \text{until} \\ \text{till} \end{array} \right\}$ / /unless/ I've read it, can I?

1

As in IV.16.4.
What is your opinion of it?
I'll have read becomes *I've read* in the
TEMPORAL or CONDITIONAL CLAUSE.
till always replaceable by *until*.

2 We shan't get to the theatre till 8.15.
The play will start at 8.
It will have started by 8.15.

  We $\left\{ \begin{array}{l} \text{won't} \\ \text{shan't} \end{array} \right\}$ find our seats till (after) the play has started.

2

In the SUBORDINATE CLAUSE, *will have
started* becomes *has started*.

3 I'll have seen the doctor by 7.
I'll tell you what he thinks /as soon as/ /immediately/ /the moment/ I've seen him.

3

immediately, *the moment*, introducing a
temporal CLAUSE.

4 *A* When I've learnt a thousand English

  words, $\left\{ \begin{array}{l} \text{shall} \\ \text{will} \end{array} \right\}$ I be able to read an

  English newspaper?

  B You'll be able to read something, [so long as][2] you *have* learnt a thousand words and so long as you've been studying properly.

4 I haven't learnt them yet. Perhaps I'll
have learnt them by the end of this year.
I'll have learnt becomes *I've learnt*.

so long as= provided, as in IV.14.1.
PROGRESSIVE in the temporal CLAUSE.

5	/By the time (that)/ /When/ you've learnt two thousand words, you'll know quite a lot.
6	Wait for me. I'm not ready yet. Wait till I've put my shoes on.
7	Don't ask me to write a letter in English yet. Wait till I've been studying it (for) a few more weeks.
8	We didn't find our seats till (after) the play {began. / had begun.}
9	I didn't want to write a letter in English till (after) I had been studying it (for) a few more weeks.

5 *By the time* (*that*) introducing a temporal CLAUSE.

6 IMPERATIVE + temporal CLAUSE.

7 IMPERATIVE + temporal CLAUSE, with PROGRESSIVE.

8 PAST equivalent of 2 above. This produces a normal use of the PAST PERFECT, as in III.27.

9 PAST equivalent of 7 above.

Lexicon
1 *after, as soon as, immediately, the moment, when*
2 *if, provided* (*that*), *providing* (*that*), *so long as*

IV.18 Unfulfilled past obligation, etc; and action taken despite obligation to the contrary; unused ability and unfulfilled wishes and intentions

Models

You should have asked me.
You shouldn't have promised.
You /ought/ /oughtn't/ to have done that.
I would like to have seen it.

Notes

1 *A* I've sent the money. I sent it yesterday.

   B You haven't asked my permission.
You didn't ask me if you could.

You {should / ought to} have asked my permission first.

You {should / ought to} have (done).

1 Fault of omission, PRESENT PERFECT.
Fault of omission, SIMPLE PAST.

Unfulfilled obligation; cp III.22.
should / *ought to*} *have done* refers to fault of omission before now or in the past.

2 *A* I've given him my promise.
I promised him I'd go with him.

  B Then you {shouldn't / oughtn't to} have {(promised). / (done so). / (done).}

2 *shouldn't* / *oughtn't to*} *have done* refers to fault committed before now or in the past.

3 I've been resting. I was resting when you called.

You {should / ought to} have been working.

You {shouldn't / oughtn't to} have been resting at that time of (the) day.

3 Fault of omission and fault committed, PROGRESSIVE ASPECT.

4   Why was (there) no one on duty?
There {should / ought to} have been someone on duty all the time.

4   {should / ought to} have (been) with *there*.

5   {Shouldn't there / Oughtn't there to} have been a message for us?

5   There wasn't a message: I think there {should / ought to} have been one.

6   We {should / ought to} have been met.
We {shouldn't / oughtn't to} have been left to find our own way.

6   PASSIVE: someone should have met us.

7   I could swim across that river once.
I managed to pass the examination.

I didn't take or pass the exam, but I could have passed it easily.
I couldn't pass it.
I couldn't have passed it.

7   As in II.17.6. I had the ability then.
As in II.17.7. I made successful use of my ability to pass it.
I had the ability but didn't use it.

I didn't have the ability.
—even if I had tried: see IV.19.5.

8   You didn't get here in time. Why not?
Couldn't you have got here earlier?

8   Didn't you have the means or ability?

9   I haven't seen that [film]. I didn't see it when it was on. It's too late now.
But I would like to have seen it.

9   *a film*, in a cinema; *a play* in a theatre.
when it was on (the programme).
I would like to have (done).

10   I meant to have seen it.

10   That was my intention; but I didn't see it. See VI.23.10.

IV.19 Conditional sentences, type 3: see IV.8

Models
He'd have come if you'd asked him.

Notes

1 *A* Ooh, I nearly dropped that vase.
  B If you *had* dropped it, the owner would have been furious.
He'd have been furious if you'd dropped it.
You would have had to pay for it, if you *had* dropped it.

1 But I didn't drop it: that is a fact.
Suppose the opposite had happened; then imagine the consequences.
In fluent speech, *he would have been* is likely to be reduced to *he'd've been*.
Similarly, *you would have* might be reduced to *you'd've*.

2 *A* We didn't ask Tom. He didn't come.
  B Why didn't you ask him?
He would certainly have come if you'd asked him.
  A Would he have come?
  B Of course he would (have).
  A Perhaps he wouldn't (have).

2 See IV.8.2.

Reducible in pronunciation to *he would've*.
Reducible in pronunciation to *he wouldn't've*.

3   If you hadn't lost the way, we $\left\{\begin{matrix}\text{'d} \\ \text{should}\end{matrix}\right\}$
have been home by now.

If you had looked at the map, we $\left\{\begin{matrix}\text{'d} \\ \text{should}\end{matrix}\right\}$
never have been so late.

4   *A*   If you had come earlier, you /could/
/might/ have met him.
   B   /Could/ /Might/ I have met him?
   A   Of course you /could/ /might/ have.
   B   Perhaps I might not (have).

5   *A*   If you had worked a little harder, you
/could/ /might/ have passed,
you might just have passed.

6   If only you had kept quiet—
if only you hadn't made that noise—
they would never have known we were
here.
We'd never have been heard.

7    $\left.\begin{matrix}\text{Suppose} \\ \text{Supposing}\end{matrix}\right\}$ he had asked you for money,
would you have given him any?

3   Unfortunately, you *did* lose the way, and
we're not home yet.

But you *didn't* look at the map, and now
we *are* late.

4

Exclude *could*.

5

See IV.18.7.
You might have got the minimum pass
mark.

6   *only* intensifies the wish that the past
had been different.

PASSIVE in MAIN CLAUSE.

7   See IV.14.5.

IV.20 Further passive constructions

Models
Hamlet was written by Shakespeare.
Mind you don't get hurt.
You must have your hair cut.
I didn't hear my name called.

Notes

1   *Hamlet* was written by Shakespeare.
My dog was bitten by a snake.
Rivers are being ruined by pollution.

2   Mind you don't get [hurt][1].
I'm sorry we're late. We got lost.
Hundreds of people get killed every year
by traffic on the roads.
Hundreds of [cars] get [smashed up][2].

3   You must have a hair-cut. You must $\left\{\begin{matrix}\text{get} \\ \text{have}\end{matrix}\right\}$
your hair cut.
Do you want to cut yourself?
Do you want me to cut your hair?
Do you want (to have) your hair cut?
No, I want (to have) my [photograph taken][3].
I must have this tooth out.

4   Is that the police? Oh, officer, I've had
all my luggage stolen.

1   The PREP PHRASE, *by* [*the agent*], included
when it supplies essential information,
ie answering such questions as *Who
wrote 'Hamlet'? What bit the dog?*

2   *Mind* = be careful. PASSIVE with *get* +
PAST PARTICIPLE, emphasising the result
of previous activity.

3   You must take action that will result in
someone else cutting your hair.
you want, *you* cut.
you want, *I* cut.
you want, *someone else* will cut.

ie taken out.

4   I've suffered the consequences of someone
else's action.

5 He was looking for the clock (that)

he $\begin{Bmatrix} had \\ 'd \end{Bmatrix}$ mended.

He was looking for the clock (that)

he $\begin{Bmatrix} (had) \ had \\ 'd \ had \end{Bmatrix}$ mended.

5

had unstressed: he had mended the clock.

He had taken action resulting in someone else mending the clock for him.

6 I didn't [hear my name called]⁴.
   I'd like my [car washed]³, please.
   She made her presence felt.
   He found himself stranded in the strange country without any money.

6 I didn't hear anyone calling my name.
   I'd like someone to wash it.
   She acted so that other people felt it.
   He had stranded himself, or someone else had abandoned him.

7 You should have these figures checked.
   You should have had them checked.

7 PASSIVE of IV.9.13.
   PAST PASSIVE of IV.9.13 and IV.18.1.

8 I want to be left alone.
   I don't want to be bothered by anyone.

8 PASSIVE INFINITIVE: I want other people to leave me alone. I don't want anyone to bother me.

9 Women like $\begin{Bmatrix} to \ be \\ being \end{Bmatrix}$ admired.

Men don't like $\begin{Bmatrix} to \ be \\ being \end{Bmatrix}$ criticised.

I don't mind being criticised by you, but I /hate/ /dislike/ being criticised by strangers.

9 Cp IV.10.3.

They don't like other people criticising them.

The PREP PHRASE *by [the agent]* is essential in this last sentence.

Lexicon
1 *burnt, drowned, hurt, killed, lost, run over*, etc
2 *broken, damaged, lost, smashed (up), torn*, etc
3 *suit cleaned, washing done, house painted, room decorated*, etc
4 */feel/ /hear/ /see/ something done*

IV.21 Review of certain sentence patterns so far presented that can be put into the passive: see also VI.11–13

Models
We are supposed to leave now.
We were made to wait.
The children were given sweets.

Notes

1 They /weighed/ /locked/ the luggage.
   The luggage /is/ /was/ weighed.
   It /is/ /was/ being weighed.

   It /has/ /had/ been locked.
   It /must/ /has to/ be examined.
   It should have been packed properly.

1 vt + DIRECT OBJECT.
   PASSIVE in SIMPLE TENSES.
   PROGRESSIVE. Exclude the PASSIVE with PERFECTIVE-PROGRESSIVE.
   PERFECTIVE, PRESENT and PAST.
   PASSIVE with MODAL.
   As in IV.18.6.

2 It has been put on the 'plane.

2 SP 6a: see I.21.4; *on the 'plane* is an ADV ADJUNCT, as in IV.5.2.

3a We told you to come at eight.
    You were [/told/ /asked/]¹ to [come at eight].
    We are supposed to leave now.
    I /am/ /feel/ obliged to admit it.

3a SP 6c: see II.15.3.
    See Appendix A2.

    = we ought to: no ACTIVE counterpart.
    No ACTIVE counterpart of this sentence.

b We expect him to come about eight.
He is expected to come about eight.

b This may mean either *We expect he will* or, especially in the PASSIVE, *we want him to*.

4 They won't let us /go/ /out/.
We won't be allowed to go.
We won't be /let/ /allowed/ /asked/ /helped/ out again.
I'll let you know the whole story.
You'll be told (the whole story).

4 As in II.14.5–6.
ACTIVE, *let us go*; PASSIVE, *be allowed to go*. But *let us* [*out*], PASSIVE *be let out*: see IV.9.1*A*.
I'll let *you* know.
You will be told: see I.28.3 and 7–8 below.

I'll let the whole story be known.

The *story* will be known.

5 We were made to wait for two hours.
6 He has never been known to behave like that before.

5 PASSIVE of IV.9.1: *be made to* [*wait*].
6 See IV.9.8: *be known* (*to*) [wait].

7a The [children] were [given][2] [sweets].
b Our car has been given a wash.
8 We [found][3] him a [seat] [at the back].
He was [found] a [seat] [at the back].
9 Sweets were [given] to the children.
A seat was found for him at the back.

7a PASSIVE of SP 10a: see I.28.2*A*.
b See II.2.8.
8
PASSIVE of SP 10b.
9 Alternatives of IV.21.7–8, emphasising the DIRECT OBJECT. Not applicable to SP 7b.

10a They have taken our luggage up.
[Our luggage] has been [taken up][3].
b We have [dealt with] this matter.
[This matter] has been [dealt with][4].
11 The safe was broken open.
The prisoner was set free.
12 He was seen to cross the road.
He was seen (to be) crossing the road.

10a See III.23.3.
Stress the PARTICLE, *up*. See Lex 3.
b See III.23.1, and Lex 4.
Do not stress the PREP *with*.
11 See III.23.5.
12 PASSIVE of model in IV.10.1.
PASSIVE of model in IV.10.2.

Lexicon
1 See Appendix A 2
2 See Appendix A 3
3 See Appendix A 4
4 PHRASAL VERBS of this type can freely occur in the PASSIVE: Examples: *bring* /in/ /out/ /up/ /down/; *give* /away/ /back/ /up/; *put* /off/ /on/ /up/; *take* /away/ /back/ /down/ /off/ /up/
5 Not all PREPOSITIONAL VERBS occur in the PASSIVE. Among those that do so occur are: *ask for, believe in, deal with, hear of, hope for, laugh at, listen to, look at, send for*. See also VI.11, Lex 1

IV.22 Past participles followed by prepositions other than *by*, and 'quasi-passives' like *I'm surprised*

Models
The lion was shot with a rifle.
I'm surprised at you.
He was surprised by a knock at the door.

Notes

1 A hunter shot a lion. He used a rifle.
He shot it with a rifle.
The lion was shot by an expert hunter.
The lion was shot with a rifle.

1

by (*the agent*) telling us who shot the lion; *with* (*the instrument*).

It was shot by a hunter, with a rifle.

Agent and instrument in the same sentence.

It was shot by a hunter with a rifle.

No pause between *hunter* and *rifle*: *with a rifle* is now a POSTMODIFIER in NP as in IV.5.2.

2 John was very disappointed by what you said. In fact, he was rather annoyed by it.

2 *disappointed*, etc, may be either a PARTICIPLE used adjectivally, as in III.7, or a part of the PASSIVE: in any case, it can be modified by *very*, etc.

3 *A* The audience $\left\{ \begin{matrix} \text{was} \\ \text{were} \end{matrix} \right\}$ obviously interested by your story of the lion.
   B Not many people were interested in the main subject. That's why so few came.

3 The story obviously interested them when you told it. Example of PASSIVE.

Partly PASSIVE, partly example of PARTICIPLE used adjectivally and followed by *in*.

4 Who was that scientist engaged by?
   A What work is he engaged in?
   B He's engaged in important experiments.

4 Who engaged him?
   What work is he doing?
   Similarly, *involved in* [*this affair*].

5a The thief was surprised by a knock on the door and jumped out of the window.

5a The knock surprised him, so he jumped out.

 b I'm surprised at you: I didn't expect you to do a thing like that.

 b = I'm shocked by [your behaviour].

6 None of us know that man. Perhaps he is known to you but he's quite unknown to any of us.

6
he's known to you = you know him; *he's unknown to us* = we don't know him.

7a We were /bothered/ /worried/ by mosquitoes all night. We hardly had a wink of sleep.

7a PASSIVE + *by*.

 b That man's a fool. I can't be bothered with /him/ /his silly stories/.
    I'm very worried about Jane. What has happened to her?

 b PASSIVE + *with*.

    worried, as in III.7.

8 I was invited to come here by Mr Jones. You were invited (to come here) (in order) to give us your expert advice. You were /appointed/ /engaged/ /invited/ to do a certain job.

8 He invited me to come: as in IV.21.3.
   to give us your advice: purpose, as in IV.6.1.
   Purpose of your appointment, etc.

IV.23 Sentence patterns in which the object has a complement

Models

They made him captain.
He regarded her as a friend.
We consider him (to be) a good officer.

Notes

1a The team [chose][1] a captain.

1a DIRECT OBJECT—*captain*.

 b They [chose][1] Tom (as their captain).

 b DIRECT OBJECT—*Tom*.

 c They [chose][1] Tom captain.

 c Both OBJECTS in the same sentence, but in the order in which they occurred in 1b.

 d /A captain/ /Tom/ was [chosen][1].

 d Either OBJECT may become a PASSIVE SUBJ.

e Tom was [chosen]¹ captain.

e In this PASSIVE structure, only the first of the OBJECTS in 1c can become the PASSIVE SUBJECT.

2a They [christened]² their son.
 b They [christened]² John last June.
 c They [christened]² their son John.
 d /Their son/ /John/ was [christened]².

 e Their son was [christened]² John.
3a and b _____

 c They [made]³ John an officer.
    They [made]³ John (the) manager of the bank.
 d _____
 e John was [made]³ /an officer/ /Manager/.

4a They left Mary a million pounds.

    Mary was left a million pounds.
    They left Mary a millionairess.
    She was left a millionairess.
 b They called him a taxi.

    They called him a coward.

5a He [regarded]⁴ her as a friend.

 b She was regarded as a friend.
6a They recognised him as a genius.

    He was recognised as a genius.

 b I knew him {to be / as} a very brave man.

    He was known {to be / as} a very brave man.
7 She [took]⁵ him for a fool.
   He was taken for a fool.
8 We [consider]⁶ him (to be) /a good officer/ /very capable/.
   He is considered (to be) /a good officer/ /etc/.
   We all [imagine]⁷ him to be a spy.
   He is known to have been a spy.
9 He /declared/ /proved/ himself to be an enemy.
   He proved to be an enemy.
   He was /declared/ /proved/ (to be) etc.

2
 b Exclude *as their son*: contrast with 1b.
 c Contrast the order with that in 1c.
 d Either OBJECT may become a PASSIVE SUBJ.
 e Contrast the order with that in 1e.
3a and b Not realised with Lex 3 below.
 c Contrast *He made me a suit* as in I.28.5. DEFINITE ARTICLE optional in the case of a specific appointment.
 d Not realised with Lex 3.

4a ie they left that money {to / for} Mary.
    PASSIVE of previous model.
    As in 3c above.
    PASSIVE of previous model.
 b = They called a taxi for him. A taxi was called.
    = He was called a coward. As in 3c above. PASSIVE as in 3e.
5a As in 1b above, but *as [a friend]* obligatory after *regard*.
    PASSIVE.
6a *as [a genius]* obligatory after *recognise*, used in this sense.
    PASSIVE.

 b Contrast *He acts as my lawyer*, ie in that capacity. *I knew him as a young man*, ie when he was young.

8 Note the difference between *We found him (to be) a good officer* and *We found him a good secretary* = *We found a good secretary for him*.
   We imagine that he is.
   We know that he /has been/ /was/.

Lexicon
1 *appoint, choose, crown, elect, label, name, nominate, proclaim*
2 *christen*
3 *call, leave, make, nickname, pronounce, vote*

4 *consider, count, recognise, regard*
5 *mistake, take*
6 *believe, consider, find, prove, think*
7 *imagine, judge, know, suppose*

IV.24 NP[1] + vt + NP[2] + adjective, *-ing* or past participle

Models

The jury found him guilty.
I found him lying on the floor.
We found all our seats occupied.

Notes

1	They built their houses well. They found the site good. I /feel/ /find/ it hot in here.	1	*well*, ADV-M. *good*, ADJ.

1 They built their houses well.
  They found the site good.
  I /feel/ /find/ it hot in here.

1 *well*, ADV-M.
  good, ADJ.

2a I [like][1] my soup (to be) hot.
   I like people to be punctual.
   I want you all (to be) ready by 8.

2a I like *my soup* when it is hot.
   I like *punctuality* (in people).

 b I want you all (to be) outside.

 b Sim. *I want my dinner upstairs.*

3 In spring, all the islanders paint their
  houses white.
  Their houses are painted white.
  They get their houses ready (for the
  summer).

3 The houses are white as a result.
  Similarly: *drive somebody mad; keep
  /somebody/ /something/ warm; make
  something dirty; wipe something clean.*

4 [The jury] [found][2] the [prisoner]
  [guilty].
  The prisoner was [found][3] guilty.

4 The jury decided he was guilty.

5 I [found][4] him [ly]ing [on the floor].
  He was [found][5] lying on the floor.

5 When I found him, he was lying on the
  floor.

6 I [caught][4] the boys climbing the fence.
  They were [caught][5] climbing the fence.

6 They were in the act of climbing when
  I came.

7a They kept us waiting all day.
   We were kept waiting all day.

7a They made us continue to wait all day.

 b We /got/ /started/ /kept/ the fire going.

8 The news [left][6] me wondering what
  would happen to us all.

8 After I heard the news, I began to
  wonder. PASSIVE: *I was left wondering . . .*

9 I /don't want/ /can't have/ you sitting
  there doing nothing.
  She soon [had][7] everyone singing.

9 Cp I don't want them to sit there:
  sitting expresses the PROGRESSIVE aspect.
  They were singing, because she made
  them sing.

10 The weather prevented us (from)
   leaving.
   It kept us from leaving.
   We were prevented from leaving by the
   weather.

10 or *stopped us (from) leaving.* Contrast
   kept us waiting as in 7 above.

11 I can't imagine flying to the moon.

   I can't imagine him flying anywhere.
   I'll [keep][8] working all night.
   I'll keep the light burning all night.

11 I can't imagine myself or anyone
   flying . . .
   I can't imagine him flying.
   I'll be working myself.
   The light will be burning.

12   We found all our seats occupied (by a
      party of children).
      Our seats were found occupied.

Lexicon
1 *like, prefer, want*
2 *find, prove*
3 *found, proved*
4 *catch, come across, discover, find*
5 *caught, discovered, found*
6 *keep, leave, set, start*
7 *get, have*
8 *go on, keep (on)*

IV.25 The *-ing* form as subject, with its own object, and in other common constructions

Models	Notes

Models
Swimming is good exercise.
Sailing a boat is good fun.
I couldn't help laughing.

Notes

1 *A* I enjoy /swimming/ /sailing a boat/.

   B I'm tired of watching television.

2 Swimming is good exercise.
   Smoking is not allowed here.
   A Smoking is bad for me.
   B Then why don't you give up smoking?

3 I like working /here/ /in this office/.
   Working /here/ /in this office/ is very
   pleasant.

4a She enjoys looking after children.
    Pointing at people is very rude.

 b I don't like getting up early.
    Getting up late is a lazy habit.

5   /Smoking/ /Driving a car/ costs a lot of
    money.

6   I've seen George again. Now I'm happy.
    Seeing him again [made][1] me happy.

7   What a funny looking man he was!
    I couldn't help laughing at him.

8   Those shoes $\left\{\begin{array}{l}\text{want}\\\text{need}\end{array}\right\}$ mending.
    They need to be mended.
    Your tyres $\left\{\begin{array}{l}\text{want}\\\text{need}\end{array}\right\}$ pumping up.
    They need to be pumped up.

1   As in III.24; *-ing* without and with an
    OBJECT.
    -ing after a PREPOSITION.

2   *-ing* as SUBJECT in SP 1.
    Cp IV.10.6.
    -ing as SUBJECT in SP 2.
    give up + -ing; PHRASAL VERB, type 3
    (III.23.3).

3   *-ing* with ADV-PLACE as MODIFIER.

4a *-ing* in PHRASAL VERB Type 1 (III.23.1).

 b *-ing* in PHRASAL VERB Type 2 (III.23.2).

5   *-ing,* and *-ing* + OBJECT, as SUBJECT of a
    VERB other than *be.*

6   The experience of seeing him made
    me happy; or *I was happy to see him*
    (III.8.3).

7   [*funny*] *looking.*
    = I couldn't prevent myself (from)
    laughing.

8   *want* replaceable by *need.*

    need not replaceable by *want.*

    Contrast: *Children /want/ /need/ someone
    to love them. They /want/ /need/ to be
    loved.*

9	What about hiding till they've gone? What about having your /shoes mended/ /tyres pumped up/?
10a	I never enjoy going for a walk alone. Going for a walk alone is very dull. It's very dull going for a walk alone.
b	I don't want to go for a walk alone. It would be much [nicer]² to go for a walk with you.

9   = Let's do that. See IV.20.3.

10a In these examples, the *-ing* generally implies that the action has been performed, by the speaker or by others, as in 6 above.

b   In contrast the INFINITIVE generally implies that the action is a new or future one. The INFINITIVE can also be SUBJECT: see IV.29.1 and VI.9.

11   It's [a pleasure]³ $\left\{\begin{matrix} \text{to be} \\ \text{being} \end{matrix}\right\}$ here.

11   Note as for 10 above.

12   John's paintings are very good.

12   *-ing* as NOUN with PLURAL ending.

Lexicon
1 *leave, make*
2 *better, more agreeable, nicer, pleasanter*
3 *an honour, a pleasure, a mistake*
4 Other *-ing* forms with plural include *doings, goings-on, happenings, readings, writings*

IV.26 Relative clauses involving the use of *whose, whom, which* and *that*

Models

That's the boy whose father is an astronaut.
Persons to whom this circular is addressed should study it carefully.
The case to which you refer is closed.

Notes

1a	Whose partner are you?
b	That's Tom. His father's an astronaut. That's the boy whose father is an astronaut.
2	The players whose names are on this list have been chosen to play against New College on Saturday.
3	Whom do you wish to see, madam?
	Who won? Who beat whom?
4	Tom and Dick are boys I knew at school. They are boys I went to school with.

1a   *Whose* as in I.4.3.

b   *the boy. His father* becomes *the boy whose father*.

2   *whose* in a RELATIVE CLAUSE postmodifying the SUBJECT of another CLAUSE.

3   *Whom*, OBJECT, in formal speech or writing.
     whom, OBJECT, in contrast with *Who*, SUBJECT.

4   Usual in informal style.
     Usual in informal style.

They're boys $\left\{\begin{matrix} \text{that} \\ \text{whom} \end{matrix}\right\}$ I knew, etc.

RELATIVE PRONOUN unnecessary in informal style.

They're the boys $\left\{\begin{matrix} \text{that} \\ \text{who} \\ \text{whom} \end{matrix}\right\}$ I went to school with.
They are boys whom I knew at school.

More appropriate in formal talk or writing.

They are boys with whom I went to school.

The boys $\left\{\begin{matrix} \text{that} \\ \text{whom} \end{matrix}\right\}$ I /knew at school/ /went to school with/ have all grown up.
The boys with whom I went to school have all grown up.

More appropriate in formal talk or writing.

Informal. RELATIVE PRONOUN unnecessary.

More appropriate for formal talk or writing. *Whom* obligatory directly after a PREP.

5   Persons to whom this circular is addressed should study it carefully.

5   Formal. Cp *Who is this addressed to?*, informal style.

6   James Russell is a man for whom I have the greatest respect.

6   *whom*, again, after a PREP.
     the greatest here = very great.

7   This is the picture we bought at the sale.
     That is the case I'm referring to.
     That is the case to which I am referring.

     The picture we bought is a masterpiece.
     The case you're referring to is closed.
     The case to which you are referring is now closed.

7   *that* or *which* optional before [we].
     that or *which* optional before [I].
     More appropriate for formal talk or writing.
     that or *which* optional before [we].
     that or *which* optional before [you].
     More appropriate for formal talk or writing. *Which* obligatory after a PREP.

8   This monument is all that remains of the ancient city.
     All that remains of the ancient city has been placed in the museum.
     I'll give you all (that) I have.

8   Use *that*, not *which*, after *all*.

IV.27 Clauses specifying the time when, the place where, the reason why, the way in which

Models
I shall never forget the day we first met.
I can't think of the reason why he came so early.
That's just the way he spoke.

Notes

1   *A* I shall never forget when I first met you.
     B It was on New Year's Day in 1969.
          That's when we first met.

     I shall never forget the [day]¹ $\left(\left\{\begin{matrix} \text{when} \\ \text{that} \end{matrix}\right\}\right)$ we first met.
     I shall never forget the day we first met.

     The day we first met will always remain in my memory.

1   As in IV.13.1b.

     See Lex 1 below.

     The link-word (/when/ /that/) is usually absent.
     The CLAUSE, eg *we first met*, acts as a POSTMODIFIER to *the day*, OBJECT or SUBJECT.

2   I remember the morning /he first came to school/ /I last saw him/.

2

A I'll show you where he worked.　　　　As in IV.13.1b.
B So that's where he worked, is it?
This is the [room]² where he worked.
The room where he worked is closed.
This is the room (that) he worked in.　　or *the /desk/ /table/ he worked at.*
The room he worked in is now closed.

3 *A* I don't know why he came so early.　　3 As in IV.13.1b.
B Perhaps he wanted a good seat.
A No, that's not why he came so early.
I can't think of the reason why he
came so early.
The reason (why) he came so early is his
own affair.

4 *A* Did you notice how he smiled at us?　　4
B Yes, like a real villain. That's how he
smiled at us.
A I didn't like the way (that) he spoke　　or *the way in which* as in 5 below.
to us a bit. That's not the way to speak.　　*the way to speak:* see IV.7.8.
The way he spoke to us was suspicious.
B Yes, that's just the way he spoke to us.

5　　You conducted this case very well indeed.　5

I congratulate you on the $\left\{\begin{array}{l}\text{way}\\\text{manner}\end{array}\right\}$ in　　Regard *manner* as more formal than *way*.

which you conducted this difficult case.

The $\left\{\begin{array}{l}\text{way}\\\text{manner}\end{array}\right\}$ in which you answered　　or *the way you answered,* as in 4 above.

the questions was admirable.
You handled the case with ease.
The ease with which you handled the case
was perfect.

Lexicon
1 *afternoon, day, evening, first day,* etc, *morning, night, time*
2 *desk, house, place, road, room, spot, street, table, town*

IV.28 The infinitive as complementation of an adjective. See also III.8 and VI.9

Models　　　　　　　　　　　　**Notes**
I'm glad to have met him.
He was foolish to do that.
That is an easy rule to remember.

1　I'm [glad] to hear the (good) news.　　1　As in III.8.3 and IV.25.6.
I'm [glad] to have met him.　　　　　I'm glad because I (have) met him.
I was [delighted]¹ to meet him.　　　　I was delighted because I (had) met him.
We weren't [sorry]² to see it.　　　　In fact, we were glad because we did.
We were [sorry]² not to see him.　　　We were sorry because we didn't.
We were /[glad]¹/ /[sorry]² not/ to.　　*glad [not] to, sorry [not] to.*

2   I'm [sorry][2] to hear the (bad) news.
    We were [sorry][2] not to be there.
    We were /[glad][1]/ /[sorry][2]/ not to be.

3a I'm [surprised][1, 2] to see you here.
 b I was surprised to see Henry.
 c I'm surprised I recognised him.
 d I'm surprised he /remembers/ /recog-
    nised/ me.

4   We're [ready][3] to make the attempt.
    We're [determined][4] to succeed.
    We're [determined][4] not to fail.

5   This tyre is [likely][5] to burst.
    Is it likely to?

6   He was being very [foolish][6].
    Don't be foolish.
    Do be sensible.
    He was foolish to do that.
    He was [rude][6] not to call on you.
    He was rude not to.

7   Would you be kind enough to do that
    for me?

8 *A* Mary's attractive, isn't she?
  B To look at, not to listen to.
    She's very attractive to look at.

9a Mary is [easy][7] to teach.
 b This car is [expensive][8] to run.
 c That rule is [easy][9] to remember.
    She's an [easy][7] pupil to teach.
    This is an [expensive][8] car to run.
    That's an [easy][10] rule to remember.

2

    glad [*not*] *to be, sorry* [*not*] *to be.*

3a I see (PRESENT TENSE) and I am (PRES).
 b I saw (PAST TENSE) and I was (PAST).
 c I recognised (PAST), I am (PRESENT).
 d He (one person) remembers etc, I
    (another person) am. Cp IV.11.13.

4   As in III.8.4.

5   = It will probably burst.
    Here, *it* = the tyre; cp IV.29.6.

6   Use the PROGRESSIVE with *be* only in the
    sense of *He /is/ /was/ acting* in such and
    such a manner.
    . . . *foolish doing that* also acceptable.

7   Another example is *Surely you're not
    foolish enough to think that?*

9   See IV.29.7a.
    See IV.29.7b.
    See IV.29.7c. Sim. *That is easy to say.*

    Sim. *That's an easy thing to say.*

Lexicon

1 III.8, Lex 2 + *content, fortunate, grateful, relieved, thankful, thrilled*
2 *annoyed, ashamed, disappointed, grieved, unfortunate, unhappy, hurt, sad, shocked, sorry, surprised*
3 III.8, Lex 3 + *determined, due, eager, fit, free, frightened, inclined, keen* (or *keen on -ing*), *prepared,
    reluctant, welcome*
4 *anxious, determined, inclined, prepared*
5 *certain, likely, sure, unlikely*
6 *brave, careful, careless, clever, clumsy, courageous, cruel, foolish, generous, good* (in the sense of *kind*
    or *well-behaved*), *(dis)honest, (un)kind, mean, nasty, nice, (im)polite, reasonable, rude, (un)selfish,
    sensible, silly, stupid, sweet, weak, wicked, wise*
7 *agreeable, amusing, difficult, easy, hard, hopeless, impossible, interesting, nice, pleasant*
8 *cheap, (in)convenient, dangerous, difficult, easy, hard, pleasant, thrilling, wonderful*
9 As in 7 and 8
10 As in 7 and 8 + *good, important*

IV.29 Further constructions beginning with *it*. See also: I.20.4, II.1.5, III.10, IV.7.9, IV.8.7, IV.11.5–6, IV.12.15, IV.25.10–11

Models

It's a pity to spoil your drawing.
It was so kind of you to come.
It took us five weeks to get there.

Notes

1   It /is/ /seems/ a [pity][1] to spoil your drawing. It would be a pity to spoil it. It /is/ /seems/ /would be/ a pity to.

1   *It + be* or *seem + NP + INFINITIVE.* It is a pity to do it, so don't let it be done. Alternatively, but less currently: *To spoil your drawing /is/ /seems/ /would be/ a pity.*

2   /Isn't it/ /wouldn't it be/ a pity to spoil it?

2   Exclude the alternative above in Q-*Yes/No.*

3   It's a [good idea][2] to save regularly.

/Is it/ /Would it be/ a good idea to open a bank account?

3   ie to save money. Alternatively, *To save regularly is a good idea.* Exclude the alternative in Q-*Yes/No.*

4   It's a great [pleasure][3] to be here.

What is it like to be here?

4   Alternatively, *To be here is a great pleasure,* less current, more formal.

5   It was /a pity spoiling your drawing like that/ /a good idea opening a bank account/ /a pleasure being here/.

5   *It + be + NP + -ing*: see note to IV.25.10a.

6   It's [certain][4] to be fine tomorrow.

6   *It + be* or *seem + ADJ + INFINITIVE.*

7a   It's [hard][5] to teach Tom anything.
 b   It's [cheap][6] to run this car.
 c   It's [easy][7] to [remember that rule].

7a   Cp *Tom is hard to teach,* IV.28.9.
 b   Cp *This car is cheap to run,* IV.28.9.
 c   Cp *That rule is easy to remember,* IV.28.9.

8a   It's [important][8] to remember to switch off the electricity.

Why is it important?
 b   It's [impossible] to work with him.

8a   Alternatively, but less currently, *To remember to switch off the electricity is important.*

9   It was [foolish][9] (of him) to do that.

It was rude (of him) not to.
It was so kind of you to ask us.

9   or *He was foolish to do that,* as in IV.28.6.
or *He was rude not to.*
or *You were so kind to ask us.*

10 *A* What does it matter (if we're late)?
 B It doesn't matter /at all/ /a bit/.
 C It matters /a lot/ /a great deal/.

10   *It + VERB* other than *be* or *seem.*

11   It took (us) five hours to get here.
How long did it take you?
It needed hard work to finish the job.

11   Cp IV.2.10.

12   It's a [pity][1] (that) he isn't here.
It's a [good thing][10] (that) he's tall.

12   *It + be* or *seem + NP* or *ADJ + that-CLAUSE.*

13   It's lucky (that) you were at home.
14   It's [likely][11] (that) the tyre will burst.
It's quite likely.

14   or *The tyre is likely to burst. It's likely to:* IV.28.5.

15   It's [obvious][12] (that) we're wrong.

15   or *Obviously, we're wrong.*

Lexicon
1 *disadvantage, disgrace, nuisance, pity, shame, silly idea*
2 *advantage, good idea, good thing*
3 *honour, pleasure*
4 *certain, (un)likely, sure*
5 As in IV.28, Lex 7
6 As in IV.28, Lex 8
7 As in IV.28, Lex 9

8 *better, desirable, essential, important, (un)necessary, (im)possible, useful, useless*
9 As in IV.28, Lex 6
10 *advantage, good thing*
11 *certain, (un)likely, sure*
12 *certain, clear, definite, evident, obvious, possible, probable*

IV.30 Constructions where *for* (+ NP) marks the subject of an infinitive clause, etc

Models

Here's a book for you to read.
It's lucky for you (that) the other car wasn't going faster.

Notes

1 It took six weeks for the travellers to reach the coast.

1 Cp IV.2.10 or *The travellers took six weeks to reach the coast.* The structure opposite emphasises *six weeks.*

2 I hope there will be a chance for us to see the museum.

2 Cp IV.7.7.

3 Here's a book for you to read.

3 I hope you will (want to) read it; IV.7.8.
Cp IV.7.9.

It's time for the children to go to bed.
It was a bad day for us to call.

4 It is a great pleasure for us to be here this evening.

4 IV.25.11. *We* find it a pleasure.

5a It's a pity for you to have to stay indoors in this weather.

5a IV.29.1. I'm sorry that you have to.

b It's a pity for there to be any disagreement in the family.

b = There is disagreement; it's a pity.

6 That story is much too long for us to read in one lesson.

6 Expansion of model in II.18.4.

7a Mr Turner was very anxious for Tom to take the examination.

7a See IV.28.4. Mr T wanted Tom to take the exam.

b He is anxious for there to be a lawyer in the family.

b = He wants there to be a lawyer.

8 It's rather difficult for the people over here to see the screen.
Would it be possible for you to move it?

8 IV.28.9. Or *The people over here find it difficult to see the screen.*

9 If you had stayed where you were, it would have been easier for the guide to find you.

9 Expansion of IV.28.9. Or *If you had stayed where you were, the guide could have found you more easily.*

10 You had a narrow escape. It was lucky for you (that) the other car wasn't going any faster.

10 Or *You were lucky (that) the other car* etc.

11 Tom has asked to come to our party. Shall we ask for Mary to come too?

11 He wants to come.
Do we want Mary to come too?

12 We long for the end of term.
We long for the term to end.

12

We ourselves *long to* go on holiday.

13 I've been to the travel agency and made arrangements about our luggage.

13

I've arranged with the agent for our
heavy luggage to be sent to the station in
in advance.

It will be sent to the station before we
go ourselves.

14   We telephoned to ask the right time.
We telephoned for a taxi to come at once.

14   That was the purpose of our call.
The purpose of the call was to ask
someone to send a taxi at once.

Summary of Stages I, II, III and IV

Stages I, II and III, plus the following:

SENTENCE PATTERNS
from the list on page 107.
B5a and b; B6; B7; B12; C5–8; D1–6
Also CONDITIONAL SENTENCES, as in IV.8 and IV.19
    that-CLAUSES after VERBS, NOUNS and ADJECTIVES
    wh-CLAUSES after VERBS and PREPOSITIONS
    CONDITIONAL SENTENCES with *provided* etc
    RELATIVE CLAUSES with *whose, whom*, etc
    sentences beginning with anticipatory *It*
    INFINITIVE CLAUSES beginning with *for* (+ SUBJECT)

NOUN PHRASE
    ABSTRACT, MASS NOUNS
    order of MODIFIERS before a NOUN
    combination and MODIFIERS of DETERMINERS
    MODIFIERS after a NOUN

VERB PHRASE
    INFINITIVE of purpose
    VERB+ bare INFINITIVE
    VERBS followed sometimes by INFINITIVE, sometimes by *-ing*
    tenses in INDIRECT SPEECH
    seem, appear, happen+ INFINITIVE
    PROGRESSIVE and PERFECTIVE ASPECTS with future reference
    unfulfilled obligation
    further PASSIVE constructions (as in IV.20)
    PAST PARTICIPLES followed by *about, at, in*, etc
    -ing as SUBJECT, OBJECT, etc

PREDICATIVE ADJECTIVES
with COMPLEMENTATION as in sentence patterns A6a and b, A7a, c, d, e

Stage V

Contents

18 More RELATIVE CLAUSES, including non-defining: *I will now introduce the candidate in support of whom I wish to speak; his speech, which went on and on, bored everybody.*

19 ADVERBS with or without the ending *-ly*: *Stand clear of the gates; I'll take you direct to your room; he aims high: he's highly ambitious.*

20 PRESENT PARTICIPLE CLAUSES with related PARTICIPLE: *Going home I saw a snake; I saw my friend George riding a bicycle; jumping into the car, he drove away at full speed.*

21 PAST PARTICIPLE CLAUSES with related PARTICIPLE: *Placed under arrest, he denied the charges brought against him; the man arrested by the police has not yet been named; the castle, built in 1360, is deserted.*

22 PREPOSITIONAL PHRASES which can replace SUBORDINATE CLAUSES: *The crops failed because of the drought; we go by air, in spite of the expense; regardless of the obstacles, we must press on.*

23 Avoiding a SUBORDINATE CLAUSE by means of a nominalisation: *Please telephone me on your arrival; you cannot do that without approval; a tendency to upset his colleagues was his only fault.*

24 Different PREPOSITIONS+ *-ing*: *They make a fire by rubbing two pieces of wood together; on entering the town, you will be greeted by the Mayor; in saying that, I am not exaggerating; I object to being kept waiting.*

25 Use of *being, not being, having been, not having been*: *I don't remember having said that; having been invited, I intend to speak; never having been there, I can't say.*

26 Different constructions with *since*: *Since leaving school in 1960, I have only met him twice; it's a long time since we('ve) met; since he left school in 1960, he must be older than thirty now.*

27 Constructions with *while* and *as*: *They slept while we kept watch over them; as you read this page again, make a note of all the new words; while I agree with you up to a point, I cannot agree to your plans as a whole.*

28 POSSESSIVE before a GERUND: *I don't like you being out so late; I cannot understand /him/ /his/ behaving like that; Susan('s) running away was the last straw.*

29 NOUN PHRASES in apposition to each other; and abbreviated CLAUSES beginning with *If* and *When*: *George Stamp, the novelist, will be there; if asked to comment, you have nothing to say; never at a loss for words, he spoke for over an hour.*

30 Statements followed by comment CLAUSES; and *that*-CLAUSES, as OBJECTS, beginning the sentence: *George has passed his examination, I hear; John has failed, I assure you; that John has failed I can't believe.*

V.I Compound[1] nouns, and noun phrases in which the head-word is modified by another noun. (Some examples of compound nouns have been introduced earlier, eg in I.12.5 and I.16.6. Unit V.1 now arranges compounds in groups)

Models	Notes
The door-handle has come off.	
Have you change for a ten-pound note?	
In sunny weather we wear sun glasses.	

A Stress on the first part of the compound

1 My /tooth/ /head/ aches. My teeth ache. I have /toothache/ /a headache/.

    1 COMPOUNDS formed of NOUN SUBJECT+ VERB: the NOUN (*tooth*) remains SINGULAR.

2 We brush our teeth with a tooth-brush. A blood test. An intelligence test.

    2 COMPOUNDS formed of OBJECT+ VERB, ie it brushes teeth, tests intelligence.

3 The door-handle has come off. | 3 That part of the door, of the window, of the television set.
The window-pane. The television screen.

4 Is this a teacup or a coffee-cup? A playground. A tool-shed. | 4 a cup for tea or coffee, ground for play, a shed for tools.

5 Give the breadcrumbs to the birds. | 5 crumbs (consisting) of bread.

6 Is his friend a boyfriend or a girlfriend? Men students. Women drivers. | 6 His friend is a boy. NB *boyfriends, girlfriends*, but *men students, women drivers*.

7 Gas makes this stove work: it's a gas stove. A motor-car. A steam engine. | 7 What makes it work? Gas, a motor, steam.

8 A coal-mine produces coal. A power station produces electric power. | 8 What produces what?

9 What will you do during the holidays? We'll go on a holiday course. | 9

A course during the holidays.

10 A train that carries goods is a goods train. A sports ground. A savings account, a post office savings account. A clothes-hanger. | 10 A train for goods (as in 4), a ground for sports, an account for savings: *s* retained when ambiguity might result from its omission. *Clothes:* no singular.

B Stress on both parts of the COMPOUND

11 A leather belt is made of leather. These shoes were made from an old rubber tyre. | 11 Stress on both parts as in IV.3.2. Contrast *made of* (II.1.8): the rubber tyre is no longer identifiable.

12 We need some dining-room furniture. | 12 Furniture usually found in a dining-room;

What is the time by the town clock? He works in a government office. | the clock in the town; an office in the government.

13 Have you change for a ten-pound note? He works in a twenty-storey building. | 13 *ten-pound note.* No *s* on *pound.* Similar comment.

C NOUN MODIFIERS *contrasted with* ADJS

14 We wear sun glasses in sunny weather. A danger signal. A dangerous road. Science lessons. A scientific method. | 14 *Sun glasses,* as in 4 above; *sunny* describes the weather; the signal gives warning of danger but is not dangerous.

15 We study law in a law school, physics in a physics laboratory, and medicine in a medical school. | 15 Regard *medical school* as exceptional, and note *medicine chest,* as in 4 above. *Physics,* no SINGULAR in this sense.

[1] As to whether a COMPOUND is spelt as one word, as two words, or with a hyphen, usage varies. Consult a good dictionary.

V.2 Use and avoidance of the genitive with apostrophe *s*

Models

That is my brother-in-law's car.
The lid of a saucepan: a saucepan lid.
You all need a good night's rest.

Notes

1a Tom has a brother. John is Tom's
brother.
Do you know all of these boys' names?
That is /my brother-in-law's car/ /the
Chairman of the Committee's seat/.
b Dick is the brother of the boy behind me.

2a The referee decided (that) it was a goal.
They accepted the referee's decision.
b The car skidded and injured Tom badly.
Tom's injuries were quite serious.
c Mining is hard work: it's a man's work.
The men spend the evening in a men's club.
3 /Keats's/ /Keats'/ poetry. Archimedes'
law.
4 What is /the weight of the box/ /its
weight/? The /height/ /colour/ of the
wall: its height.
All the windows of the house were locked.
5a We sat down by the /side of the road/
/roadside/. The /top of the tree/ /treetop/.

b The lid of a saucepan—a saucepan lid.
The leg of a chair—a chair leg.
6 You all need a good night's rest.
Then we need three weeks' holiday
in a week or two's time.
7 /The future of Africa/ /Africa's future/.
/The world's greatest writers/ /the
greatest writers in the world/.
The area of /our country/ /the world/.

8a Hunger and disease are world problems.
b You can't solve all the world's problems.
9 Caring for children was her life('s) work.
10 The earth's surface.
The water's edge.
At our journey's end.
At the /end of the week/ /week-end/.

11a He's at his wits' end.
b For goodness' sake, stop it.
c We all want our money's worth, don't we?
d A dangerous man: keep him at arm's
length.
e A useful book: I want it within arm's
reach.
f He lives within a stone's throw of my
house.
g The ship's /company/ /doctor/.

1a Tom's brother implies 'Tom has a . . .'

ie the names of *all these boys*.

b Avoid *'s* when, eg *boy* is postmodified
except by *of* + NP.
2a The referee /made/ /took/ a decision.

b He suffered injuries.

c The kind of work a man does.
In a club for men.
3 See I.3.5. Either form for short names
ending in *s*. For long names, only *s'*.
4 Exclude *'s*, though allow *its*, when
referring to the measurements, parts,
etc, of inanimate objects.

5a *roadside*, stress on road. Sim. *mountain-*
/*side*/ /*top*/; river-/*bank*/ /*side*/, etc.
Special case: *the seaside*, two stresses.
b *saucepan lid*, stress on 1st part;
sim. *chair leg*, and examples in V.1.3.
6 Use *'s*, not a phrase beginning with *of*,
when referring to periods of time.
Note: *a week or two's time*.
7 Use either form with geographical
names or with places of human
habitation when referring to human
activity: use only *of* . . . when referring
to physical attributes, eg size.
8a = problems throughout the world.
b = all the problems of or in the world.
9 Again, reference to human activity.
10 or *The surface of the earth*.
or *The edge of the water*.
or *At the end of our journey*.
week-end, two stresses = Saturday and
Sunday.
11a Fixed idiomatic expression.
b Fixed idiomatic expression.
c Fixed idiomatic expression.
d Fixed idiomatic expression.

e Fixed idiomatic expression.

f Fixed idiomatic expression.

g Fixed idiomatic expression.

V.3 'Active' prefixes, ie those in common use and often found in new-coined words

Models

The whole house must be re-painted.
The work was left uncompleted.
Pre-cooked, post-war, anti-anything.

Notes

1   We must repair the walls, then re-paint them. The whole house must be re-painted.

1   *re-* /ri/, as part of a word; *re-* /ri:/ as an 'active' prefix, = again.

2a   We can prepare meals more quickly if the ingredients are pre-cooked.

b   Forewarned is forearmed.

2a   *pre-* /pri/, as part of a word; and *pre-* /pri:/ as an active prefix, = before.

b   Proverb. *Fore-= before*, a less active prefix.

3   The restoration of the ruined church was postponed till the post-war period.

3   *post-* as an active prefix, and *post-= after*, as part of a word.

4   Many poisons have their own antidotes.

A   Is Vivian an anti-vivisectionist?

B   He's not anti-anything, really.

4   *anti-* as an active prefix, and *anti-= against*, as part of a word. For -*ist*, see V.4.8.

5   A relative pronoun has an antecedent. We waited outside in an ante-room.

5   *ante-= before*, in front of; ie in a room outside another room.

6   I'm neither pro-Jack nor anti-Jack. I'm still weighing the pros and cons.

6   *pro-= for, in favour of;* I'm still considering arguments for and against.

7a   Don't do that. It's unnecessary. I'll only have to undo it all later.

b   Defrost your refrigerator regularly.

7   *un-= not*, very active prefix before ADJ. *un-* before a VERB indicates reversal of a process. *De-* indicates reversal also.

8   The work was left uncompleted. Your coat is undone. Do it up.

8   *un-* (*= not*) very active before a PAST PARTICIPLE. *Do stg up:* reverse, *undo it.*

9   incomplete, inconvenient, innocent; immobile, impolite, impossible; illegal, illegible, illegitimate; irregular, irrelevant, irresponsible.

9   *in-, im-, il-* and *ir-*, instead of *un-*, depending on the first consonant sound on the root word. Note: *incomplete, uncompleted.*

10   Someone who disobeys is disobedient. These wires are unconnected: connect them up. Now they are connected; disconnect them. They are disconnected.

10   *dis-*, not as common as *un-= not*. There is no VERB **unconnect, *uncomplete;* but *disconnect* is available.

11 A You are too tired. You're overtired.

B   Yes, they overwork me and underpay me: I'm overworked and underpaid.

A   I think they underestimate your ability.

11   *over-* before VERB or ADJ= *too (much)*. *under-* before VERB or ADJ= *not enough*.

12   automatic; co-operation; counteract; He /was the President/ /is the ex-President/. I've misled you. You'll outlive me.

self-service; semi-conscious; subnormal; subway; supermarket; Vice-Chairman. uniform; monosyllable; bifocal; tripartite; multi-racial.

12   *auto-=* by itself; *co-=* with; *counter-=* against; *ex-=* formerly, no longer; *mis-=* wrongly; *out(live)=* (live) beyond.
self-= without help; *semi-=* half; *sub-=* under; *super-=* very large; *vice-=* instead of; *uni-* or *mono-=* one, *bi-=* two; *tri-=* three. *Sub-+* ADJ: stress *sub-* and ADJ; *sub-+* NOUN: stress *sub-* only.

V.4 'Active' suffixes, ie those in common use and often found in new-coined words

Models	Notes
Examiners and examinees.	
Three spoonfuls of sugar.	
Obtainable everywhere.	

1 In an examination, there are examiners and examinees.
trainers, trainees; refugees.

1 -er, unstressed, = one who does;
-ee, stressed, = one who is [examin]ed.
refugees = those who (try to) take refuge.

2 shopkeepers, wage earners, fruit growers; factory workers.

2 Those who keep shops, earn wages, grow fruit; those who work in a factory.

3 visitor, stamp collector; beggar.

3 -or, -ar, instead of -er, in a few words.

4 manageress, waitress, actress.

4 Feminine of manager, waiter, actor; but note woman driver (V.1.6), lady cashier.

5 To strain the liquid, pass it through a strainer.
A cigarette-lighter is an object.

5 -er is also used for the object that performs a function.

6 A fearless man has no fear.
A gearless car has no gears.

6 -less, = without, as part of a word, and -less as an active suffix.

7 Three spoonfuls of sugar, please.

7 -ful, plural -fuls, can be added to a NOUN referring to stg that contains.

8 A Are you a realist or an idealist?
  B I believe in /realism/ /idealism/.

8 -ist, one who believes in, or practises.
-ism, what is believed in, or practised.

9 Your room is beautifully sunny.
Mine is draughty and noisy.

9 -y added to many NOUNS, especially monosyllables, to form ADJS. Regular spelling: draught(y), sun(ny), noise, noisy.

10 He is being foolish and childish.
She was wearing a short-ish dress, with a reddish, whitish scarf.

10 -ish, as part of a word, = like (a).
-ish, added to ADJS of degree (II.20.1) or colour to mean 'somewhat'; spelling as in 9.

11 This product can be obtained anywhere.
It is obtainable everywhere.
It can't be beaten: it's unbeatable.
A space ship must be steerable.
It is (un)desirable to appoint him.
The company was most agreeable.
(un)manageable. (un)noticeable.
unforgettable. (un)reliable.

11 -able, a very active suffix, meaning can be [obtain]ed, worthy of being [admir]ed.
Prefix un- + ROOT WORD + suffix -able.
Example of 'active' use of the suffix -able.
Final e usually omitted when -able added.
Final ee: both e's retained.
After g and c, the e is retained.
Sim.: regrettable, undeniable.
NB inflammable = (very) burnable.

12 visible evidence. The Invisible Man.
(in)audible; (in)edible; (in)soluble.

12 A closed set of ADJS end in -ible; not an active suffix. Note solve, soluble.

13 shorten, fatten, widen, lengthen.

modernise, publicise, legalise.

13 = make or become (more) short, fat, wide, etc.
-ize or -ise, = make modern, etc.

14 We'll go round the table clockwise.
Weather-wise, the news is better.

14 -wise, active suffix meaning 'in that way'.
= as far as the weather is concerned: this is a current colloquialism.

15 The homeward journey. Homeward bound. On our way home- ward(s).	15 *-ward*, ADJ, or *-ward*(*s*) ADV meaning 'towards'.

V.5 *-ing* and past participle as premodifiers in a noun phrase

Models

Boiling-point; boiling oil.
Housewives need housekeeping money.
The fire was caused by a lighted match.

Notes

1 Mind! This is boiling /oil/ /water/.
Don't go out in the pouring rain.

2 Modern rooms have sliding doors.
Read the following sentence.

3 Hardworking students. Fast-moving
traffic. Long-playing records.
Good-looking men. Incoming post.

4 Housewives need housekeeping money.
Lifesaving equipment saves lives.

5 Cooking apples are (used) for cooking.
Writing paper is (used) for writing.
The swimming pool is where we swim.
The boiling-point of water is the tempera-
ture at which water will boil.

6 You must wear a bathing-costume in the
sunbathing area.

7 I heard the tramp of a marching army.
I saw an army marching to war.

8 This rose has faded. It's a faded rose.
That tree has fallen down: a fallen tree.
Its leaves have gone.

9 Two men were injured. The injured men
were taken to hospital.
This talk was recorded. It was a recorded
talk.
He has been /trained well/ /well trained/.
These goods have been /damaged badly/
/badly damaged/.
Badly damaged goods are valueless.

10 These shoes were made by hand. They are
hand-made. Hand-made shoes are rare now.

11 I appeal to you on bended knees.
What shall we do with a drunken sailor?
The fire was caused by a lighted match.
The wood is rotten. It's rotten wood.
He's a tall, clean-shaven man.
A sunken ship lay in the channel.

1 The oil etc, SUBJECT of *-ing*, is boiling.
Stress on [*boil*]*ing* and the HEAD-WORD.

2 The doors, SUBJECT of *-ing*, slide open
or shut. Stress as above.

3 The students etc, SUBJECT of *-ing*, work
hard etc. Primary stress on first and
third elements, secondary stress on
[*mov*]*ing* etc.

4 *house* etc, OBJECT of *-ing* in this type.
Stress only on *house*, *life*.

5 In this type, stress falls on [*cook*]*ing*,
not on the HEAD-WORD.

6 *bathing costume* as in 4.
sunbathing = bathing in the sun.

7 *marching army* as in 1 above.
See V.6.1.

8 *faded, fallen*, are in the ACTIVE VOICE.
Normally, avoid ACTIVE PAST PARTICIPLES
as ATTRIBUTIVE ADJS. Stress [*fad*]*ed* and
rose.

9 *injured* is part of a PASSIVE VERB PHRASE.
The PASSIVE PAST PARTICIPLE occurs frequently as an ATTRIB ADJ. Stress
[*injur*]*ed* and *men*.
Avoid *very* as a PAST PARTICIPLE MODI-
FIER except with the type of ADJ dealt
with in III.7.

10 *hand-made* = made by hand. Stress on
hand and *made*.

11 But: *It is bent*. Bend, bent, bent.
But: *He is drunk*. Drink, drank, drunk.
But: *It is lit*. Light, lit, lit.
It has rotted. Rot, rotted, rotted.
He has shaved. Shave, shaved, shaved.
It has sunk. Sink, sank, sunk.

V.6   Postmodifiers in the noun phrase

Models

I have a friend living in London.
This is only for the people concerned.
The stupidest thing imaginable.

Notes

1   They are real people—living people.

X is the greatest $\begin{cases}\text{living writer.}\\\text{writer living.}\end{cases}$

He is the greatest writer living today.
I have a friend living in London.

1   *living people* as in V.5.1.

Position of *living* optional in this case; *living* = alive.
POSTMODIFIER usual here.
No option when *-ing* itself is modified: *living* = who lives.

2   Students wishing to attend the meeting /are/ /were/ free to do so.
Everything belonging to you should be clearly marked with your own name.

2   *Students wishing* = students who wish or students who wished.
= Everything that belongs . . . Note that STATIVE VERBS can be used in this way.

3   There were several uninvited guests.
There were hundreds of guests invited to the reception.

3   *uninvited* as PREMODIFIER.
invited + PREP PHRASE as POSTMODIFIER.

4   We struck a ship sunk in the channel.

4   Cp V.5.11. Normal PARTICIPLE.

5   This document should only be sent to the people /interested/ /concerned/ /involved/.

5   *the interested party* or *the party interested*. Exclude *concerned* and *involved* as PREMODIFIERS.

6   The present situation concerns all students present.

6   *The present situation* = the situation now; *students present* = those who are here.

7   The Secretary-General.

The President-elect.

7   More dignified title than 'General Secretary'.
The person elected, not yet in office.

8   The proper way into the city proper.

8   *city proper* = city itself.

9   I've just said the stupidest thing imaginable.
This is the finest [cloth] obtainable.
X was the last man (to be) chosen.

9   Structure frequently found with a SUPERLATIVE.
or *the finest obtainable cloth*.
= who was chosen.

10a Every fire-engine available was rushed to the scene.

10a or *every available fire-engine*.

b   Venus is a clearly visible star.
It is the only star visible now.

b   You can always see it clearly.
It is the only star you can see now.

11a Tom is the $\begin{cases}\text{easiest boy}\\\text{boy easiest}\end{cases}$ to teach.

11a Variation on the pattern in IV.28.9.

b   I can tell you a $\begin{cases}\text{much funnier story}\\\text{story much funnier}\end{cases}$ than that.

b   Option.

c   I can tell you a story quite as funny as that.

c   No option.

12 /Any boy/ /Anyone/ brave enough to swim in that sea deserves a medal.

12 *who is* could be inserted before *brave*.

V.7 Replacing a verb by a noun. See also IV.7

Models

What was the cause of the explosion?
Their arrival was unexpected.
Give a brief description of what you see.

Notes

1   Gas was escaping from a pipe.
There was an escape of gas from a pipe.
A lighted match caused the gas to explode.
The explosion was caused by a lighted match.
What was the cause of the explosion?

1   *Gas:* MASS NOUN.
an escape, NOUN, *of gas.*
lighted (not *lit*) ATTRIB ADJ.
explode, VERB; *explosion,* NOUN.
cause, VERB: *cause,* NOUN.

2   We did not expect /that they would/ /them to/ arrive. We were surprised when they did.
Their [arrival][1] /was unexpected/ /was a surprise/ /took us by surprise/ /came as a surprise/.
Their arrival was unavoidably delayed.

2   *arrive,* VERB; *arrival,* NOUN.

surprise, VERB; *surprise,* NOUN.
See Lex 1 below.
un-+ avoidable+ -ly.

3a   We did not expect them to be so excited.
Their [excitement][2] was simply unbelievable.

3a   *excited,* PARTICIPLE used as ADJ.
See Lex 2.

b   We did not imagine they would be dismissed.
Their [dismissal][3] was reported in the press.

b   *dismissed,* part of PASSIVE VERB.

See Lex 3.

4   Our aim is /to protect historic buildings/ /the [protection][4] of historic buildings/.

4   *protect*+ DIRECT OBJECT.
the protection of+ DIRECT OBJECT.

5a   John has applied for the post (of Director).
His application for the post (of Director) is being carefully considered.

5a   *apply,* VERB, *for*+ NP.
application, NOUN, *for*+ NP.

b   I know you're interested in the job.
I know (of) your interest in the job.

b   *interested,* as an ADJ, *in*+ NP.
interest, NOUN, *in*+ NP.

c   I can't allow you to interfere with my staff.
I can't allow interference with my staff.

c   *interfere,* VERB, *with*+ NP.

interference, NOUN, *with*+ NP.

6   They did not complain to us about the food.
They made no [complaint(s)][5] to us about it.
We had no complaint(s) about it from *them.*

6   *complain,* VERB; *complaint,* NOUN.

/make/ /have/ /receive/ a complaint.

The order of the PREP PHRASES is a matter of emphasis.

7   We congratulated them on their success.
We offered them our [congratulations][5] (on it).

7   *congratulate* somebody *on*+ NP.
offer congratulations on+ NP.

8   Describe briefly what you see in the picture.
Give a brief [description][5] of what you see.

8   For position of *briefly,* see VI.14.10.

Give a description.

9	You are forbidden to export art treasures. The export of art treasures is forbidden.	9	*ex*PORT, VERB. EX*port*, NOUN: see Lex 6.
10	Our expenses have /increased/ /decreased/. There has been an /increase/ /decrease/ in our expenses.	10	*in*CREASE, *de*CREASE, VERBS. IN*crease* (in), DE*crease* (in), NOUNS.

Lexicon

1 *arrival, departure; approval, disapproval; acceptance, refusal; agreement, disagreement; success, failure; appearance, disappearance; attendance, absence* (corresponding to *be absent*)
2 See III.7: *amusement, annoyance, astonishment, delight, disappointment; disgust; embarrassment, excitement, interest, pleasure, satisfaction*
3 *appointment, dismissal; promotion; nomination, election*
4 *protection, preservation, restoration, destruction, replacement*
5 See Appendix D
6 The following words are NOUNS when stressed on the first syllable and VERBS when stressed on the second: *accent, ally, combine, conduct, conflict, contest, contract, contrast, convert, convict, decrease, desert, digest, discount, envelope, escort, exploit, export, extract, import, increase, permit, produce, progress, prospect, record, torment*

V.8 Special uses of *will, would* and *shall*: see also II.13, II.15, III.20 and V.9

Models

You will leave that door open.
He *would* do a thing like that.
You shall have your money soon.

Notes

1a	*A* Can I help you? *B* Yes please, if you will. *A* Of course I /will/ /'ll help you/.	1a	*will* suggesting willingness and occurring in a CONDITIONAL CLAUSE. See IV.8.1.
b	I shall be grateful if you will reply as soon as possible.	b	Cp 9 below.
2	You will do what I tell you.	2	*will*, reducible to '*ll*, = *must* in this case.
3	You will leave that door open.	3	*will*, stressed and not reducible. Meaning: *you keep, or insist, on doing it.*
4a	He's obstinate. He won't obey me.	4a	*won't* = refuses to.
b	Something is wrong with the machine: it won't start.	b	Refusal imagined in an INANIMATE OBJECT.
5	When the cat's away, the mice will play.	5	Proverb. That is characteristic of mice: *will play* replaceable by *play* or *are apt to play.*
6	Uncle John will sit there for hours.	6	Habit. *Will sit* replaceable by *sits.*
7	Iron will rust in a damp atmosphere.	7	Prediction based on experience. *Will rust* replaceable by *rusts.*
8	Would you help me? I $\left\{\begin{array}{l}\text{'d}\\ \text{would}\\ \text{should}\end{array}\right\}$ be grateful if you $\left\{\begin{array}{l}\text{'d}\\ \text{would}\end{array}\right\}$ help me.	8	Cp 1a above. This is a less direct expression of willingness.
9	I should be grateful if you would let me know as soon as possible.	9	Structure commonly used in formal correspondence, more courteous than 1b. Say *I should* to avoid repeating *would.*
10	He would leave things lying about.	10	Past equivalent of 3 above: stress *would.*

11	He wouldn't obey. It wouldn't start.	11	Past equivalent of 4 above.
12	Uncle John would sit there all day. He'd sit there for hours.	12	Past equivalent of 6 above, often used in telling a story about the past.

13 *A* I'm afraid I've lost my key again.
    B You would. You would do a silly thing like that, wouldn't you.
    A Well, Dick lost *his* yesterday.
    B He would have. That was the kind of thing Dick would /do/ /have done/.

13

That is characteristic of you (cp 10 above). Stress *would*.

He would've in fluent speech: *would have done* as the PAST of *would* in this sense.

14 *A* When are you going to pay me?
    B Don't worry. You shall have your money soon, I promise you.

14

shall can be used with 2nd and 3rd persons in this situation.

15 So we agree, Gentlemen, that the new Secretary shall receive £1500 a year.

15 *shall* conveying an official decision.

16 We are determined that there shall be no more war.

16 This is intended as an expression of hope rather than a prediction.

17 You will be sitting on my right.

Shall we be seeing you this evening?

17 Plain FUTURE, avoiding the command-ing tone of 2 above.
Plain FUTURE, avoiding the idea of suggestion, as in II.15.6.

V.9 Modals used to express the speaker's assessment of a situation

Models

That will be George, no doubt.
You must be very tired.
You must have been hungry.

Notes

1 *A* Who is that man over there?
    B That will be George, no doubt.
      That would be George, I expect.

1

I assume it is or will prove to be.
I assume less confidently that it is.

2 That /won't/ /wouldn't/ be the house we're looking for, surely.
/Will/ /Would/ *that* be the one?

2 I imagine it isn't.

Can I assume that it is?

3 Now you'll understand why I had to refuse.
I've no doubt (that) you do.

3 I assume you do understand.

4 *A* Who was that? Who has done it?
    B That will have been George.
      That would have been George.
      Dick will have done it, I suppose.
      Dick would have done it, perhaps.

4

I assume it was. Contrast IV.16.4.

I assume Dick has done it.

5a *A* Am I right? Was I right?
    B I don't know. You /may/ /might/ be.

You /may/ /might/ have been right.

5a

It is /possible/ /less definitely possible/ or it is not: both possibilities exist.
It is /possible/ /etc/ that you were or have been; or it is possible you weren't.

  b He /may/ /might/ be pulling our leg.
He /may/ /might/ have been pulling our leg.

  b Perhaps he is, perhaps he isn't.
Perhaps he was, perhaps he wasn't.

6   Forget anything you /may/ /might/ hear.

Forget anything you /may/ /might/ have heard.

6   Anything that you perhaps will hear.

Anything that you perhaps (have) heard.

7   A That's not mine. Whose can it be?
     B It /can/ /could/ be anyone's.
     A /Can/ /Could/ it have been John's?
     B It /can/ /could/ have been.

7

That one possibility is, more or less, definitely open: cp note 5 above.
That possibility (has) existed.

8   Come in. You must be very tired.
     You must have been hungry.

8   I'm sure you are.
I'm sure you were: contrast *had to*, II.17.11.

9   If they're coming by car, they
$\begin{Bmatrix} \text{should} \\ \text{ought to} \end{Bmatrix}$ arrive about seven.

There $\begin{Bmatrix} \text{should} \\ \text{ought to} \end{Bmatrix}$ be some instructions on the lid, if I'm not mistaken.
Should they have arrived by now?

9   According to my calculation, I expect they will arrive then.

I expect you will find some.

Do you think, according to your calculations, that they have?

10   A They must be hungry.
     B They *can't* be (hungry). They had an enormous breakfast.
     A They must have been tired.
     B Oh, they can't have been (tired).

10   As in 8 above.
Firm denial of previous statement.

Firm denial.

11   A They must be waiting at the other door.
     B They can't be (waiting) there.
     A They must have been waiting a long time, then.
     B They can't have been (waiting, etc).

11   I've no doubt they are: that's the only solution.
I'm sure they are *not*.
I've no doubt they have been, or were, waiting.
I'm sure they have not been, or were not, waiting long.

12   A Was there an answer to my telegram?
     B John says there must have been one.
     C And I say there /can't/ /couldn't/ have been.

12

couldn't is not so firm as *can't*.

V.10 Ways of referring to the future other than those dealt with in II.12 and II.13

Models
He's leaving tomorrow.
He'll be leaving tomorrow.
The train leaves in ten minutes.
The President is to arrive at three.

Notes

1a Mr T is going to leave tomorrow.
 b I'm going to sneeze in a moment.

 c It's going to rain later.

1a As in II.12.2: present intention or plan.
 b As in II.12.6: no intention, but I feel signs.
 c As in II.12.6: no intention, but we see signs.

2 Mr T proposes to leave tomorrow.	2 *be going to*, typical of conversational style, replaced in formal style by /*propose*/ /*plan*/ /*intend*/ *to*, or simply *will*.
3 Mr T is leaving tomorrow. What time is he leaving? He's seeing Mr X on Monday.	3 Economical alternative to 1a above, available for reference to human plans, but not for 1b or 1c.
4 He'll be leaving at about four.	4 Cp IV.16.1. This is an alternative to 3 above, with less emphasis on present plan and more on future action.
5 We /may/ /might/ /must/ /have to/ /should/ /ought to/ be leaving at the same time.	5 The same pattern as 4 above, the pre-dicted action now having a MODAL colouring.
6 The train leaves in ten minutes. What time does Mr T leave tomorrow?	6 The departure is fixed by schedule. Again, not available for 1b or 1c.
7 It's my birthday next week. I'm busy tomorrow—I can't see you.	7 My birthday is a fixed date. I already have engagements for tomorrow: cannot replace, eg *You'll be tired tomorrow*.
8 The ship is (just) about to sail. It's on the point of sailing. It may be /about to sail/ /on the point of sailing/.	8 Reference to immediate future. Cp II.12.3b. Reference to immediate future. *may* + *be about to*.
9a I'll post your letter now. b Newcastle will now play Hereford next Thursday.	9a I'll do it in the immediate future. b According to information now at hand, that will happen. Structure frequently found in journalism, which tends to avoid 1a above.
10a The President is (due) to arrive in Rome at three o'clock this afternoon. b PRESIDENT TO ARRIVE AT THREE.	10a According to plans now made. Struc-ture frequently found in news items. b Headline summarising 10a above.
11 You are to stay here till I return. You are not to move.	11 This is an order. Prohibition.
12a The President is not to arrive /this afternoon/ /until tomorrow/. b The new hotel is not to be opened (till next year). c This door is not to be opened. You are not to open it.	12a Plans cancelled or postponed. See V.11.5a. b Plans cancelled or postponed. c Prohibition. No one must open it. See V.11.5b.
13 The poor old lady is not to be comforted.	13 No one can comfort her.

V.11 Structures that compensate for the ambiguities and defectiveness of the modals

Models	Notes
We may be able to help you. We have been obliged to cancel your appointment. It's a pity to have to leave.	

1a Tom can pilot the aeroplane.

b   He $\left\{\begin{array}{l}\text{is able}\\\text{has the ability}\end{array}\right\}$ to pilot it.

c   He $\left\{\begin{array}{l}\text{is allowed}\\\text{has permission}\end{array}\right\}$ to.

d   He is free, or available, to.

2a He can be very stupid at times. =

b   He $\left\{\begin{array}{l}\text{is apt}\\\text{tends}\end{array}\right\}$ to be (stupid).

3a He may pilot the aeroplane.

b   He $\left\{\begin{array}{l}\text{is allowed}\\\text{has permission}\end{array}\right\}$ to.

c   It is likely that he will.

4a May he pilot the aeroplane?

b   /Is he/ /Will he be/ allowed to?

5a The President's plans are that he will
    not arrive till tomorrow.

b   You are forbidden to open it.

6a You must go. = You are obliged to (go).
    You are bound to (go).

b   You needn't go= You're not obliged to.

c   You mustn't go= You're forbidden to.

7   We have been obliged to cancel your
    appointment.

8 A Can you help me, please?
  B Not now. I may be able to later.

  A You /must/ /$\left\{\begin{array}{l}\text{should}\\\text{ought to}\end{array}\right\}$/ be able to.

9 A /Must we/ /Have we (got) to/ /Are we
    to/ go?

  B We may have to (go).
    We may (not) be /allowed/ /forbidden/
    to.

10 They $\left\{\begin{array}{l}\text{can}\\\text{are able to}\end{array}\right\}$ reach the top.

    They $\left\{\begin{array}{l}\text{could}\\\text{were able to}\end{array}\right\}$ reach it.

    They have been able to reach it.

    We heard that the climbers had been
    able to reach the top before the clouds
    came down.

11 The surgeon must operate at once.
    He had to operate that night.
    He has had to operate.

1a This can be paraphrased by 1b, 1c or 1d.

    NEG: *He isn't able to, hasn't the ability to,
    isn't allowed to*, etc.

    Q-*Yes/No : Is he able to? Has he the
    ability to?* etc.

2

b   =a.

3a This may be paraphrased by 3b or 3c.

4a Only paraphrased by 4b. Exclude *May
    he pilot it?* to mean *Is it likely that he
    will?*: see II.16.4, note.

5a
    Paraphrase of V.10.12a.

b   Paraphrase of V.10.12c.

6a See III.21.
    be bound to go; no ACTIVE: = cannot
    avoid going: it is inevitable.

b   ie you have a choice.

c   ie you have no choice.

7   Polite way of saying *We've had to do it.*
    as in 11 below.

8   Two MODALS, eg *may* and *can*, cannot
    be used in the same VERB PHRASE; but
    may be able to, etc, are available instead.

9   *may* cannot occur in the same VP as
    must, have got to or *be to*; but *may have
    to* is available.

10 *can* is available for the present.

    could is available for the past; see
    II.17.7.
    Use *have been able to* for PRESENT
    PERFECT.
    Use *had been able to* for PAST PERFECT.

11 *must* available for the PRESENT.
    had to available for the PAST.
    have had to for PRESENT PERFECT.

<table>
<tr><td colspan="2">

12   It's a pity /to have to leave now/ /not to be able to stay longer/.
      /Being able to swim/ /Not having to stand in a queue/ is a great advantage.

</td><td colspan="2">

12   MODALS have no INFINITIVE or *-ing*; but *to have to*, *to be able to*, etc, and *having to*, *being able to*, can be used used instead.

</td></tr>
</table>

V.12   Further uses of *need*; and *dare* as full verb and modal (see III.21.4–10)

Models	Notes
I need hardly remind you of it.	
You needn't have taken it.	
I daren't speak to him.	

1   He needs a new suit, doesn't he?
     The horses needed water.
     Did they need anything to eat?

1   *need* + NP. As full VERB, *need* has the inflexions of a regular VERB like *mend*, and forms the NEGATIVE and INTERROGATIVE with *do, does, did*.

2   *A* We need to ask you something.
     B What do you need to know?

2   *need* + INFINITIVE with *to*: full VERB.

3a   *A* What will he say when he knows?

3a

     B $\left.\begin{matrix} \text{Need we} \\ \text{Do we need to} \end{matrix}\right\}$ tell him?

     need as MODAL or full VERB.

     We $\left\{\begin{matrix} \text{needn't} \\ \text{don't need to} \end{matrix}\right\}$ tell.

     needn't, used as in III.21.4. *need*, as MODAL, in NEGATIVE and INTERROGATIVE only.

     He need never hear about it.

b   He $\left\{\begin{matrix} \text{needn't} \\ \text{doesn't need to} \end{matrix}\right\}$ be told.

b   *need* + PASSIVE INFINITIVE, personal SUBJECT.

4a   I hardly need remind you of the facts, need I? I need hardly remind you.
     or I hardly need to remind you, do I?

4a   MODAL, with SEMI-NEGATIVE /*hardly*/ /*scarcely*/; *I need hardly* or *I hardly need*. *I need hardly to is unacceptable.

b   We need think only of the main facts.

b   = We need not think of anything else: implied NEGATIVE.

5a   I'm sure you all need to know.

5a   AFFIRMATIVE, full VERB only.

b   I'm not sure you $\left\{\begin{matrix} \text{need all know.} \\ \text{all need to know.} \end{matrix}\right.$

b   The NEGATIVE in the MAIN CLAUSE may produce a MODAL in the subordinate.

6   You /needn't/ /won't need to/ worry about accommodation when you arrive; but you'll need to get some cash.

6   MODAL, NEGATIVE, or full VERB, referring to the future.
     '*ll need to*, full VERB only, AFFIRMATIVE.

7   *A* Did you take your overcoat?
     B No, it wasn't cold. I didn't need to take it.

7

     It wasn't necessary at that time.

     or Yes, I did, but it wasn't cold.
     I didn't need to take it.
     I needn't have taken it after all.

     It wasn't necessary at that time.
     I took it unnecessarily.

8   This work $\left\{\begin{matrix} \text{needn't} \\ \text{doesn't need to} \end{matrix}\right\}$ be done today.

8   *need* + PASSIVE INFINITIVE; NON-PERSONAL SUBJECT.

9	I didn't dare (to) look down the cliff-face. It was so steep. I've never dared (to) ask him. Don't (you) dare (to) say that again. Nobody would dare (to) denounce him. She hesitated, not daring to go on.	9	*dare (to)*, full VERB. Used with PRESENT PERFECT. Also *Who would dare (to)?* *to* obligatory in this case.
10	I dare you to climb up that cliff.	10	*dare* (= challenge) somebody to do something.
11	Dare we ask him if he can go? I'm not sure that I dare go in. How dare you [smoke in here]? I won't speak to him: I daren't. I didn't speak to him: I daren't. I dare say you're right.	11	*dare* as MODAL, without *to*. Commonly used utterance. *daren't* referring to PRESENT or FUTURE. *daren't* referring to PAST. *dare say*, used with 1st person only. Meaning: I'm prepared to believe [you're right].
12	We $\begin{Bmatrix} \text{daren't} \\ \text{don't dare to} \end{Bmatrix}$ be seen in a bar.	12	*dare* + PASSIVE INFINITIVE: cp 3b above. *dare* not used as in 8.

V.13 Use of the past tense in expressing wishes, etc

Models

I wish I could give you the answer.
It's time we /went/ /were leaving/.
I'd rather you stayed a little longer.

Notes

1	*A* I hope you know the way. *B* I wish I /knew it/ /did/. If only I had a map /./ /,/ I could show you where to go.	1	Note the tense sequence with *hope*. *I don't know: I wish I knew. I wish I did.* The utterance often ends at the end of the CLAUSE, or it can go on as in IV.8.
2	*A* I hope you take enough exercise. *B* I wish I /took/ /could take/ more.	2	 *I wish I /did/ /could/* (first PERSON).
3	I hope he'll come more often in future. I wish he would come more often. I wish he could be more sociable.	3	Exclude *I wish I would.* Use *would* or *could* with third PERSON.
4	*A* I hope you're enjoying yourselves. *B* I wish we were (enjoying ourselves).	4	*we aren't* + *-ing: I wish we were* + *-ing.*
5	I hope you're going to the dance. *B* I wish I /was/ /were/ going.	5	*going to* used as in II.12.2. For this use of *were*, see IV.8.9.
6	*A* I won't get myself a new suit yet. *B* I wish you would get one soon.	6	*I hope you will: I wish you would.*
7	*A* I hope you /told/ /could tell/ him. *B* I wish I /had/ /could have/ told him, but I /didn't/ /couldn't/. If only I had had a map /./ /,/ I could have told him how to get there.	7	*I didn't tell him: I wish I had (told him);* *I couldn't: I wish I could have (told him).* Note as for 1b above. Sequence as in IV.19.
8	*A* I hope you don't regret your action. *B* I wish I didn't (regret it). *A* I hope you're not sitting in a draught.	8	*I do regret it: I wish I didn't.*

B I wish I /wasn't/ /weren't/ feeling so bad.   *I'm feeling bad. I wish I /wasn't/ /etc/.*
    I wish we couldn't hear that radio.   *I wish we couldn't.* cp *I hope you can't.*
    I wish you wouldn't /make that noise
    now/ /leave me this evening/.   *I wish you wouldn't.* cp *I hope you won't.*
    I wish you hadn't spoken like that.   *I hope you didn't : I wish you hadn't.*

9   It's time we were /in bed/ /leaving/.   9   We aren't: it's time we were.
    It's /about/ /high/ time you were earning   *about time, high time* + PAST TENSE.
    your own living.

10   I'd /rather/ /sooner/ you didn't wait.   10   See IV.9.9. *I'd rather wait* = *I'd rather*
    I'd prefer you not to (wait).   *you waited :* use the CLAUSE, not the
    I'd prefer it if you didn't (wait).   INFINITIVE, when the SUBJECTS are
       different.
    I'd rather you hadn't told him.   Unfortunately you did tell him.
    I'd have preferred it if you hadn't.

11   He behaves as $\begin{cases} \text{if} \\ \text{though} \end{cases}$ the house   11   See IV.15.10. Obviously it doesn't
    belonged to him.   belong to him.

V.14 *What*, meaning 'the thing(s) which'; and *whatever, whoever*, etc

    Do /what/ /whatever/ you like.
    Borrow whichever (book) you want.
    Whatever you did has been forgiven.

1a   A   What are you doing?   1a   *what I'm doing :* this can be an indirect
    B   I'll tell you what I'm doing.   *Wh*-question as in III.2.6.
  b   A   What shall I do with these books?   b
    B   Do what you like with them.   Here, *what* = the thing which. *Wh*-
       CLAUSE.
    Do /anything/ /whatever/ you like.   OBJECT. *Whatever* = anything which;
       Wh-CLAUSE, OBJECT.

  c   I don't want anything whatever.   c   *anything whatever* = anything at all.
2   I'll give you /what (little)/ /whatever/   2   *whatever* + NOUN.
    help I can.

3   A   Which of these books may I borrow?   3
    B   Take the /one/ /ones/ you want to read.   = the book(s) which, the one(s) which.
    Take whichever /one/ /ones/ you want.   *whichever* = any one(s) of that selection.

4   A   Who shall I give these papers to?   4
    B   Give them to the /person/ /people/   Do not use *who* alone in place of 'the
    (who /is/ /are/) likely to be interested.   person who'; cp *what* in 1b above.

  a   Give them to anyone (who is) likely to   a
    be interested = Give them to whoever
    is likely to be interested.   *anyone interested* = *whoever is interested.*
  b   Don't tell that to anyone whatever.   b   *anyone whatever* = anyone at all.

5   Come when you're free, when you can.   5   = /at the hour/ /on the day/ when or
       that.
    When you're free, come and see me.
    Come $\begin{cases} \text{any time} \\ \text{whenever} \end{cases}$ you can.   *whenever* = *any time whatever.*
    Whenever you can, come for supper.

6   Park where you like.

    Park $\begin{Bmatrix} \text{anywhere} \\ \text{wherever} \end{Bmatrix}$ you like.

6   *where* = in the place that . . . .

    wherever = anywhere, *in any place whatever.*

7a   Some people drive how they like.
    They drive however they like.

b   They drive anyhow.

7a   *how* = in the way that.
    however = in any way.

b   *anyhow* = according to no method or system.

8a   *A*   I did a terrible thing.
    What I did was unforgivable.
    What I did was (to) break my promise.

    B   I've forgotten what you said.
    Anyhow
    Anyway $\Big\}$, whatever you said has not
    In any case
    made any difference.

8a   I did something DEFINITE.
    Wh-CLAUSE as SUBJECT.

    Uncertainty, preparing for *whatever.*
    Anyhow, anyway, informal: cp 7b above
    = anything you may have said (see
    V.9.6).

    b   *A*   What shall we do if anyone comes late?
    B   Whoever comes late can't be admitted.

b

    Whoever not replaceable by *who.*

9   What /in the world/ /on earth/ are you doing? What ever are you /doing/ /talking about/? Who ever told you I could play the piano? Where ever have you been all this time? When ever did you find time to do all that? How ever did they find out our secret? Why ever didn't you tell me you'd been ill?

9

    In such questions, typical of colloquial style, *ever* is spoken with a high intonation rise and is replaceable by *in the world, on earth, in heaven's name,* etc: it can be used with *why,* whereas **whyever* is not available.

V.15   Continued from V.14. More clauses beginning with *whatever, however,* etc

Models
Whatever you did, I'll forgive you.
We'll go out whatever the weather.
However we go, it makes no difference.

Notes

1a   Whatever you did, I'll forgive you.
    I'll forgive you, whatever you did.

b   Whoever comes now, I won't let him in.
    I won't let him in, whoever he is.

c   Whichever book you borrow, you must return it within a week.

d   You must leave your membership card here, whichever book you borrow.

e   Wherever I park my car, I get fined.
    I get fined wherever I park my car.

f   However you drive, the roads are always dangerous.

g   You are likely to have an accident however you drive.

h   Whenever you're free, come and see me.
    Come and see me whenever you're free.

1a   Contrast *What I did* in V.14.8a: *whatever* not replaceable by *what* here.

b   Contrast V.14.8b: *whoever* not replaceable by *who* here.

c   *Whichever* not replaceable by *which* here. See 2 below.

e   ie anywhere: contrast *Where I park my car, there is plenty of shade.*

f   *However* not replaceable by *how.*

g   NB In all the models in 1, *-ever* = it doesn't matter what, who, etc.

h   *Whenever* replaceable by *when,* but *whenever* means 'any time whatever'.

2a Whichever book you borrow must be
   returned within a week.
 b Whichever book you borrow you must
   return within a week.
3 We'll go out whatever the weather is like.
   We'll go out whatever the weather.
   Whatever the weather, we'll go out.
4 Give the full address, where (it is)
   possible.
   Where (it is) possible, give the full address.
   You must park your car wherever possible.
 A When do you defrost your refrigerator?
 B (I do it) whenever possible.
   /When/ /Whenever/ (I am) in doubt, I
   look up a word in the dictionary.
5a However experienced you /are/ /may be/,
   driving fast is always dangerous.
   However well you (may) drive, someone
   else may involve you in an accident.
   You run a risk every time you go on the
   road, however skilful you /are/ /may be/,
   however skilfully you (may) drive.
 b Every driver, however skilful (he /is/
   /may be/), must pass a test.
 c However the damage was done, it must be
   repaired at once.
6 However, we must find out who was
   responsible for it.

2a *Whichever*-CLAUSE as SUBJECT of *must be*.

 b *Whichever*-CLAUSE as OBJECT of *you must
   return*.
3 *Whatever* not replaceable by *what*;
   be+ COMPLEMENT optional.

4 PRONOUN+ *be* optional: *where possible*=
   where it is possible to give it.

   it is optional in the *-ever* CLAUSE.

   it is optional.

5a *However*+ ADJ.

   However+ ADV.

 b *however*-CLAUSE, with SUBJECT and VERB
   optional.
 c The cause of the damage does not alter
   the fact that it must be repaired.
6 *However*, as a CONJUNCT ADVERB: see
   VI.17.

V.16 *Wh*-clauses as subject of the verb in another clause, as object of a verb or preposition, or as adverbials

Models
What we need is more time.
It doesn't matter what you think.
Tell us about when you fell in the river.

Notes

1 I can't imagine what he was doing.

   What he was doing, I can't imagine.

2 I can't tell you $\left\{ \begin{array}{l} \text{if} \\ \text{whether} \end{array} \right\}$ he's coming
   or not.
   Whether he's coming or not, I can't tell
   you.
3 We won't wait, whether he's coming or not.
   Whether he's coming or not, we won't
   wait.

1 *Wh*-CLAUSE as OBJECT, following MAIN
   CLAUSE.
   Wh-CLAUSE as OBJECT, preceding MAIN
   CLAUSE.

2 *if* replaceable by *whether* when the SUB-
   CLAUSE follows the MAIN.
   Wh-CLAUSE as OBJECT, preceding the
   MAIN CLAUSE: *Whether* not replaceable
   by *if*.

4   Whether he's coming or not is still un-
    certain.
    What we all need is more time.
    What is needed is more ready cash.

    What $\begin{Bmatrix} is \\ are \end{Bmatrix}$ needed $\begin{Bmatrix} is \\ are \end{Bmatrix}$ books.

    Why he did it remains a mystery.
    Where he goes on Sunday(s) is his own
    affair.

4   *Wh*-CLAUSE as SUBJECT of *is*: *Whether*
    not replaceable by *if*.
    Wh-CLAUSE as SUBJECT.

    What is needed are books is acceptable.
    but not **what are needed is books*.

5   It's still uncertain $\begin{Bmatrix} if \\ whether \end{Bmatrix}$ he's coming
    or not.
    It remains a mystery why he did it.
    It's his own affair where he goes on
    Sunday(s).

5   *It* standing for the *Wh*-CLAUSE.

6a What you think doesn't matter.

    It doesn't matter $\begin{cases} \text{what you think.} \\ \text{who goes first.} \\ \text{which one you take.} \end{cases}$

    It doesn't matter $\begin{cases} \text{where we go next.} \\ \text{when we get up.} \\ \text{whether I go or not.} \end{cases}$

6a

    Or *Who goes first doesn't matter*, etc.

 b What we do next is very important.
    It's very important what we do next.
7   Does it matter who goes first?
8   What you told me isn't true.
    Is what you told me really true?
9   What we want to know is how much it
    will cost.
10 Tell us about when you fell in the river.

    It all depends on whether he is coming
    or not.
    Were you surprised at what I said?
    I can't make up my mind (about) who
    should be asked to speak first.
    I can't make up my mind (about) who(m)
    we should ask to speak first.

9   *Wh*-CLAUSE as SUBJECT and as COMPLE-
    MENT.
10 *Wh*-CLAUSE as OBJECT of a PREPOSI-
    TION.
    whether not replaceable by *if* after a
    PREPOSITION.

    who SUBJECT of *should be asked*.

    who(m) OBJECT of *we should ask*.

V.17 Further examples of subordinate clauses, especially those concerned with purpose, cause and result: see IV.6

Models

He spoke through a microphone so that
everyone /would/ /could/ hear him.
He spoke very clearly, so that everyone
/could hear/ /heard/ him.

Notes

1 *A* Stand up so (that) I can see you.
  B Why do you want me to stand up?
  A So (that) I can see you.

1

    This assumes that speaker *B* is not
    subordinate in rank to *A*.

2a We've come early so (that) the meeting can begin promptly.

b We're all here now, so (that) the meeting can begin at last.

c /Now (that)/ /Seeing (that)/ we're all here, the meeting can begin.
The meeting can begin, /now (that)/ /seeing (that)/ we're all here.

3a He spoke through a microphone /so as to be heard/ /so that he would be heard/ /so that he could be heard/ in every room.

b He spoke through a microphone in order that everyone should hear him.

c So /as to/ /that he would/ /that he could/ be heard, etc, he spoke through a microphone.

A Why did he use a microphone?

B So /as to/ /that he would/ /etc/ be heard.

4 He spoke through a microphone /so that/ /with the result that/ everyone /heard him/ /could hear him/ /was able to hear him/.

A Why was everyone able to hear him?

B Because he spoke through a microphone.

5 *A* Why did he speak so loudly?

B He spoke /so loudly/ /in such a loud voice/ so that the people at the back could hear.

6 *A* He speaks /so clearly/ /with such a clear voice/ /such good English/ that we understand every word he says.

7 *A* Why did the dog run away?

B It must have been frightened.

A Yes, it must have been frightened, for it ran away and hid in the bushes.

She was clearly upset, for her eyes filled with tears.

8 Hurry up, /or else/ /otherwise/ you'll be late. You'll be late otherwise.
Come early, /or else/ /otherwise/ you won't get a seat. You won't get a seat otherwise.

2a We've come early for that *purpose*: SUB-ORDINATE CLAUSE can precede the MAIN.

b It can begin as a *result* of our all being here: SUB-CLAUSE cannot precede.

c *that* often omitted in conversational style.

3a *so as to be heard* = so that he himself could be heard. Retain *that* in formal style. *Should* also possible: see VI.24.

b *so that* can be replaced by *in order that* in formal style.

c The SUBORDINATE CLAUSE can precede the MAIN CLAUSE.

The SUBORDINATE CLAUSE states that the purpose of his using the microphone.

4 The SUBORDINATE CLAUSE of result cannot precede the MAIN CLAUSE.

The SUBORDINATE CLAUSE states the *result* following a *cause*.

5

Put the MAIN CLAUSE with *so* + ADV first. Purpose of his speaking so loudly.

6 The MAIN CLAUSE must come first.

Result of his speaking clearly.

7

As in V.9.10.
(Assumed) *cause* of action.
Evident result. The *for*-CLAUSE cannot precede the MAIN CLAUSE.
(Obvious) *cause*, she was upset, leading to a *result*, tears. This structure is typical of narrative style.

8 The result of your *not* hurrying will be that you'll be late. The /or else/ /otherwise/ CLAUSE cannot precede the MAIN CLAUSE.

V.18 More relative clauses (see III.13, III.14 and IV.26), including non-defining clauses

Models

I will now introduce the candidate in support of whom I wish to speak.
His speech, which went on and on, bored everybody.

Notes

1   I will now introduce the candidate in support of whom I wish to speak.

1   Formal style, as in IV.26.

2   The house which he bought in 1968, and which he sold two years later, is again on the market.

2   The first *which* might be omitted informally: in formal style its inclusion, if *and which* follows, is obligatory.

3   You're the only girl I know who can really play chess.

3   *who*, unavoidably separated from *girl*; though the NP *the only girl I know* might be considered as the ANTECEDENT.

Is there anything else you'd like that you don't see on the shelves?

that unavoidably separated from *anything else.*

4a I turned to the Chairman, who was the first to speak. The Chairman, who spoke first, sat on my right.

4a Non-defining RELATIVE CLAUSE.
Non-defining RELATIVE CLAUSE.

b   His speech, which bored everyone, went on and on.

b   Use *which*, not *that*, in a non-defining CLAUSE, when antecedent is non-personal.

c   His wife, whom you met at my house, was bored too.

c   RELATIVE PRONOUN obligatory in a non-defining CLAUSE, even when it is OBJECT.

d   The speech, which he had written on little bits of paper, seemed endless.

d   The last comment applies here also.

e   The Chairman's daughter, whose name is Ann, gave me a patient smile.

e   POSSESSIVE, person.

f   My tea-cup, the handle of which was broken, was upturned in its saucer.

f   POSSESSIVE, thing.

g   Ann, beside whom I was sitting, told my fortune from the tea-leaves.

g   OBJECT of PREPOSITION, person.

h   I now hoped that the speech, to which we were no longer listening, would go on all the evening.

h   OBJECT of PREPOSITION, thing.

5   We were all given boxes of chocolates, which was even kinder.
What was even kinder, we were all given boxes of chocolates.

5   *which*, referring to the whole previous CLAUSE.
what not replaceable by *which* when the CLAUSES are in this order.

6   He tried to stand on his hands for five minutes, which—as you know—is rather a difficult thing to do.

6   *which* referring to the whole performance.

7   I have /two/ /three/ grammars, /both/ /all/ of which are rather poor.
They have four children, all of whom are now at school.
I have two brothers, neither of whom can speak English.

7   *both of which, all of which;* sim. *some of which*, etc.
both of whom, all of whom.

neither of whom: sim. *either of whom, neither of which,* etc.

V.19 Adverbs with or without the ending *-ly*. See II.23.6

Models
Stand clear of the gates.
I'll take you direct to your room.
He aims high: he's highly ambitious.

Notes

1   This /pen writes/ /knife cuts/ cleanly.
The bullet went clean through the wall.

1   *cleanly*, ADV = in a clean way.
clean through = right through.

2   A windscreen is made of clear glass.
     Keep it clear; you must see the road
     clearly.
     Stand clear of the gates.

3   The new law concerns us all (in)directly.

     Let's meet $\left\{ \begin{array}{l} \text{directly} \\ \text{straight} \end{array} \right\}$ after lunch;

     then I'll take you $\left\{ \begin{array}{l} \text{direct} \\ \text{straight} \end{array} \right\}$ to your
     room.

     I'll tell you directly he comes.

4 *A* I can carry this table easily.
   B Yes, but go easy with it. It's an antique.

5   That's not fair: you must play fair.
     I've marked your essay fairly, and I can
     assure you (that) it's fairly good.

6   The enemy is advancing. Stand firm.
     Speak to them firmly.

7   He's very ambitious: he aims high.
     He's highly intelligent, highly trained.

8   Don't speak so loud(ly). They'll hear
     you.
     They shouted loudly for help. No one
     came.

9   Aim low. Tackle him low; grab his legs.
     He occupies a /high/ /low(ly)/ position.

10   Mary dances very prettily. She's pretty
     good. She dances pretty well.

11   Please report to me at ten o'clock sharp.
     At the crossroads, turn sharp (to the)
     left.
     The car turned sharply and drove off.
     The policeman spoke to the driver
     sharply.

12   Go slow(ly). Go $\left\{ \begin{array}{l} \text{slower.} \\ \text{more slowly.} \end{array} \right.$

     I can understand you when you speak
     slowly.

13   We're just starting. Hold tight.
     Sit tight. Hold on to your seats tightly.

14   He's an elderly, friendly, kindly man.
     He speaks to everyone in that elderly,
     friendly, kindly /way/ /manner/ /voice/.

15   The road is very dangerous. Go dead
     slow.

     Don't touch that. It's $\left\{ \begin{array}{l} \text{deadly.} \\ \text{deadly poisonous.} \end{array} \right.$
     I can't read this. It's deadly dull.

2   *clear* as ADJ.
     clear, ADJ, as in IV.24.1; *clearly*, ADV.

     clear of it = away from it, ADV.

3   *(in)directly* = in /a/ /an/ (in)direct way.

     directly, straight = immediately.

     direct, straight = without deviation.

     directly = as soon as (informal).

4   *easily* = without difficulty.
     go easy = don't be rough.

5   *fair*, after *play* as vi; otherwise, use
     fairly as an ADV of manner or as replace-
     ment for *rather* before ADJS, expressing
     a positive quality.

6   Cp *stand clear*.

7   Sim. *fly high, fly low*.
     Sim. *highly delighted, amused*, see VI.16.3.

8   Sim. *speak louder*, or *more loudly*.

     Use only *loudly* before the PREP PHRASE.

9   *low* as ADV; cp *high*.
     Use *lowly* as an ADJ meaning 'humble'.

10   *prettily*, ADV manner; *pretty*, (informal)
     modifying ADJ or ADV, meaning *rather*.

11   = punctually at ten o'clock.
     = at an acute angle.

     = suddenly.
     = in an abrupt, firm manner.

12   *slow(ly)* with *go*. Regard *slow* and *slower*
     as ADVS, as more informal, otherwise
     slowly.

13   *tight*, as ADV after vi.
     tightly after vt + OBJECT.

14   *elderly, friendly, kindly* as ADJ.
     Note devices for using an equivalent
     ADV manner.

15   *dead* as ADV.

     deadly, ADJ, or as ADV modifying an ADJ.

V.20 Non-finite, present participle clauses; related participles; see V.6.1 and 2

Models	Notes
Going home I saw a snake.	
I saw my friend George riding a bicycle.	
Jumping into a car, he drove away at full speed.	

1a /Going home/ /On my way home/ I saw a snake.

1a *I* was going and *I* saw the snake. *Going* related to *I*.

 b I saw my friend George riding a bicycle.

 b *I* saw him; *he* was riding. *Riding* related to *George*.

2 Grazing on the hills (there) were herds of black cattle.
 We saw herds of black cattle grazing on the hills.
 Standing at a safe distance, we watched them grazing.

2 The herds were grazing.

 The herds were grazing.

 We were standing, *we* watched them. Exclude **Grazing on the hills, we ...*

3 Lifting the weight, he sprained his back.
 He sprained his back lifting the weight.

3 *He* sprained it while *he* was lifting.
 He sprained it while *he* was lifting: obviously, his back was not lifting.

4 Shouting with joy, we rushed into the sea.
 We rushed into the sea, shouting with joy.
 Rushing into the sea, we shouted with joy.
 We shouted with joy, rushing into the sea.

4 The *shouting* and the *rushing* occurred simultaneously, but the VERB in *-ing* provides a background for the SIMPLE PAST.

5 He jumped into the car and drove away at full speed.
 Jumping into the car, he drove away at full speed.

5 The two actions are consecutive, and in that case the PARTICIPLE CLAUSE must precede the MAIN CLAUSE.

6 As ⎱ he was backing his car out of the
 While ⎰
 garage, Tom knocked down a pedestrian.
 Tom knocked down a pedestrian while backing his car out of the garage.
 When (you are) paying by cheque, always give your address.

6 *While -ing.*

 Contrast 1b. Tom knocked while Tom was backing. Exclude **as -ing.*
 When -ing: when *you* are paying *you* should give, etc.

7 Before you go to bed, brush your teeth thoroughly. Clean your teeth thoroughly before going to bed.
 After you have used the brush, put it in its proper place. After using the brush, etc.

7 *Before you go* becomes *Before going.*
 All the *-ing* phrases in 6 can follow or precede the MAIN CLAUSE.
 After you use or *After you have used* becomes *After using.*

8 Considering the heat, I think we should stay indoors. (ie when I consider it . . .)
 Considering how hot it is outside, this room is surprisingly cool.
 Supposing a fire broke out, what would you do?
 Supposing a fire broke out, what would be the first thing to do?

8 *Considering* and *supposing* both agreeing and not agreeing with the SUBJECT of the MAIN CLAUSE. Allow non-agreement with these two PARTICIPLES, despite the implications of the notes to 2 above. The *-ing* phrases could also follow the MAIN CLAUSE.

9 He looked down at the ground, his face burning with shame.

9 His face was burning as he looked, etc.

10 All those (who are) standing at the back, please come and sit here.

Anyone $\left\{\begin{array}{l}\text{who wishes}\\\text{wishing}\end{array}\right\}$ to buy a ticket should do so today.

10 RELATIVE CLAUSES reduced to a PARTICIPLE CLAUSE, even when the VERB, eg *wish*, is STATIVE.

V.21 Non-finite, past participle clauses, with related participles

Models

Placed under arrest, he denied the charges brought against him.
The man arrested by the police has not yet been named.
The castle, built in 1360, is deserted.

Notes

1 Arriving at the gate, we were challenged by a smart young sentry.

1 We arrived and were challenged. *Arrived*, INTRANSITIVE and ACTIVE, cannot replace *arriving* here.

2 Challenged by a smart young sentry, we produced our identity cards.

2 *Challenged*, TRANSITIVE and PASSIVE, related to *we*.

3 Charging Cuthbert with theft, the policeman placed him under arrest.

3 *Charging*, TRANSITIVE but ACTIVE, related to *the policeman*.

4 Charged with theft, Cuthbert insisted that he was innocent.
Cuthbert, placed under arrest, denied the charges brought against him.

4 *Charged*, TRANSITIVE and PASSIVE, related to *Cuthbert*.
placed under arrest, PARTICIPLE CLAUSE, following the SUBJECT of the MAIN CLAUSE.

5 Considered as a work of art, the building is rather disappointing.
If we consider it as a work of art, the building is rather disappointing.

5 As in V.20.2, the PARTICIPLE in this model is related to the SUBJECT of the MAIN CLAUSE.

6 We found our old house completely destroyed by fire.
We found none of the neighbouring houses left.
We found all our old neighbours gone.
We found (that) they had all died.

6 This is an example of the pattern given in IV.24.12.
none left: they had all gone.

Exceptionally, *gone* (vi) can occur in this structure. Use a different structure with eg *died*.

7 The hotel walls looked hideous painted blue.
We thought the walls looked hideous painted blue.
Painted blue, the walls looked hideous.

7 They had been painted blue.

But not **Painted blue, we thought ...*

8 Tired out, we were glad to find even the humblest shelter.
The children, exhausted, fell asleep at once. They fell asleep, quite exhausted.

8 Non-finite CLAUSES consisting simply of PARTICIPIAL ADJECTIVES, as in III.7.3.

9a One of the houses (that had been) wrecked by the storm belonged to my grandfather.

9a Defining RELATIVE CLAUSE, with deletable RELATIVE PRONOUN + *be*.

 b The castle, (which was) built in 1360, is now a deserted ruin.

 b Non-defining RELATIVE CLAUSE (V.18), deletable.

10   He lay there, perfectly content, his head   10   Cp V.20.8.
      cradled in his mother's arms.

V.22 Prepositional phrases which can replace subordinate clauses

Models   **Notes**

The crops failed because of the drought.
We go by air, in spite of the expense.
Regardless of obstacles, we must press on.

1a   The crops failed because there had been   1a   Can be re-written, as in the next model.
     no rain for a long time.
     The crops failed because of the drought.   *because of* + NP, replaceable by *owing to*,
     Owing to the drought, the crops failed.   before or after the MAIN CLAUSE.
  b He resigned, because of what you said.   b   *because of* + *Wh*-CLAUSE.
2   The failure of the crops was due to the   2   Use *owing to* + NP as an ADV ADJUNCT,
     long drought.   and *due to* + NP to modify an NP,
     The poor harvest, due to the long drought,   eg *harvest*.
     proved to be a national disaster.
3a   We go by air, though it's expensive.   3a   Can be re-written as in next line.
     We go by air, in spite of the expense.   *in spite of* + NP, replaceable by
     We travelled by air, despite the expense.   *despite*, which is more formal.
  b In spite of ⎫   b   In spite of ⎫
     Despite   ⎭ what you said to him, he   Despite   ⎭ + *Wh*-CLAUSE.
     still made the same mistake.   Note the reinforcing *still*.
4   He lives miserably, for all his wealth.   4   *for all*: even though he has plenty.
5   With all his money, he could surely afford   5   *with all*: he had plenty, so he could
     a decent suit of clothes.   afford . . .
6   There are obstacles ahead of us. Whether   6   Can be re-written as in next model.
     there are or not, we must press on.
     Regardless of obstacles, we must press on.   *regardless of* + NP.
7   May I refer to your letter of 13th July?   7
     The information you require is as follows:
     With reference to your letter, etc, the . . .   *with reference to* + NP.
8   You asked about a suitable hotel.   8
     The ⎰enclosed brochure⎱ will give you full
         ⎱brochure enclosed⎰
     particulars.
     With regard to ⎫
     Regarding   ⎭ a suitable hotel, the   Consider *regarding* here as a PREPOSI-
     enclosed brochure etc.   TION, not as a PARTICIPLE.
9a   As for bookings on the ferry, you should   9a   Used in continuation of the kind of
     apply to your local travel agents.   statement made in 8.
     Concerning bookings on the ferry, you   Formal, commercial.
     should apply, etc.
9b   As for George, he ought to be ashamed   9b   Conversational.
     of himself.
10   /As to the question of costs/ /As to how
     much it will cost/, you will find details
     on page 16.

11 According to the rules, subscriptions must be paid in advance.

11 That is what the rules state.

12 In accordance with Rule 19, as you are in arrears with your fees I cannot allow you to use the club.

12 *in accordance with* + NP: I am acting in the way that Rule 19 allows.

Lexicon
according to, apart from, as a result of, as for, as to, concerning, despite, due to, except, except for, for all, for fear of, in accordance with, in comparison with, in spite of, in view of, owing to, regarding, regardless of, with all, with reference to, with regard to

V.23 Avoiding a subordinate clause by means of a nominalisation: see V.7

Models

Please telephone me on your arrival.
You cannot do that without approval.
A tendency to upset his colleagues was his only fault.

Notes

1 Before his illness, he was very thin.

After his promotion, he was much happier.
During your absence, we made a few changes in the office.

1 *Before he was ill* can become *Before his* + NP.
After he /was/ /had been/ promoted can become *after his* + NP.
While you were /away/ /absent/ can become *During your* + NP.

2 When you arrive, please telephone me. Please telephone me immediately on your arrival (at your hotel).

2 *on your arrival (at).*

3 When we receive your application, we shall send you further particulars.
On receipt of your application, we etc.

3 *When we receive* + NP can become *On receipt of* + the same NP.

4 /When/ /As soon as/ the experiment had been completed, we wrote our report.
On completion of the experiment, etc.

4 *When* + NP + PAST TENSE or PAST PERFECT becomes *on completion of* + the same NP.

5 We all believed (that) he was /loyal/ /innocent/ /truthful/ /trustworthy/.
We all believed in his loyalty, innocence, truthfulness, trustworthiness.

5 *believe (that) he was* + ADJ can become *believe in his* + NP.

6a He tended to upset his colleagues. That was his only fault.

6a Less formal than 6b.

b A tendency to upset his colleagues was his only fault.

b More formal than 6a.

7a Passengers who travel on any train without a ticket when they don't intend to pay will be prosecuted.

7a Less formal than 7b.

b Passengers travelling on any train without a ticket and with the intention of avoiding payment will be prosecuted.

b Formal announcement on public transport.

8	What you achieved was remarkable.	8	*Wh*-CLAUSE as SUBJECT.

8   What you achieved was remarkable.
     Your achievement was remarkable.
9   You cannot do that unless /someone
     approves/ /I approve/.
     You cannot do that without /approval/
     /my approval/.
10   *A* Shall we close the factory down?
     B I think we must decide that later.
     A decision was therefore postponed.

8   *Wh*-CLAUSE as SUBJECT.
     Wh-CLAUSE nominalised.

V.24 Different prepositions + *-ing*

Models
They make a fire by rubbing two pieces
of wood together.
On entering the town, you will be greeted
by the Mayor.
In saying that, I am not exaggerating.
I object to being kept waiting.

Notes

1   They make a fire by means of two pieces
     of a certain kind of wood.
     They do it by rubbing these two pieces
     of wood together.
     You cannot get rid of a plague of monkeys
     simply by shooting at them.
2   In saying (that) it was the finest perform-
     ance I have seen, I am not exaggerating.
     Even in (the process of) stirring a cup of
     coffee you are generating a certain amount
     of heat.
3a   By giving that talk on television he gained
     a great advantage over his opponent.
 b   In allowing himself to appear in such a
     programme, he lost a good deal of support.
4   (On) entering the town, turn sharp left.
     (On) entering the town, you will be greeted
     by the Mayor.
     On being taken to the scene of the crime,
     he broke down and confessed everything.
5   We have ⎰got ⎱ quite used to /cooking
            ⎱become⎰
            ⎱grown ⎰
     our own meals/ /being criticised/.

     We have ⎰got ⎱ quite accustomed to
            ⎱become⎰
            ⎱grown ⎰
     /driving/ /being driven/.
     I object to having to wait in the rain.
     I object to being kept waiting.

1   *by means of* + NP.

     by -ing, the means by which a result is
     achieved.
     You cannot achieve that result by such
     means.
2   I am not exaggerating in that little
     speech.
     You are (unintentionally) generating
     heat in that process.

3a   He secured that result by those means.

 b   He lost it, incidentally, in the process.

4   *On* optional.
     On entering = at the moment when you
     enter.
     On less likely to be optional before a
     PASSIVE.

5   *get* is more informal than *become*.
     Contrast *used to do* as in III.5, with
     the PREP *used to* + *-ing*.

     object to -ing.
     object to being -ed.

He admitted to $\begin{Bmatrix}\text{stealing} \\ \text{having stolen}\end{Bmatrix}$ the purse.

I look forward to meeting you again.   *look forward to -ing.*

6 He did not hesitate but picked up the   6
   'phone. Without hesitating, he picked   *Without -ing.*
   up the 'phone.
   He left last night. He didn't (even) say
   good-bye. He left without (even) saying
   good-bye.

7 He was surprised to find us here.   7 As in III.8.5. The meaning of the two
   He was surprised at finding us here.   sentences is substantially the same.

8 He insisted (that) he must see the Manager. 8 As in IV.11. Meaning of the two senten-
   He insisted on seeing the Manager.   ces substantially the same.

V.25 Use of *being, not being, having been, not having been*, etc

Models   ### Notes

I don't remember having said that.
Having been invited, I intend to speak.
Never having been there, I can't say.

1 You're a professor. You ought to know.   1 Re-write as on next line.
   Being a professor, you ought to know.   *Being*, PARTICIPLE, agreeing with *you.*
   Being a professor is not an easy job.   *Being* (+ NP) as NOUN, SUBJECT of *is.*

2 I'm not a professor. I can't explain it. 2 Re-write as on next line.
   Not being a professor, I can't explain it.   *Not being.*

3 *A* Having a telephone at your side, you 3 *Having*, PARTICIPLE, agreeing with *you.*
      can easily ring him up.
      Not having a telephone, I shall have   *Not having*, PARTICIPLE, agreeing with *I.*
      to write to him.

  B Having a telephone can be a nuisance.   *Having* (+ NP), as NOUN, SUBJECT of *can.*
  A Not having one has its disadvantages.   *Not having* (+ NP), as NOUN, SUBJECT of
                                             has.

4a I [regret] $\begin{Bmatrix}\text{saying} \\ \text{having said}\end{Bmatrix}$ that.   4a $= I$ [regret] (*that*) I (*have*) *said it.*

   I don't recall ever $\begin{Bmatrix}\text{saying} \\ \text{having said}\end{Bmatrix}$ such
   a thing.

   I regret not $\begin{Bmatrix}\text{seeing} \\ \text{having seen}\end{Bmatrix}$ him sooner.

 b Imagine /travelling/ /having travelled/   b meaning 'Imagine that you might travel
    all that way for nothing.   or (have) travelled'.

5 He has travelled round the world, so he   5 Re-write as on next line.
   ought to know where Cape Horn is.
   Having travelled round the world, he
   ought to know where etc.
   /Not/ /Never/ having been to Peking,
   I can't tell you what it looks like.

6a Passengers boarding any train without   6a Formal announcement. Cp V.23.7;
    having previously paid the fare are   PREP + *having -ed.*
    liable to be prosecuted.

b   I (have) interrupted you. Forgive me.

Forgive me for $\begin{Bmatrix} \text{interrupting} \\ \text{having interrupted} \end{Bmatrix}$ you.

b   Re-write as on next line.

7   I have been invited to speak and I intend
     to do so.
     Having been invited to speak, I intend
     etc.
     /Not/ /Never/ having been invited to his
     house, I can't describe it to you.

7
     Re-write as on next line.
     Having been -ed before the SUBJECT.

8   Having been refused permission to stay
     in the country, we had to return home by
     the first available aircraft.

8   *Having been -ed* + NP before the SUBJECT.

9   Several of our customers complain of
     having been /treated/ /spoken to/ very
     rudely.

9

     PREP + *having been -ed*.

V.26 Different constructions with *since*: see II.9.7 and III.15.7

Models

Since leaving school in 1960, I have
only met him twice.
It's a long time since we met.
Since he left school in 1960, he must
be older than thirty now.

Notes

1a   We've been here (ever) since /ten
     o'clock/ /then/.

1a   As in II.9.7: *since* + a point in time.

b   I've lived here (ever) since I was a boy.

b   As in III.15.7: *since* + CLAUSE, PAST
     TENSE.

c   I've lived here (ever) since my child-
     hood.
     Since /ten o'clock/ /our arrival/ /we
     arrived/, there have been some impor-
     tant developments.
     Ever since we arrived, he has been
     pestering us.

c   *since* + NP. PRESENT PERFECT in main
     CLAUSE in models a, b and c.
     The *since*-PHRASE or *since*-CLAUSE can
     follow or precede the MAIN CLAUSE.

     Ever since = throughout the whole
     time from then till now.

2   Since I left school in 1960, I have only
     met him twice. = Since leaving school
     in 1960, I have only met him twice.

2   *Since -ing* can precede or follow the
     MAIN CLAUSE, but is only available
     (a) if the SUBJECTS of both CLAUSES are
     the same, and (b) if *since* is used in a
     temporal sense, not as in 6b below.

3   I left school in 1960 and haven't seen
     George since.
     I met him in 1960 and we've been
     friends ever since.

3
     since as an ADV in final position only.

     ever since as ADV.

4   It $\begin{Bmatrix} \text{is} \\ \text{has been} \end{Bmatrix}$ a long time since

     we $\begin{Bmatrix} \text{met} \\ \text{have met.} \end{Bmatrix}$

4   PRESENT PERF may occur in the *since*-
     CLAUSE, following the MAIN CLAUSE, in
     this type of utterance.

5a	He left New York in 1860. He had lived there since /1839/ /his childhood/ /he was a boy/.	5a	*since* + a point in time, with the PAST PERFECT in the MAIN CLAUSE and PAST TENSE in the SUBORDINATE.
b	Since arriving in New York in 1839 (till 1860), he had worked as a carpenter.		
6a	Since he left school, as long ago as 1960, I have only seen him twice.	6a	*Since* used as in 2 above.
b	Since ⎤ ⎬ he left school as long ago as 1960, As ⎦ he must be over thirty now.	b	*Since* replaceable by *as* and also by *seeing that* (V.17.2).
7	We'll have to stop soon, since we're almost out of petrol.	7	*we're out of* = we've none left; *since* replaceable by *as* or *because*.
A	Why do we have to stop?		
B	(Because) we're almost out of petrol.		*Since* unlikely in this short answer.
8	Since we have to stop for petrol, let's have something to eat at the same time.	8	*Since* replaceable by *seeing* (*that*) and *as*.
9	Since we are all here now, the meeting can begin.	9	In this case, *since* is replaceable by *now* (*that*) and *seeing* (*that*), V.17.2, and by *as*.
10	Since you knew that man was coming, why didn't you warn me?	10	*Since* replaceable by *as* or *seeing* (*that*).

V.27 Constructions with *while*, *when* and *as*

Models

They slept while we kept watch over them.
As you read this page again, make a note of all the new words.
While I agree with you up to a point I cannot agree to your plans as a whole.

Notes

1a	He arrived /while/ /when/ we were playing chess.	1	*while*, as in III.18.7, meaning 'during the time that'; *when* meaning 'at a time that'. MAIN CLAUSE not likely to follow if very short.
b	/While/ /When/ we were playing chess, someone called and left this note for you.		
2a	Mary was cooking the lunch /while/ /when/ we were playing chess.	2a	PROGRESSIVE aspect, stressing activity in progress, in both CLAUSES.
b	She has been doing all the work /while/ /when/ we've been sitting here talking.	b	Could mean 'She's been working': in contrast with 'we've been sitting'.
3a	We'll wait while you /put/ /'re putting/ your shoes on.	3a	*while* not replaceable by *when* here.
b	Wait here while I fetch your coat. Wait here while I /do/ /'m doing/ the shopping.	b	SIMPLE PRESENT focuses on the act as a whole, PROGRESSIVE on the duration of the activity.
4	They slept while we kept watch over them.	4	Note as for 3b above.
5a	While waiting, I /read your article/ /was reading some old magazines/ /have been studying my notes/.	5a	*While waiting* here could mean '*While I was waiting*', or '*while I have been waiting*'.
b	When opening the can, be careful not to spill any of the liquid.	b	*When* replaceable by *in* as in V.24.2.

6 He arrived just $\left\{\begin{array}{l}\text{when}\\ \text{as}\end{array}\right\}$ we were going out.
   He arrived just as we stepped into a taxi.

6 Exclude *while* when the meaning is 'at the point of time when'.

7a $\left.\begin{array}{l}\text{While}\\ \text{As}\end{array}\right\}$ we read this page again, make a note of all the new words.

7a The two activities, *reading* and *making notes*, will proceed together.

 b While reading this page again, make a note etc.

 b Exclude **As reading*.

8a $\left.\begin{array}{l}\text{While}\\ \text{Though}\end{array}\right\}$ I agree with you up to a point, I cannot agree to your plans as a whole.
   $\left.\begin{array}{l}\text{While}\\ \text{Though}\end{array}\right\}$ agreeing with you up to a point, . . .

8a *While* replaceable by *(al)though*;

   agree to a plan.

   Contrast *while agreeing* here with *while waiting* in 5a above.

 b I've written ten pages $\left\{\begin{array}{l}\text{while}\\ \text{whereas}\end{array}\right\}$ you've written only eight.

 b Again, the meaning 'in contrast'.

9 $\left.\begin{array}{l}\text{As}\\ \text{Seeing that}\end{array}\right\}$ we agree on so many points, can we not now agree on a resolution?

9 *As* as in V.26.8. Note the formal NEGATIVE INTERROGATIVE, and *agree on* a subject.

10 There are good people and bad in our country, (just) as (there are) in every country.

10 *good people and bad* (*people*). Note *as in every country*.

11 English does not have a regular system of spelling, /as certain other languages do/ /like certain other languages/.

11

   as + CLAUSE; *like*, PREPOSITION + NP.

12 I am returning the photographs, as you requested.

12 = in accordance with your request.

V.28 Possessives before a gerund

Models

I don't like $\left\{\begin{array}{l}\text{you}\\ \text{your}\end{array}\right\}$ being out so late.

I cannot understand $\left\{\begin{array}{l}\text{him}\\ \text{his}\end{array}\right\}$ behaving like that.

Susan('s) running away was the last straw.

Notes

1 We caught him climbing the fence.
   I dislike $\left\{\begin{array}{l}\text{you}\\ \text{your}\end{array}\right\}$ climbing the fence.

1 As in IV.24.6. Use *him*, not *his*.

   Here, *climbing* has NOUN function and can be preceded by *your*.

2a I don't like $\left\{\begin{array}{l}\text{you}\\ \text{your}\end{array}\right\}$ being out so late.

   I'll never forget $\left\{\begin{array}{l}\text{you}\\ \text{your}\end{array}\right\}$ falling into the river.

2a *you* rather than *your* is likely to occur in informal style.

b	I cannot understand his behaviour. I cannot understand his behaving in such an irresponsible manner.	b	In formal speech and writing, the analogy is likely to be drawn between *his behaviour* and *his behaving*.

b
I cannot understand his behaviour.
I cannot understand his behaving in such an irresponsible manner.

b In formal speech and writing, the analogy is likely to be drawn between *his behaviour* and *his behaving*.

3
I object to smoking in my office.
I object to anyone('s) smoking in here.

I object to $\left\{\begin{array}{l}\text{you}\\\text{your}\end{array}\right\}$ smoking cigars.

We can't agree to $\left\{\begin{array}{l}\text{you}\\\text{your}\end{array}\right\}$ going yet.

We cannot agree to $\left\{\begin{array}{l}\text{you}\\\text{your}\end{array}\right\}$ taking part in such a function.

3 The GERUND, and POSSESSIVE + GERUND, after a PREPOSITION. As a general rule, use the POSSESSIVE, eg *your*, with a PERSONAL PRONOUN before a GERUND in formal style. Regard the POSSESSIVE with any other NP as possible but not necessary.

4
Do you remember Mary and her mother coming to see us last June?

4 POSSESSIVE most unlikely in this sentence.

5a
She was worried about the little bird: she was frightened of $\left\{\begin{array}{l}\text{it}\\\text{its}\end{array}\right\}$ building a nest in the chimney.

5a
it, its refers to the little bird.
its possible though rather old-fashioned.

b *A* Look at the time. It's eight o'clock.
B I'm surprised at it being so late.

b
Exclude *its* here.

6 I object to that being said about me.

6 Exclude **that's* as a POSSESSIVE.

7a His being a doctor helped them to make friends with the neighbours quickly.

7a Avoid **Him being* as SUBJECT.

b $\left.\begin{array}{l}\text{You}\\\text{Your}\end{array}\right\}$ falling into the river was the climax of the whole trip.

b *You falling . . .* would be typical of informal style.'

c Susan('s) running away from home was the last straw.

Proverb: *It's the last straw that breaks the camel's back.*

8 It's not worth (while) $\left\{\begin{array}{l}\text{you}\\\text{your}\end{array}\right\}$ coming all that way just to see us.

It's strange $\left\{\begin{array}{l}\text{him}\\\text{his}\end{array}\right\}$ leaving like that.

8 Cp *worth buying*, III.24.4.

9 It was the last straw Susan running away from home.
It helped them to make friends quickly, his being the only doctor in the village.

9 The construction beginning with *It*, as in 8, can also replace the models in 7.

V.29 Noun phrases in apposition to each other; and abbreviated clauses beginning with *If* and *When*; see also V.20.6, V.21.8, V.26.2 and V.27.8a

Models

George Stamp, the novelist, will be there.
If asked to comment, you have nothing to say.
Never at a loss for words, he spoke for over an hour.

Notes

1 I met my friend George Stamp today.

1 *My friend* and *G.S.* in apposition.

2 Sailing a boat, his chief hobby, cost him most of his salary.

2 His chief hobby was sailing a boat. It cost him etc. See IV.25.

3 Her parents gave Mary /just what she wanted, a silk scarf/ /a silk scarf, just what she wanted/.

3 The two DIRECT OBJECTS could also be separated by a dash.

4a George Stamp, a novelist, booked in at the Grand Hotel last night.

4a *a novelist* could be expanded into a non-defining RELATIVE CLAUSE: see V.18.

b George Stamp, the novelist, will be the Guest of Honour at our next dinner.

b This assumes that G.S. is well-known as a novelist.

5a Mr John Spratt, /(the) Manager of the National Bank/ /Manager of the National Bank since 1965, is to retire next month.

5a Cp IV.23.3c.

b The Manager of the National Bank, Mr John Spratt, will /preside/ /take the chair/.

b The initial *The* and the commas might be absent in journalistic style.

6a When in Rome, do as Rome does.

6a Proverb. The 'ABBREVIATED CLAUSE' could be expanded by adding (a) *you are*; (b) *he was*; and (c) *people do*.

b While at school, he scarcely read a book.

c They go to sleep in the afternoon, as in most Mediterranean countries.

d If in doubt, ask a policeman.
Never at a loss for words, he stood up and spoke for over an hour.

d Expandable by adding *you are*.
Expandable by adding *being* after *never*.

7 If asked to comment, you should insist that you have nothing to say.
He threw himself down from his horse, as if shot.
When pressed to go into politics, he firmly declined.

7 Expandable by adding *you are*.

ie as if he had been shot.
Expandable by adding *he was*.

8a Mr Richard Temple, a lawyer by profession, made the following comment.

8a Expandable by adding *who was*.

b (Though) a lawyer by training, he proved himself (to be) a great soldier.

b = Though he had been trained as a lawyer. See IV.23.9.

9 There he was, /with no money in his pocket/ /without a cent in the world/, in a city where he had no friends, not even a roof over his head.

9 *and he had no money in his pocket, he didn't have a cent, . . . and he had no friends, not even a roof . . .*

10 At the end of the hall (there) /was/ /stood/ a knight in armour.

10 *there* often omitted when an ADVERBIAL PHRASE begins the sentence. Note the position of *stood*: see VI.30.3.

11 The numbers were smaller than expected.

11 = than the numbers that had been expected.

12 I am returning the photographs, as requested.

12 See V.27.12: *as requested* = as I have been requested to do.

V.30 Statements followed by comment clauses; and *that*-clauses, as objects, beginning the sentence

Models

George has passed his examination, I hear.
John has failed, I assure you.
That John has failed, I can't believe.

Notes

1a I hear (that) George has /passed/ /failed/ his examination.
b I'm afraid (that) John has failed.
c I admit (that) John has failed.
d I'm sure (that) George has passed.
e I can't believe (that) John has failed.
2 George has passed his examination, I [hear]¹.
  He passed with honours, I [would add]¹.
3 John has failed his examination, I'm [afraid]².
4 John has failed, I [admit]³.

5 George has passed, I'm [sure]⁴.
6 That John has failed, I [can't believe]⁵.

7 'We've run out of petrol,' he [explained]⁶.
  He explained that they had run out of petrol.
8 'Where is the nearest garage?' he [asked]⁷.

9 'Where is the nearest garage, I [wonder]⁸?'

1a As in IV.11. The speaker is making a plain statement.
b See III.8.8. Plain statement.
c The speaker is making a concession.
d A re-assurance.
e Denial, doubt or contradiction.
2 Exclude *that*. *I* [*hear*]¹, spoken with a low, one-level tone, is a COMMENT CLAUSE.
3 Same note as for 2 above. Lex 2.
4 Exclude *that*. *I admit*, spoken with rising intonation on the stressed syllable, followed by falling tone, is a COMMENT CLAUSE making a concession, as in 1c.
5 Note as for 4 above. See Lex 4.
6 *That* obligatory. *I can't believe* spoken with rising intonation on stressed *can't*, followed by falling tone. See Lex 5.
7 DIRECT SPEECH, followed by [*the speaker*] [*said*] spoken with the same intonation as in 2 above. See Lex 6.
8 Direct question, followed by [*the speaker*] [*asked*]: same low level tone.
9 *I wonder* added to the actual speech on the same low level tone, as in 2 above.

Lexicon

1 *would add, assume, assert, believe, consider, decided, expect, fancy, fear, feel, find, gather, guess, hear, hope, imagine, insisted, learn, mean, note, notice, observe, realised, recall, recollect, recommend, would remind you, reply, report, request, reveal, (would) say, state, suggest, (don't) suppose, tell [you], think, trust, understand*

2 *I'm afraid;* also *I'm* $\begin{Bmatrix} ashamed \\ pleased \end{Bmatrix}$ *to say*

3 *admit, agree, assure sby, confess, grant, know, own (= admit), promise, realise.*
4 *certain, positive, sure*
5 */can't/ /refuse to/ /find it hard/ to believe, deny, doubt ;* also *admit, agree, concede, confess, grant, realise* when the speaker is making a concession to his audience
6 *answer, argue, assert, beg, boast, call out, claim, complain, confess, cry, declare, exclaim, explain, inform sby, object, order, pretend, promise, recall, recommend, reply, request, remark, remind sby, say, shout, tell sby, threaten, urge, warn, propose*
7 *ask, demand, enquire, want to know, wonder*
8 */want/ /would like/ to know, wonder*

Summary of Stages I, II, III, IV and V

Stages I, II, III, and IV, plus the following:

SENTENCE PATTERNS
  B 8
    SUBORDINATE CLAUSES of purpose, cause and result
    RELATIVE CLAUSES, non-defining
    CLAUSES beginning with *Whatever, However*, etc

Wh-CLAUSES as SUBJECT
non-finite PARTICIPLE CLAUSES
abbreviated CLAUSES of the type *Since leaving school*
COMMENT CLAUSES, as in V.30

NOUN PHRASE

apposition
COMPOUNDS, and NOUN + NOUN, as in V.1
use and avoidance of apostrophe *s* with INANIMATE NOUNS
structures of the type *boiling water, boiling-point*
POSTMODIFIERS of the type (*the people*) *concerned*
NOMINALISATIONS of the type *on arrival, during your absence*
(*I object to*) *your saying that*

VERB PHRASE

VERBS
MODAL uses of *will, would, shall, must, can*, etc
special uses of *need* and *dare*
compensating for defectiveness and ambiguities in the MODALS
PAST TENSE in expressing wishes and non-fact
use of *being, not being,* (*not*) *having been*, etc
ADVERBS
stand clear in contrast with *speak clearly*
PREPOSITIONAL PHRASES
by rubbing, on entering, in opening
owing to the rain, in spite of the expense

OTHER ELEMENTS

CONJUNCTIONS
Different uses of *as, since* and *while*
ACTIVE prefixes and suffixes

Stage VI

Contents

18 Further examples of the four types of PHRASAL VERB with an indication of how ADVERBIALS are combined with them: *We walked slowly across it; we must go into it carefully; we took it down quickly.*

19 NOUNS derived from PHRASAL VERBS: *There has been a break-down; where is the holdup?; he had a strict upbringing.*

20 CONDITIONAL sentences with tense sequences other than those in Types 1, 2 and 3: *If he sent the letter off on Friday, why hasn't it arrived by now?; if you would care to take a seat, I'll let the Manager know you're here.*

21 CONDITIONAL sentences with PROGRESSIVE ASPECT in one of the CLAUSES: *If you are looking for that new grammar book, you'll find it on my desk; if you do that, you'll be breaking the law.*

22 Special uses of the SIMPLE PRESENT TENSE and of the PRESENT PROGRESSIVE: *Astronauts reach Mars; I'm hoping you can come and have lunch with me.*

23 Unfulfilled or suspended intentions, hopes and wishes: *I was going to phone him tomorrow; I was to have seen him, but . . .*

24 Special uses of *should* and the SUBJUNCTIVE: *We propose that somebody neutral (should) take the chair.*

25 Special uses of *would* and *might*: *Anyone would have thought . . . ; you might have told me.*

26 Special uses of *as, so* and *such*: *He resigned, as was right and proper; he never so much as said good-bye; books such as these . . .*

27 Reported statements, using the PAST TENSE: *He never doubted that they would succeed; he doubted whether they would be able to help.*

28 Reporting the essential points of a dialogue: *Asked how long he intended to stay, the Minister was non-committal.*

29 Variation on the form of *if*-clauses: *If it weren't for this rain . . . ; but for this rain . . . ; had it not been for your knowledge of the language, . . . ; should you be interested, . . .*

30 Inversion of the normal sentence order, other than in questions: *Never have I seen such a magnificent performance; only then did I realise the trouble he was in.*

VI.1 Special uses of, and absence of, the definite article with count nouns and with proper nouns

Models
The price of food concerns the house-wife.
Take care of the sick.
Do you mean *the* Shakespeare?

Notes

1a	Who work harder, coal-miners or farm labourers?	1a This can be replaced by 1b.
b	Who works harder, the coal-miner or the farm labourer?	b *the coal-miner* = that class of person.
2	The price of food concerns { housewives. / the house-wife.	2 *the housewife* = that class of person.
3	The Inca reached a high state of civilisation.	3 *The Inca* = that race of people.
4a	In that warm climate, the olive and the vine grew abundantly.	4a that kind of tree or plant.
b	Peace reigned; and the lion lay down with the lamb.	b that class of animal.

5a Our team $\begin{cases}\text{plays best on its}\\\text{play best on their}\end{cases}$ own ground.

5a Collective NOUN (eg *team*) with SINGULAR or PLURAL CONCORD.

b Deer, wild duck, tiger are plentiful in this region.

b SINGULAR form used for collective PLURAL.

6 Man has always fought. Woman has been the preserver.
The young child learns his own tongue with apparent ease.

6 *Man* = men or mankind in general.
Woman = women in general.
The child = children in general.

7a Speak well of the dead.
Take care of the sick.
The young have a whole life before them.
He was popular with both young and old.
I know both father and son.

7a *the dead :* only use this structure to mean those who are dead, and with a restricted set of ADJS: see Lex 1 below.

the usually absent in both [*young*] and [*old*] and in pairs on this pattern.

b Have you heard the latest?
Prepare for the worst. Hope for the best
From the sublime to the ridiculous.

b A few ADJECTIVES, particularly SUPERLATIVES, can be used in the sense of *the* [*latest*] *abstract thing*.

8 The United States of America.
The Soviet Union. The Netherlands.
The $\begin{cases}\text{Philippine Islands.}\\\text{Philippines.}\end{cases}$

8 Exceptionally, the names of a few countries begin with *The* when followed by a COUNT NOUN, eg *states, union, lands, islands*.

9 The (River) Nile.
The Atlantic (Ocean). The North Sea.
The Rocky Mountains.   The Rockies.
The New York Times. The Guardian.
The Grand (Hotel). The Rex (Theatre).
The (liner) Queen Elizabeth.

9 Names of rivers, seas, mountain ranges, newspapers, hotels, theatres, ships, usually begin with *The*. The words *Ocean* and *Mountains* may be omitted if meaning is clear without them.

10 *A* Where do the Robinsons live?
B Next door to the Bowmans; next door but one to the Berrys.

10 *the* with a family name followed by *s*, to mean the family of that name. Note *bowman, bowmen* but *Bowman, Bowmans; berry, berries*, but *Berry, Berrys*.

11 *A* Byron played cricket against Shakespeare.
B Do you mean *the* Shakespeare?
A No, not the Shakespeare who wrote 'Hamlet'!

11

the, stressed and pronounced /ði:/.

12 His son is studying at Oxford University.
The Vice-Chancellor of the University of Oxford.

12 *Oxford University*.

The University of Oxford sounds more ceremonial.

Lexicon

1 *able-bodied, blind, brave, dead, deaf, dumb, unemployed, guilty, injured, innocent, living, old, poor, rich, sick, wise, wounded, young*. Similarly *the British* (= *the British people*), *the Chinese, the Dutch, the English, the French, the Irish, the Japanese, the Maltese, the Portuguese, the Swiss, the Vietnamese, the Welsh*, ie nationality ADJECTIVES ending in a SIBILANT. Cp *the Americans, the Germans, the Italians*, etc, not ending in a SIBILANT

VI.2 Absence or use of *the* and *a* with mass nouns referring to substances and materials

Models

(Crude) oil has many uses.
The crude oil you see here . . .
This is a very good butter.

Notes

1 Oil is essential to modern life.
Plastic is often used instead of wood (in) these days.

1 Absence of ARTICLE, or 'ZERO' ARTICLE, before a MASS NOUN referring to a substance or material in general. See I.16.

2 Crude oil has many uses.
Cheap plastic is often used instead of beautiful, natural wood.

2 A descriptive ADJECTIVE before a MASS NOUN does not, by itself, entail the use of an ARTICLE.

3 The oil in this barrel is crude oil.
The plastic (that) people leave behind them after a picnic spoils the beauty of the countryside.

3 *The*, + MASS NOUN, signalling a particular example of the substance or material. The PREP PHRASE (*in this barrel*) and the CLAUSE (*that people leave . . .*) are POST-MODIFIERS in an NP and help to identify the particular example referred to.

4 The fire destroyed everything. It burned the wood and even melted the plastic.

4 Such a sentence can only occur in a fuller context which would definitely answer the questions *What fire? What wood?* etc.

5 The crude oil you see here will later become the refined oil you use in your cars.

5 *The*+ ADJ+ MASS NOUN referring to a particular example.

6 Oil in the Middle East costs less than it does here.
Fire at sea can be terrifying.
Plastic, which has made so much difference to our lives, is cheap.

6 Cp 3 above. The PREP PHRASE is here an ADVERBIAL and could come after *less*: oil in general costs less in the Middle East. Similarly, a non-defining RELATIVE CLAUSE (V.18) is not sufficient to attract the DEFINING ARTICLE.

7a /Oil in Greece is plentiful/ /Oil is plentiful in Greece/.
 b The oil in Greece is lighter than this.

7 In a, the PREP PHRASE is an ADJUNCT and can be separated from the MASS NOUN. In b, the PREP PHRASE is a POST-MODIFIER and must come immediately after *oil*.

8a /Olive oil/ /Greek oil/ is delicious.
 b This oil is dark green, whereas the Greek oil is lighter in colour.

8a /Olive oil/ /Greek oil/ in general.
 b Despite 7a, *the* may occur before a MASS NOUN to distinguish one class of substance from another: cp VI.2.1.

9 Oil can be either a (kind of) fuel or a (kind of) food—a fuel or a food.

9 The INDEFINITE ARTICLE can occur before a MASS NOUN to mean *a kind of*.

10a This is a very good /butter/ /cheese/.
 b I'll keep these two seats. Will you get two rolls, two coffees, two butters and six sugars?

10a ie a kind of /butter/ /cheese/.
 b The speaker is in a cafeteria and is asking his companion to get two rolls of bread, two cups of coffee, two little packets of butter, etc.

11 You have egg all over your chin.
    I can taste onion in this soup.

11 On the other hand, a COUNT NOUN (egg, onion) will occur without an ARTICLE when reference is to substance rather than the whole unit.

VI.3 Absence or use of articles with abstract nouns. See IV.1

Models

Knowledge is power.
A good knowledge of English is desirable.

Notes

1 A doctor's first duty is to preserve life.
    Men fear death, as children fear to go into the dark.

1 MASS NOUNS (*life*, *death*) referring to abstractions, used without an ARTICLE when reference is made to the idea in general. *The dark*, as distinct from *the light*.

2 I've just been reading the life of Mozart.
    Dangerous driving causes the death of thousands of people every year.

2 *the* signalling a particular example, as in VI.2.3. Note that the MASS NOUN (*life*, *death*) in these examples is modified by a PREP PHRASE (*of Mozart*, etc).

3a Knowledge, they say, is power.
  b The knowledge that he would never see her again drove him to despair.
  c Philosophy is, literally, love of wisdom; or it is knowledge that deals with general causes and principles.

3a *Knowledge, power* in general.
  b That particular example of knowledge; despair in general.
  c *Philosophy, love, wisdom*, in general; *knowledge*, an unspecified part of knowledge as a whole.

4 A tooth for a tooth, a life for a life—that is a philosophy of violence.

4 *a life*—one example, unspecified.
    a philosophy = one kind of philosophy.

5 [Linguistics][1] is the study of language.
    English is a language. You are studying /English/ /English language/.
    I can't understand why the English language is {used so widely. / so widely used.}

5 *Linguistics*, the science in general.
    language in general; *a language*, one example; *English language* in general.
    the English language, that class, as distinct from other classes (see VI.1.1).

6 /Advice/ /Information/ /Music/ is not always good.
    Here is some /advice/ /information/ /music/; a piece of /advice/ /information/ /etc/.
    The advice he gave me was useful.

6 Examples of ABSTRACT NOUNS used as MASS NOUNS and not occurring with *a*, nor in the PLURAL. For other such NOUNS see Lex 2 below.

7 Education is widely regarded as the responsibility of the state.
    He has had an expensive education.
    A good knowledge of English, and a lively imagination, are desirable.

7 *Education* and *knowledge*, other MASS NOUNS (see Lex 3 below) can occur with *a*, to mean 'a kind of', but not in the PLURAL.

8 Experience is the name everyone gives to their mistakes.
    The experience of seeing ourselves as others see us can be disturbing.
    An interesting experience, interesting experiences.

8 *Experience* in general; but /an experience/ /experiences/, particular examples. See Lex 4 for other words used in this way.

9	We are studying $\begin{cases}\text{Chinese history.}\\ \text{the history of China.}\end{cases}$	9	[Chinese] [history], the [history] of [China].

10   (Modern) industry plays a dominant role in twentieth-century civilisation.
The making of cars is an industry.
The [car] [industry]⁵ is no longer booming.

10   *industry* in general.

an industry, as in 8 above.
The car industry, stress on *car*, as in VI.1.8.

Lexicon
1 See IV.1, Lex 3
2 *advice, fun, information, laughter, music, news, progress, safety*
3 *education, hunger, importance, imagination, knowledge, thirst*
4 *business, failure, health, history, industry, injustice, kindness, love, success, suggestion, thought, vice, virtue*
5 *the |car| |steel| |etc| industry; the |silk| |wine| |etc| trade*

VI.4 *Any* and *some* as identifiers, and other uses of determiners not covered in 1.17 and 11.5

Models
There must be some book on this subject.
You can get that at any chemist's.
Every such case will be examined.

Notes

1   We need some petrol, some stamps.
Have you got /any/ /some/ money?
No, I haven't any at all.

1   *some* and *any* as quantifiers, answering the question *How much* (mass)? or *How many* (units)? *Some* in AFFIRMATIVE, *any* in NEGATIVE.

2   /I deny/ /It isn't true/ that he offered her any.

2   The (implied) NEGATIVE in the MAIN CLAUSE produces *any* in the SUBORDINATE CLAUSE.

3 *A* I can't find any book on the subject you were talking about.
   B There must be some book on it.
        There must be one somewhere.
        Someone must have it. There must be something on the subject.

   C Someone isn't telling the truth.
        Something in this machine isn't working properly.

3   *any*, as quantifier or identifier, answering *How many books?* or *What book?*
some, stressed and pronounced /sʌm/, as identifier giving an indefinite answer to the question *What book?* Similarly, *some |one| |thing| |where|*, with *some-* stressed.
Some-, identifier, in a NEGATIVE sentence.

4   You can get that at any chemist's.

You can go anywhere and ask anybody any questions you like.

4   *any*, giving an indefinite answer to the question *What chemist's?* as in an AFFIRMATIVE sentence.
Similarly, *any |one| |thing| |where|*.

5   Come and see me any day.
Come and see me some day next week.
It happened on a certain day in June, 1966.
Certain people have written to me complaining about your conduct.

5   The maximum of indefiniteness.
Less indefinite.
Less indefinite still: the speaker probably knows which day it was.
The speaker obviously knows which people, but he is not naming them.

6a	I don't lend books to anyone, not even to you.
b	I don't lend books to *anyone*, but I'll lend some to you.
7a	Many a man has told the same tale.
b	Such a speech has not been heard for many a long /day/ /year/.
8a	He is one of my /many/ /few/ friends. You may have some of the little money I have left.
b	He is one of the /lucky/ /fortunate/ few.
9 *A*	Will my case be considered soon?
B	All such cases Every such case } will be examined in due time. Any such case will be examined on its merits.
10	He is a mere child. That is a sheer waste of time.

6a *anyone* = any single person.

b = I don't lend to any of *all*, only to a selected few.

7a More currently, *many men*.

b *for many a long day* = for very many days.

8a As in IV.4.5.

b One of the few examples of ADJECTIVE before a DETERMINER.

9

Any as in 4 above.

10 = only a child. ATTRIB ADJ only.
= a complete waste of time. ATTRIB only.

VI.5 Further constructions with *it*. See III.10, IV.29

Models

It's strange how often the lights fail.
We find it rather dull living here.
We thought it wrong not to tell her.

Notes

1a	It is [important]¹ to [remember the amount of work involved in this exercise].
b	It is [important]¹ to [remember to sign your name at the bottom of the form].
c	It is [important]¹ to [add that this examination cannot be taken again].
d	It is [important]¹ to [ask]² { if / whether } your name is on the list of candidates.
2	It is [important]¹ that I should add, etc.
3a	It is [strange]³ how often the lights fail.
b	It is a mystery how he came to have such a valuable painting.
4a	It worries me to see you looking so ill.
b	It worries me that he hasn't written.
5	It doesn't matter to me where we go.
6	It depends on you whether we go or not.
7a	It is said that he lives entirely alone.
b	It is regretted that we have to ask you to leave.
8a	It is /wrong/ /a pity/ that you should feel that way about it.
b	It is deeply regretted that you should feel obliged to resign at this point.

1a *It* + *be* + *important to* vt + NP.

b *It* + *be* + *important to* vt + INFINITIVE.

c *It* + *be* + *important to* vt + *that*-CLAUSE.

d *It* + *be* + *important to* vt + { if. / whether. }

2 Alternative to 1c: see VI.24.7.

3a *It* + *be* + ADJ + *wh*-CLAUSE.

b *It* + *be* + NP + *wh*-CLAUSE.

4a = To see you looking etc worries me.

b As in VI.10.5.

5 Cp V.16.6.

6 Cp V.16.10.

7a See VI.13.1.

b See VI.13.15.

8a See VI.24.5.

b See VI.24.5.

9   We find it rather dull living out here.   9   = We find living out here rather dull.
10a We thought it [wrong]⁴ (not) to tell her.   10a Cp IV.24.1.
  b We thought it wrong that she should be
    left in complete ignorance.
11a We must leave it to /you/ /your   11a *it* = to decide what must be done.
    conscience/ to decide what must be done
    now.
  b We owe it to the community to see that   b *it* = to see that such men etc.
    such men are kept out of harm's way.
  c We owe it to you that there wasn't a   c *it* = that there wasn't etc.
    serious accident.
  d I put it to you that Roberts offered you   d *it* = that Roberts offered you etc.
    money for that information.
  e I will take it upon myself to see that   e *it* = to see that justice etc.
    justice is done.
  f I will see (to it) that you get your reward.   f *to it* optional in this case.
  g I will make it my business to help her.   g *it* = to help her.
  h Can we depend upon it that you will keep   h *it* = that you will keep etc. See VI.9.13.
    this matter strictly confidential?

Lexicon
1 *convenient, desirable, essential, important, natural, necessary, useful, useless*
2 *ask, enquire, find out, know, see*
3 *curious, odd, strange*
4 *odd, proper, right, rude, wrong*

VI.6 'Cleft' sentences bringing into prominence certain parts of sentence structure—not verbs, adjs or advs of manner

Models   **Notes**

It was an envelope that he handed to
Roberts.
It was Roberts that he handed it to.
It was to Roberts that he handed it.

1 *A* Who was it that met Roberts in the   1 *Who was it who:* stylistically weak.
    bank?

    Was it Turner { who / that } met Roberts?   Prefer *who* after personal name.

  B It was Taylor { who / that } met Roberts.   Focus on SUBJECT of the sentence.

2 *A* Who was it that Taylor met in the bank?   2 *Who* SUBJECT of *was.*

  B It was Roberts { (whom) / (that) } Taylor met.   *whom* OBJECT of *met.* Focus on OBJECT.

3 *A* Where exactly was it that they met?   3
  B It was just inside the bank (that they   Focus on PREP PHRASE, ADV of place.
    met).

4 *A* When was it that this meeting took   4
    place?
  B It was on July 14th (that it took place).   Focus on ADV of time, date.

5 *A* Did you say it was at 7.20 that they   5
    met?
  B Yes, it was at 7.20 (that they met).   Focus on ADV of time, hour.

6 A What was it that Taylor handed to Roberts?

6

   B It was an envelope (that he handed to R.).

Focus on OBJECT, non-personal.

      What Taylor handed to Roberts was an envelope.

Pseudo-cleft sentence, putting the focused part at the end.

7 A Was it to Richards (that) he handed it?

7 More formal than the next model.

   B No, it was Roberts (that) he handed it to.

Less formal than the previous model.

      or It was to Roberts that he handed it.

More formal than the previous model.

8 A Why was it that Roberts turned away?

8

   B I think it was because he had noticed me watching him (that he turned away).

Focus on *because*-CLAUSE.

9 A When was it that Taylor went to the door?

9

   B It was /when/ /as soon as/ Roberts turned away (that Taylor went to the door).

Focus on temporal CLAUSE.

10 A Was it you /who/ /that/ gave the alarm?

10

    B Yes, it was I /who/ /that/ gave the alarm.

Focus on PERSONAL PRONOUN, SUBJECT.

11 A And was it you /whom/ /that/ Roberts struck?

11

    B Yes, it was me (that he struck).

Focus on PERSONAL PRONOUN, OBJECT.

12 A /Who gave the alarm/ /Whom did he strike/?

12 In a simple sentence like *It was you*, use either *I*, *we* etc or *me*, *us*.

    B It was me.

13 A How was it that you did not give the alarm at once?

13 *How was it that . . .?* requires an explanation for a certain event or course of action.

    B (It was) because I was dazed by the blow (that I did not etc).

14 It was on a dark evening in December that I first met James Warburton.

14 Typical beginning of a narrative with focus on time.

15 It is not because we do not trust you but because of your inexperience that we have decided not to offer you this difficult task.

15 *not because . . . but because.*

16 It is not that we doubt your loyalty, but rather that we need someone with more experience.

16 *It is not that* + CLAUSE.

    What we doubt is not your loyalty to us { but / so much as } your experience.

Another example of a 'pseudo-cleft sentence'; cp 6 above.

VI.7 'Existential' *there* (see I.11.4) and *have*, or another device for focusing attention on a certain part of sentence structure (see VI.6)

Models	Notes
There's no escaping the fact.	
We were surprised at there being a deputation to meet us.	
I have someone outside waiting to see me.	

	Models		Notes
1a	There is a dog in the garden.	1a	As in I.11.4: *a dog*, INDEFINITE.
b	There are plenty of difficulties in the way.	b	*Plenty of difficulties are in the way*: the model opposite is more idiomatic.
c	There is no easy solution to the problem.	c	No easy solution exists.
d	There is no doubt about it: he's mad.	d	No doubt exists.
e	There is no escaping the fact that we have made a great mistake.	e	Sim. There is no /denying/ /getting over/ the fact that . . .
2a	The light is on in your room.	2a	*The light*, DEFINITE.
b	There's a light on in your room.	b	*a light*, INDEFINITE.
3a	There is something that worries me.	3a	= Something worries me: focus on *something*; b = I must speak to some people over there; focus on *some people*.
b	There are some people over there (/that/ /who/) I must speak to.		
c	There must be very few cities that are not threatened by pollution.		
4	There exist many ancient temples of this kind on the shores of the Mediterranean.	4	Typical of literary, historical, descriptive prose.
5	There came a time when the people felt the need to settle down and live in peace.		
6	There occurred at that moment a most remarkable incident.	6	Dramatic.
7	I want there to be no mistake about this: we expect there to be no argument.		
8a	We were surprised at there being such a large deputation to meet us.	8a	Cp V.28. We were surprised that there was . . .
b	We have no objection to there being a meeting here, so long as it is peaceful.	b	= no objection to anyone('s) holding a meeting.
c	Were you disappointed at there not having been more applause?	c	= disappointed because there had not been more.
9	/There is/ /George has/ a car waiting for us.	9	*George has* makes it clear who is responsible for the car's being there.
10	/There are/ /You have/ several splashes of mud on the back of your coat.	10	You may not be responsible, but the coat is yours.
11a	There is something important I want to say to you *or* I have something important to say to you.		
b	It is fortunate for you that there is a doctor so near *or* You are fortunate to have a doctor so near.		

12 /There is a friend of mine in the Ministry/ /I have a friend in the Ministry/ who could tell us what to do next.

12 I have a friend who is in the Ministry.

13 I can't attend to you now. /I have/ /There is/ someone outside (who is) waiting to see me.

13 I have an appointment with someone who is waiting outside.

14 *A* Is there a table free?
    B /There is/ /I have/ a table free over there by the window.

14 = a table that is free.
    Cp I.12.2.

15 *A* Have we forgotten anyone?
    B Yes, there's the man with a stick. Where is he?

15 The *there is* structure normally has an INDEFINITE SUBJECT, as in 2b above.

VI.8 Structures involving comparison

Models
The more you earn, the more you spend.
The older I am, the younger I feel.
Rather than go there, I'd prefer to stay here on my own.

Notes

1 The harder a task is, the more interesting I find it.

1 Two ADJS in the COMPARATIVE degree.

2 The $\left\{\begin{array}{c}\text{sooner}\\\text{earlier}\end{array}\right\}$ we start, the $\left\{\begin{array}{c}\text{sooner}\\\text{earlier}\end{array}\right\}$ we shall get there this evening.

2 Two ADVERBS in the COMPARATIVE degree.

3 The harder it is, the more I like it.

3 ADJ in one CLAUSE, ADV in the other.

4a The more (money) you earn, the more (money) you spend.

4a *more* (+ NP) in both CLAUSES.

b The more money some people earn, the less pleasure they get out of it.

b *more* + NP in one CLAUSE, *less* + NP in the other.

5 The older I am, the younger I feel.

5 Contrasting ADJS both in COMPARATIVE.

6a The quicker you finish what you're doing, the sooner you can go home.

6a *quicker*, ADVERB: see V.19.

b The quicker you finish the better.

b *the better* = the better it will be for you or somebody else.

c The sooner the better.

c No VERB in this common saying.

7 The more the merrier.

7 = The more people there are, the merrier the company will be: common saying.
Proverb.

The nearer the bone the sweeter the meat.

8 $\left.\begin{array}{l}\text{Rather}\\\text{Sooner}\end{array}\right\}$ than go there, I'd (much) prefer to stay here on my own.
I'd prefer to give them what they're asking, $\left\{\begin{array}{l}\text{sooner}\\\text{rather}\end{array}\right\}$ than let this dispute drag on for weeks, possibly months.

8 Cp IV.9.9.

9 He receives a $\left\{\begin{array}{l}\text{salary lower than average.}\\\text{lower than average salary.}\end{array}\right.$

10a We were both treated $\begin{cases} \text{in the same way;} \\ \text{alike;} \end{cases}$ 10a *alike.*

he was treated (in the same way) as I was.

b Our conclusions were about the same:
he reached a conclusion similar to /the
one/ /what/ I found.

c Our objections are /the same/ /similar/.   c
I object on procedural grounds: you
object likewise. I object to /much/   *likewise.*
/about/ the same things as you object to.

d Our objections are different: you're
objecting to something different from
what I am complaining about.

e Some one else must decide: I can't.   e
Some one other than me must decide.   *other than* + NP.

f We need a plan other than the one we
have just been discussing.

g We think differently: I /think as George   g
does/ /share George's opinion/. You
think otherwise.   *otherwise.*

VI.9 Further uses of the infinitive: see I.22.2, II.15.3, IV.6, IV.7, IV.23.8, IV.28, IV.29

Models   **Notes**

To know the main facts is sufficient.
The key to the safe was nowhere to be
found.
You are not to blame for what happened.

1a He was very happy to see you again.   1a As in IV.28.1.
b He must be very [happy]¹ to sing like   b He sings because he is happy.
that.

2a He was foolish /to do/ /doing/ that. =   2a See IV.28.6.
b He was a fool to do it.   b Few NOUNS are available for 2b, but
one can say *He's a brave man to* etc.

3a That rule is easy (for me) to remember. =   3a See IV.28.9.
b It is easy (for me) to remember that
rule. =
c I find it easy to remember that rule.
d He's impossible to work with.   d = *It's impossible to work with him.*
4 He is [quick]² to see the essential points.   4 = He sees them quickly.
5 To /begin with/ /tell you the truth/   5 Fixed expressions, usually at the
/speak frankly/ /cut a long story short/, I   beginning of a sentence, but also at the
asked him to go.   end; or between commas, in the middle.

To hear him talk (now), anyone would   See VI.25.2.
think he owned the whole town.

6 $\begin{matrix} \text{To know} \\ \text{Knowing} \end{matrix}$ the main facts is sufficient.   6 INFINITIVE or *-ing* as SUBJECT.

7a Who can tell the shape of things to come?
Do not despair. The best is yet to be.

   b If we are to win, we must all pull our
weight.

8 That was in 1491. He was to reach the
New World in the following year.

9 I don't know him to speak to.

10a /I have//There are/several letters to
type.
/I have/ /There are/ several letters to be
typed.

   b There is so much work $\begin{cases} \text{to do.} \\ \text{to be done.} \end{cases}$

   c I have several letters for you to type.

   d Your work leaves much to be desired.

11a The key to the safe was nowhere to be
found.
You are to be congratulated on your
success.
The doctor is more to be feared than the
disease.

   b You are not to blame for what happened.
This house is to let. That one is to be
sold.

12a We arrived to find a huge meal ready for
us.
We came home to find the house burgled.
We got there only /to find the door locked
/to be told it was too late/.

   b He /grew/ /grew up/ to be a very unsociable man.

13 We can $\begin{cases} \text{count} \\ \text{depend} \\ \text{rely} \end{cases}$ (up)on you to do the
right thing.

7a *to come* = that will come.
is yet to be = has not happened yet.

   b Cp V.10.10.

8 Historical narrative style. /*Was*/ /*were*/
to [*reach*], future-in-the-past.

9 *but I know him* /*by sight*/ /*by name*/.

10a Someone must type them.

They must be typed (by someone).

   b PASSIVE or ACTIVE may be used.

   c *You* have to type them. ACTIVE only.

   d PASSIVE only.

11a No one could find it anywhere.

You should be.

Proverb.

   b *to be blamed*, possible, unnecessary.
to be let, possible, unnecessary.

12a A pleasant consequence.

An unpleasant consequence.
An unforeseen, frustrating consequence.

   b *He grew to be* = he got to be.
He grew up to be = he became an adult
and (a very unsociable man).

13 We know you will do it.

Lexicon

1 *happy, hopeful, hungry, ignorant, ill, important, lazy, lonely, mad, optimistic, rich, serious, skilful,
strong, stupid*

2 *prompt, quick, reluctant, slow*

VI.10 *That*-clause as subject, in apposition, as object, etc

Models

That they had forgotten to fill up with
petrol was obvious.
The explanation, that they had forgotten to fill up, had not occurred to
the driver at first.

Notes

1 *A* Why have we stopped here, driver?   1

  B The explanation is simple. We have run
    out of petrol.

    a The [explanation][1] is (that) we have   *that*-CLAUSE as complement in SP 1: *that*
      run out of petrol.   optional in conversational style here.

    b The fact is (that) we've run out (of
      petrol).

2a We have to face the fact that the   2 *face the fact* could be added to IV.11,
    nearest filling station is thirty   Lex 1. Include *that* immediately after
    kilometres away.   a NOUN.

  b The fact that . . . away has to be faced.
    or The fact has to be faced that . . .
    away.

3 The obvious explanation, that they had   3 *that*-CLAUSE in apposition: *that*
  run out of petrol, had not occurred to   obligatory.
  the driver at first.

4a That they had forgotten to fill up (with   4a *that*-CLAUSE as SUBJECT: *that*
  petrol) before they started was /obvious/   obligatory.
  /the simple explanation/.

  b It was [obvious][2] (that) they had for-   b Prefer this to 4a.
    gotten . . .

  c The simple explanation was that they   c As in 1a above.
    had forgotten . . .

  d It was a [good thing],[3] in the circum-   d Include *that* when the CLAUSE is delayed.
    stances, that [the weather was com-
    paratively mild].

  e We decided that, in the circumstances,   e Compare the position of *that* in 4d and
    the best thing to do was to wait for help.   4e.

5a That he forgot to fill up (is what)   5a SP 1 with *that*-CLAUSE as SUBJECT,
  [amaze]s[4] me.   *wh*-CLAUSE as COMPLEMENT, etc.

  b What amazes me is that he forgot to
    fill up.

  c It amazes me that he forgot to fill up
    before we left.

6 *A* How did it happen that he forgot to fill   6
    up?

  B It (so) happened (that) there was no one
    on duty.

  C It [stands to reason][5] that if you don't   Do not use VERBS in Lex 5 in structure
    fill up you'll soon run out.   5a above.

  D Does it surprise you that we've run out
    now?

7 The passengers took it for granted   7 Add *take it for granted* to IV.11, Lex 1.
  (that) they would have to spend the
  night on the mountainside.
  The [realisation][6] that they would have
  to spend the night on the mountain
  came as a shock to the two old ladies.
  The idea /that they would spend/ /of
  spending/ the night . . .
  The thought of spending the night . . .

8   The fact remains (that) there is no filling station here.

8   *The fact remains . . .*

9a   The breakdown was due to the fact that the driver had forgotten to fill up with petrol.

b   The passengers were surprised at the driver's mistake: they were surprised (that) the driver had made such a mistake.

c   Take care of the luggage: take care that none of it gets wet and that all the suitcases are locked.

9   *that*-CLAUSE cannot come directly after after a PREPOSITION, eg *to, at, of.* Include *that* as in 9c, when more than one *that*-CLAUSE occurs.

10   We have failed in that some of you remain unconvinced.
We have finished this book, except that a few of the notes have still to be corrected.

10   *in that,* and *except that* SUBORDINATING CONJUNCTIONS.

Lexicon
1   *assumption, [my] belief, explanation, fact, (latest) information, news, position, theory*
2   *clear, definite, evident, (un)fortunate, obvious, plain, positive, regrettable*
3   *comfort, good thing, nuisance, pity, relief*
4   *alarm, amaze, amuse, bother, delight, disappoint, disgust, fascinate, impress, interest, intrigue, please, puzzle, satisfy, scare, shock, upset, worry*
5   *appear, follow, seem, stands to reason, turn out ; chance, come about, happen*
6   *announcement, decision, idea, information, knowledge, news, realisation, report, statement*

VI.11   Further passive constructions. See III.28–30, IV.2 and IV.20–23

Models
No conclusion was arrived at.
He was looked on as a father.
Where they went was never discovered.

Active	Passive	Notes
1a No one slept in Tom's bed last night.	1a Tom's bed was not slept in last night.	ACTIVE: vi+ PREP PHRASE. Actual usage of this kind
b Someone has sat on my hat.	b My hat has been sat on.	may be imitated; but beware of inventing new
c They did not arrive at any conclusion.	c No conclusion was arrived at.	examples. Use *was arrived at* metaphorically only.
2 I am glad that someone appreciates me.	2 I am glad to be appreciated.	See IV.28.1 and VI.9.1.
It's nice that people appreciate you, isn't it?	It's nice to be appreciated.	See IV.29.13.
It is a shame that people treat her like that.	It is a shame for her to be treated like that.	See IV.30.4.
3 John married Mary. A priest married them.	3 Mary was married to John. They were married by a priest.	Not *married by John.*
4 He aimed the gun at the target.	4 The gun was aimed. The target was aimed at.	Beware of inventing examples of this kind.

5	They attended to /the patient/ /my application/ immediately.	5	/The patient/ /My application/ was attended to immediately.	For a selection of PREPOSITIONAL VERBS (III.23.1) commonly found in the PASSIVE, see IV.21.5 and Lex 1 below .

5 They attended to /the patient/ /my application/ immediately.
We have gone over this ground already.
They looked on him as a father.
Can we rely on him (to support us)?

5 /The patient/ /My application/ was attended to immediately.
This ground has been gone over already.
He was looked on as a father.
Can he be relied (up)on (to support us)?

For a selection of PREPOSITIONAL VERBS (III.23.1) commonly found in the PASSIVE, see IV.21.5 and Lex 1 below .

See VI.9.13.

6 No one ever discovered where the elephants went.

6 Where the elephants went was never discovered.

Wh-CLAUSE, OBJECT in the ACTIVE sentence.

7 They say that the whole Committee has resigned.

7 It is said that the whole etc. The whole Committee is said to have resigned.

This important PASSIVE construction is dealt with separately in VI.13.

8 We thanked him warmly for his help.

8 He was thanked warmly for his help.

Lexicon
1 *add to, allow for, apply for, approve of, comment on, count on, depend on, dispose of, enlarge on, go into* (used metaphorically), *go over* (metaphorically), *hint at, look after, look for, look on* (= *consider*), *refer to, rely (up)on, see to* (= *attend to*), *speak about, speak of, speak to, talk about, talk of, talk to, think about, think of*. See also IV.21, Lex 5

VI.12 More passive constructions. Continuation of VI.11

Models
I expect them all to be typed.
Careful attention has been paid to it.
These shirts wear very well.

Active	*Passive*	*Notes*
1a How would you like me to cook the fish?	1a How would you like the fish cooked?	Cp IV.20.6: in those examples, *to be* is not normal before the PARTICIPLE.
b I [expect]¹ you to type all my letters promptly.	b I expect all my letters to be typed promptly.	
c	c Publishers expect all material sent to them to be typed.	
2 I asked for the doctor to come.	2 I [asked]² for the doctor to be sent. The doctor was sent for.	
3	3 Little birds that can sing but won't sing should be [made]³ to sing.	Proverb. An ACTIVE version of this sentence would be very clumsy.
4a We have paid careful attention to your complaint.	4a Careful attention has been paid to your complaint.	
b I am satisfied that my client took proper care of your furniture.	b I am satisfied that proper care was taken of your furniture.	Two possible PASSIVE transformations; regard the second as more informal than the first.
... We took good care of your things.	Don't worry. Your things were taken good care of.	

5 They assured us that the bridge was safe. They will inform me when you /arrive/ /will arrive/.	5 We were assured that the bridge was safe. I will be informed when you /arrive/ /will arrive/.	See IV.11.2 and accompanying Lexicon. *when you arrive* is a temporal CLAUSE (III.17.5B); *when you will arrive* as in III.17.5A.
6 They showed (me) where they had hidden the treasure. The police warned (us) (that) the road was bad.	6 I was shown where they had hidden the treasure. We were warned (that) the road was bad.	The INDIRECT OBJECT, eg *me*, may be absent after *show* and *warn* in the ACTIVE.
7 They asked (me) whether I wished to accompany them.	7 I was asked whether I wished to accompany them.	
8 They explained (to me) /that I could not stay in the hotel/ /where I could find accommodation/. I [suggest]⁴ that the meeting (should) be adjourned.	8 It was explained to me /that I could not etc/ /where I could etc/. It is suggested that the meeting (should) be adjourned.	*I was explained* would be unacceptable.
9 You'll have to get rid of all this waste paper.	9 All this waste paper will have to be got rid of.	More formally, say something like *will have to be burnt*.
10 These shirts [wear]⁵ very [well]. I always [photograph]⁶ [badly].	10 Actually, the shirts are worn. Actually, I am photographed.	A few VERBS, as in Lex 5 and 6, can be used in the ACTIVE with PASSIVE sense.

Lexicon
1 *allow, expect, prefer, want, wish, would like*
2 *arrange, ask*
3 *force, make, oblige, urge*
4 *propose, suggest*
5 *sell, wash, wear*
6 *film, photograph*

VI.13 Passive transformations of the pattern *They say that he is . . .*

Models   Notes
It is known that he is an expert.
He is known to be an expert.

Passive   *Active*
1 It is [known]¹ that he is an expert.   1 They know (that) he is an expert.
   He is known to be an expert.
2 /It is [thought]¹ that he is/ /He is thought   2 They think he is travelling abroad.
   to be/ travelling abroad.
3 /It is [reported]¹ that thousands are/   3 According to news reports, thousands
   /Thousands are reported to be/ starving.   (of people) are starving.

4 /It is [believed]¹ that many/ /Many are believed to/ have died.

4 Some people believe that many have died *or* died.

5 /It is [said]¹ that the disease has/ /The disease is said to have/ been spreading.

5 They say that the disease has been spreading.

6 /It was [thought]¹ that skill at sums was/ /Skill at sums was thought to be/ the best.

6 Teachers thought that skill at sums was the best.

7 /It was [supposed]¹ that you were/ /You were supposed to have been/ working.

7 They supposed that you were working.

8a It is [understood]¹ that he /will go/ /is going/ next week.

8a They understand that he /will go/ /is going/ next week.

 b He is understood to be going next week.

 b (Exclude *will go* in 8b opposite.)

9a It is [expected]¹ that the Court will submit its recommendations next Friday.

9 The people concerned expect that the Court will submit its recommendations next Friday.

 b The Court is expected to submit etc.

 c The Court's recommendations are expected to be submitted next Friday.

10 /It is not [considered]¹ that he is/ /He is not considered to be/ an expert.

10 They do not consider that he is an expert.

11 /It is considered that he is not/ /He is considered not to be/ old enough.

11 They consider that he is not etc.

12 Who /is [alleged]¹ to have stolen it/ /is it alleged, stole *or* has stolen it/ ?

12 Who do they allege /stole/ /has stolen/ it?

13 What /are they [thought]¹ to have stolen/, /is it thought, have they stolen *or* did they steal/ ?

13 What do you think they have stolen *or* stole?

14a It is [supposed]¹ that there was a battle.

14a People supposed that there was a battle.

 b There is supposed to have been a battle.

 b People supposed that there was a battle.

 c It is supposed that a battle took place.

 c They suppose that a battle took place.

 d A battle is supposed to have taken place.

 d They suppose that a battle took place.

15 It was [admitted]² that the gate had been left unlocked.

15 They admitted that the gate had been etc. (Exclude *The gate was admitted . . .)

16 It is suspected that he is a spy.
    He is suspected of being a spy.

16 They suspect that he is a spy *or* They suspect him of being a spy.

Lexicon

1 *acknowledge, allege, believe, consider, declare, expect* (for 9 above), *fear, feel, imagine, know, observe, prove, recognise, report, say, show, suppose, think, understand*: all, except *expect*, usable as in 1–13 inclusive

2 *admit, agree, announce, argue, assert, confirm, deny, explain, insist, mention, note, notice, point out, realise, regret, remark, remember, take for granted*

VI.14 Types and position of adverbial adjuncts

Models

I only wrote to Mr X this morning.
I absolutely agree with you.
The job was well done.

Notes

1 /From a [legal]¹ point of view/ /[legally]/, you are in a strong position.

1 This kind of ADVERBIAL can also come at the end of the sentence.

2a I [only]² wrote to Mr X about that picture this morning.

2a Ambiguous in writing. The exact meaning could be made clearer in speech by intonation; or, in speech and writing, as in 2b – e below.

b I wrote only to Mr X about that etc.

b I wrote to no one else.

c I wrote to Mr X only, this morning.

c Same meaning as b. Tone fall on *only*.

d I wrote to Mr X only about that etc.

d and about nothing else.

e I wrote to Mr X only this morning.

e and not until then, or as recently as then.

3a You can find out the right time [just]³ by picking up the phone and dialling 123.

3a ADV before the element focused on. That is all you have to do.

b What [exactly]⁴ do you think you're doing? =
[Exactly]⁴ what do you think you're doing?

b This kind of ADV occurs after or before *wh*-question-words.

c I can see ten misprints on this page alone.

c *alone* comes after the element focused on.

4a I [clearly]⁵ remember the incident.

4a 'EMPHASIZER', preceding the VERB.

b You [obviously]⁶ remember it yourself.

b 'EMPHASIZER', preceding the VERB.

5a *A* Do you agree with me?
B [Absolutely].⁷ I [absolutely]⁷ agree with you.

5
'Maximizers'.
I take that positive position 100%.

b I [utterly]⁸ reject his accusation.

b I take that NEGATIVE action 100%.

6a I badly need a hair-cut.

6 'BOOSTERS'. Contrast 9 below.

b I like this room [very much]⁹.

c I [much]¹⁰ prefer it to the other room.

d I [deeply]¹¹ appreciate your kindness.

e I [deeply]¹² resent his criticism.

7a We [scarcely]¹³ know him.

7 'Minimizers' occupying the same position as ADVERBS of frequency.

b We can scarcely hear you.

c He is scarcely moving his lips.

c See 1.29.

d We little knew what the result would be.

d Use *little* in this way only with a one-word VERB. See VI.30.5.

8 I didn't enjoy it [in the least]¹⁴.

8 'Minimizer', normally final.

9 He did the job [well]¹⁵.
It was /done well/ /well done/.

9 But not *He well did the job. Here, *well* is an ADV-manner: cp 4a above.

10a I remember that morning very clearly.

10a ADV of manner, coming after the OBJECT. Cp 4a above. In 10b, ADV of manner comes, exceptionally, before the OBJECT for the sake of balance and clarity.

b I remember very clearly the morning that George first came to school.

11a He spoke to me very kindly.

11a He spoke in a kind way.

b He [kindly]¹⁶ offered me a lift home.

b He was kind to do it. See IV.28.6 and VI.9.2.

12 The Thompsons have gone [abroad]¹⁷. They went away to Paris yesterday. They'll be back [presently]¹⁸.

12 ADV place in final position. Note order: general ADV of place (*away*),+ particular ADV of place (*to Paris*)+ ADV of time (*yesterday*). *Presently*= soon.

Lexicon

1 *academical(ly)*, *commercial(ly)*, *educational(ly)*, *financial(ly)*, *ideal(ly)*, *legal(ly)*, *moral(ly)*, *physical(ly)*, *scientific(ally)* etc

2 *also, only*
3 *just, merely, purely, simply*
4 *exactly, precisely*
5 *actually, certainly, clearly, definitely, really, well*
6 *certainly, clearly, obviously, surely*
7 *absolutely, completely, entirely, fully, quite, thoroughly*
8 *absolutely, completely, entirely, totally, utterly*
9 *enormously, tremendously, very much*
10 *much, very much*
11 *deeply, greatly, heartily, (very) much, sincerely*
12 *bitterly, deeply, very much, strongly*
13 *barely, hardly, scarcely*
14 *at all, a bit (colloquial), in the least*
15 *badly, beautifully, carefully, carelessly, expertly, nicely, perfectly, sensibly, stupidly, thoroughly, well*
16 See IV.28.6 and accompanying Lexicon, thus: *bravely, carefully, carelessly, foolishly*
17 *aboard, abroad, ahead, ashore, away, downstairs, home, indoors, inside, outdoors, outside, overseas, upstairs*
18 *afterwards, before, later, presently, soon, in a few weeks' time, directly (=immediately) after lunch*

VI.15 Position of, and negation with, adverbs of frequency and of relative time. See 1.29

Models

He never has finished a job yet.
He was sometimes not accurate enough.
He still isn't eating.

Notes

1 *A* George was often late.
   He was [often][1] wasting his time.
   He has never finished a job yet.
   He has never been properly trained.
   He [usually][2] /stopped/ /gave up/ half way.
   He was late /at least three time a week/.[3]

1 ADV-F following *be*.
   ADV-F between the AUXILIARY and *-ing*.
   ADV-F between AUXILIARY and PAST PART.
   ADV-F after first of two AUXILIARIES.
   ADV-F before simple one-word VERB.

   ADV-F final when it consists of a phrase.

2 *B* I think you're maligning George.
   A I'm not. He often was late.
   He usually was wasting his time.
   He never has finished a job yet.
   He never has been properly trained.
   He always did /stop/ /give up/ half way.

2 Variations in the position of ADV-F in emphatic contradiction. Stress *be* or the AUXILIARY in such cases.

   do, does, did supplied in simple tenses.

3 *B* Surely he finished a job sometimes.
   In fact, he did /very/ /quite/ often.
   A /Sometimes/ /Often/ /Usually/ he stayed in bed till half past eight.

   B I will support him always.

3 *sometimes* and *often* may occur in final position for emphasis.
   sometimes, often and *usually* in initial position for the sake of contrast with a previous statement.
   always, final, for emphasis. Keep *never* and *seldom* in medial position, except as in VI.30.4.

4 *A* You know, he was not always truthful.
   B I agree, he was sometimes not accurate in some of his statements.
   A He was not often ill; but he was often not fit enough to do his work properly.

4 Exclude **always not*.
   Exclude **not sometimes*.

   Include *not often* (= seldom) and *often not fit enough* (= often too unfit).

B That is so. He was not usually very active, and usually not very attentive.

There may be little difference in meaning between *not usually* (=comparatively rarely) *active* and *usually not active* (=usually inactive).
Exclude *not* with *never, seldom, rarely.*

5a He isn't still eating: he has finished.
 b He has been on hunger strike for a week: he still isn't eating.

5a As in I.29.2.
 b He hasn't begun to eat again yet.

Lexicon
1 *continually, frequently, often, repeatedly*
2 *generally, normally, occasionally, usually*
3 *again and again, now and again, on several occasions, three times a week, every two weeks, every other day*

VI.16 Modifiers other than *very* before past participles; and constructions of the type *bald-headed*

Models
We were deeply disappointed.
His action was well-meant.
A bald-headed man.

Notes

1 We were very amused.

1 *very* can modify PARTICIPLES used as ADJS, as in III.7.

2 /You were/ /it was/ (very) much admired.

2 *much* occurs as a MODIFIER before certain PARTICIPLES: see Appendix H.

3 He was absolutely amazed, completely forgotten, deeply disappointed, entirely lost, fully insured, greatly mistaken, highly delighted, keenly interested, thoroughly exhausted, widely known.

3 Other MODIFIERS: see Appendix H.

4a I like a cooked meal, a [well-cooked][1] [meal]. I don't like a [badly-cooked][2] one, nor a [half-cooked][3] one.

4a PARTICIPLE (eg *cooked*) without a MODIFIER, and with *well, badly, half.* Cp VI.14.9; exclude **cooked half.*

 b This house was /well built/ /built well/. It is a [well-built][house].

 b But exclude **a built house.* See Lex 1 below.

 c John behaves /well/ /badly/. He's a /well-behaved/ /badly-behaved/ boy.

 c
   But exclude **a behaved boy.*

5a He meant his action to be good. His action was well-meant. /He/ /His action/ is well-intentioned.

5 =He meant or intended to do good. Exclude **His action was meant; but* allow *It was meant to be good.* PARTICIPLE formed on a NOUN.

6a He is (a) good-humoured, good-natured, good-tempered (man).

6a =He is usually in a good humour, in a good temper; a man of good nature.

 b Some people are ill-/natured/ /tempered/, or bad-tempered.

 b They are usually in a bad temper.

7a Such behaviour is [unheard of][4], uncalled for. It is unheard of, uncalled for (behaviour).

7a But exclude *heard of* and *called for* used adjectivally.

 b A built-in cupboard.

 b =one that is built into a wall.

8 Your plans were well thought out.
They were well-thought-out plans.

8 PASSIVE of *think out*.
But exclude *thought out* as an ADJ.

9a A man with a beard is a bearded man.
A man with a bald head is bald-headed.
A dark-haired girl. A blue-eyed baby.
He is round-shouldered and pot-bellied.

9a PARTICIPLE-type ADJS are often formed
from NOUNS referring to parts of the
body, usually on the pattern *blue-eyed*.

b A dog is a four-legged animal.

b Pronounce *legged* with two syllables.

c A boat with a flat bottom is flat-bottomed.
A three-wheeled car, a four-engined
plane.
A half-hearted effort. An ill-starred
attempt.
A $\begin{Bmatrix} \text{deep} \\ \text{deeply} \end{Bmatrix}$-rooted prejudice.

c This type of ADJ can also be applied to
things

and to abstractions.

10 A self-made man. A self-appointed
leader.

10 Someone who has made his own career,
who has appointed himself.

Lexicon

1 *well-behaved, well-built, well-cooked, well-disposed, well-done, well-dressed, well-educated, well-informed, well-kept, well-made, well-organised, well-paid, well-planned, well-spoken*
2 *badly-behaved, badly-built, badly cooked, badly done, badly dressed, badly kept, badly made, badly organised, badly paid, badly planned*
3 *half-built, half-cooked, half done, half educated, half-warmed*
4 *uncalled for, undreamt of, unheard of*

VI.17 Position of adverbs according to whether they are adjuncts, disjuncts or conjuncts

Models
George was behaving quite naturally.
Naturally, I was aware of this.
However, I pretended not to notice.

Notes

1a George was behaving quite naturally.
b He answered every question frankly.
c He described the situation generally.
d He kept strictly to the point.

1 *naturally, frankly, generally, strictly*, are
here used as ADJUNCTS, telling us how
he behaved and answered; he described
the situation in general terms; etc.

2a Naturally, I was aware of this.
b Frankly, I was impressed by his manner.
c Generally, I thought he did very well.

d Strictly, the lawyer who was cross-examining him was at fault.

2 The same ADVERBS as in 1 above are now
used as DISJUNCTS expressing the
speaker's attitude to what he is about to
say.
naturally = of course; *frankly* = to speak
frankly; *generally* = speaking generally;
strictly = if I may be strict about it.
Cp *generally* as used in VI.15.

3a I was aware of this, naturally.
I was, naturally, aware of this.
b I am naturally afraid of snakes.

3a This sentence and the next one mean the
same as 2a above.
b Ambiguous, since *naturally* here might
be an ADJUNCT, as in 1a, or a DISJUNCT,
as in 2a and 3a.

4 I was aware of what was going through
George's mind. However, I pretended not
to notice it.

4

However is a CONJUNCT making a logical
link between the two sentences opposite.
Though I was aware . . ., I pretended . . .

5a He punished the culprits properly.	5a *properly*, ADJUNCT: in a proper manner.
b Quite properly, he punished them.	b *Quite properly*, DISJUNCT: the speaker is commenting on what he is about to say.
c He answered all the questions correctly.	c *correctly*, ADJUNCT: in a correct way.
d They were, quite correctly, in bed without their boots on.	d *quite correctly*, DISJUNCT, as in 5b.
6a I cannot answer you definitely yet.	6a *definitely*, ADJUNCT; *yet*, ADJUNCT.
b [Definitely]², I think he's right.	b *Definitely*, DISJUNCT.
c I interviewed him personally.	c *personally*, ADJUNCT.
d Personally, I think he is very good.	d *Personally*, DISJUNCT.
e He faced the problem honestly; (and) yet he was afraid of the consequences.	e *honestly*, ADJUNCT; (and) *yet*, CONJUNCT, providing a logical link.
f Honestly, I think you are mistaken.	f *Honestly*, DISJUNCT.
7 Let us consider this matter carefully. [Firstly]³, this site is very valuable. We must therefore either regard it as an investment, or sell it now and invest the proceeds. Suppose we hold on to it for another year. Meanwhile, property values will rise. Moreover, ...	7 *carefully*, ADJUNCT. *Firstly*, CONJUNCT. *therefore*, CONJUNCT. *Meanwhile*, CONJUNCT. *Moreover*, CONJUNCT.
8 Suddenly it became dark.	8 See III.10.2–3.

Lexicon

1 ADJUNCTS include all the ADVERBS in VI.14 and VI.15 and phrases of the type *as politely as possible, in a strange manner, to a considerable extent, with great charm*

2 DISJUNCTS include *actually, apparently, briefly, certainly, definitely, evidently, (un)fortunately, frankly, honestly, naturally, obviously, of course, perhaps, personally, positively, really, strictly, with the greatest respect*

3 CONJUNCTS include *accordingly, consequently, finally, firstly, furthermore, however, in consequence, moreover, nevertheless, none the less, on the contrary, on the other hand, otherwise, similarly, therefore, thus, yet*

VI.18 Further examples of verb + prepositional phrase and of the four types of 'phrasal verb' with an indication of how adverbials are combined with them

Models

We must go into it carefully.
He turned up punctually.
He brought them up strictly.
We must put up with it patiently.

Notes

1a He walked across /the road/ /it/ slowly. He walked slowly across /the road/ /it/.	1a See III.23.1a. Alternative order, highlighting *slowly*.
b I refer to /the dictionary/ /it/ frequently. I {frequently refer / refer frequently} to /the dictionary/ /it/.	b See III.23.1b and Lex 1 below for other 'PREPOSITIONAL VERBS' of this type.
c We must go into /this matter/ /it/ carefully.	c See III.23.1c and Lex 2 below. See also VI.11.5 for possible PASSIVE transforms.

2a Come in quietly.

  b Pull up /at once/ /over there/.

  c He turned up (at the meeting) punctually.

3a Take /that notice/ /it/ down at once.
     Take down that notice at once.
     We took /the notice/ /it/ down quickly.
     We quickly took /the notice/ /it/ down.
     We quickly took down the notice.
     We took down the notice quickly.

  b The policeman pulled /the driver/ /him/
     up sharply.

  c He brought /his children/ /them/ up
     strictly.

     They were $\begin{cases} \text{brought up strictly.} \\ \text{strictly brought up.} \end{cases}$

  d Don't answer your parents back.
     The doctor brought the patient to.

4a Go up to the top floor immediately.

     Go $\begin{cases} \text{up immediately} \\ \text{immediately up} \end{cases}$ to the top floor.

  b This will lead up to my main point
     eventually.

  c We must /put up with these difficulties
     patiently/ /patiently put up with them/.

5   They set /the prisoner/ /him/ free at last.

2a See III.23.2a.

  b See III.23.2b: *Pull up* = stop (in a car).

  c See III.23.2c: see Lex 3.

3a See III.23.3a.

  b See III.23.3b.

  c See III.23.3c.

     No restrictions on the PASSIVE with
     PHRASAL VERBS of this type. See Lex 4.

  d In *answer back*, the PARTICIPLE *back*
     normally follows the OBJECT. In *bring to*
     (= revive), the PARTICLE only follows the
     OBJECT.

4a See III.23.4a. As in 1 above, the
     ADVERB will not come between the
     PREPOSITION (*to*) and the NP following.

  b ADVERBS can occupy the same positions
     as in 4a. See Lex 5.

  c It is not recommended that an ADVERB
     should be inserted into a completely
     idiomatic expression like *put up with*.

5   See III.23.5. Position of ADVERBS as in
     3 above.

Lexicon

1 *account for, allow for, apply for, approve of*, etc, as in Appendix A.5

2 *go into* (= *investigate*), *part with* (= *give away*), *run into* (= *meet by chance*), *run over* (= *knock down in the road*), *see to* (= *attend to*), *take to* (= *become accustomed to*), etc, as in Appendix C (Type I)

3 *catch on* (= *become a fashion* or, colloquially, *understand*), *pull up* (= *stop*), *turn up* (colloquial = *appear on the scene*), etc as in Appendix C (Type 2)

4 *back up* (= *support*), *bear out* (= *confirm*), *put off* (= *postpone*), as in Appendix C (Type 3)

5 *do away with, fall back on*, etc, as in Appendix C (Type 4)

VI.19 Nouns derived from phrasal verbs: see VI.18 and Appendix C

Models
There has been a break-down.
Where is the hold-up?
He had a strict upbringing.

Nouns derived from Type 2 phrasal verbs

1 Money that comes in is income. What goes out are outgoings, or expenditure.

2 The outgoing (= retiring) Chairman. The incoming (= newly elected) Chairman.

3 What will come out of the present situation? What will be the outcome of it?

4 What of the future? What are the prospects—what is the outlook?

5 Look out (for an attack). Keep a sharp look-out. Man the look-out post.

6 People who look on (ie spectators) are onlookers.
7 People who pass by are passers-by.
8 Someone whose health has broken down has had a breakdown.
   Our car has broken down. We have had a breakdown and need the breakdown service.
   Negotiations have broken down. We hope the breakdown is only temporary.

Nouns derived from type 3 phrasal verbs
 9 You will find full details—a complete breakdown—of our expenditure on page 15.
10 The army has been mobilised. There has been a general call-up.
11 What is holding up the traffic? Where is the hold-up?
12 *No stopping on the motorway. Lay-by five kilometres ahead.*
13 How is this work laid out? What is the layout?
14 Do you leave your car out in the street or in a lock-up garage?
15 What organisation have you set up? What is the set-up? (*rather informal*)
16 We must try the new machine out. We must have a try-out. (*rather informal*)
17 An intake is a place where water is taken into a channel or river.
18 An outlet is where the water is let out. What is an inlet?
19 What a factory produces every year is its annual output.
20 To maintain, or keep up, this property costs money. The upkeep is expensive.
21 Children brought up strictly have had a strict upbringing.

Nouns derived from Type 4 phrasal verbs
22 Look-out: *see 5 above.*
23 Someone who stands in (= deputises) for you is a stand-in.

Lexicon
Other examples: *outgoing mail; the break-up of an empire; a cut-off point; an actor's make-up; an industrial lock-out; the input of a computer; a students' sit-in; a radio pick-up; go to the doctor for a check-up*

Note on PLURAL
When one of the elements of the above compounds is felt to be a NOUN, that element usually has the PLURAL ending, thus: *onlookers, passers-by.* Otherwise, if a PLURAL is appropriate, the ending falls on the second or final element, thus: *outlets, check-ups, hold-ups, sit-ins*

VI.20 Conditional sentences with tense sequences other than those in types 1, 2 and 3 (III.16, IV.8 and IV.19). NB Any tense sequence is possible in such sentences: it depends on the exact meaning intended

Models
If he sent the letter off on Friday, why hasn't it arrived by now?
If you would care to take a seat, I'll let the Manager know you're here.

Notes

1a If I drop this stone in water, it will sink.
 b If you drop a stone in water, it sinks.

1a Normal example of Type 1 (III.16).
 b 1a replaceable by 1b when reference is made to proven experience.

 c If we /forget/ /'ve forgotten/ to do our homework, our teacher gets very angry.
2a If you broke your leg in the match today, you couldn't play again this season.

 c PRES PERFECT emphasises the idea 'if we come to class having forgotten it'.
2a Normal example of Type 2 (IV.8). You haven't broken it, but if . . .

b If Tom broke his leg in the last match, he won't play again this season.

b If it is true that he did, . . .

c It was certainly my brother you saw, if he had a large black dog with him.

c If it is true that he had, . . .

d If he sent the letter off on Friday, why hasn't it arrived by now?

d If it is true that he sent it, . . .

e If you saw him yourself, surely you can tell us what he looks like.

e If, as you say, you did see him, . . .

3a If George were here now, would you speak to him politely?

3a Type 2, as in IV.8.9. Contrast *If he were* with *if he was* on 3b.

b If he was at the meeting yesterday, why didn't you speak to him then?

b If, as I understand, he was there, . . .

4a It would be better if you /saw/ /were to see/ him yourself.

4a Variation of Type 2, *were to* stressing supposition about the future.

b If I were to be punished for something I hadn't done, I'd object very strongly.

b Suppose that happened in the future.

c I realised that if I was to be punished, I could only blame myself.

c ie if I had to be punished in the past.

5a I'd be grateful if you would come a little earlier in future.
It would help us if you would fill up the form in duplicate.

5a Polite rebuke.

Polite request.

b If you would care to take a seat, I'll let the Manager know you're here.
I'll ring up his secretary now, if you'd prefer to make a later appointment.

b *would* /care/ /like/ /prefer/ as a polite formula.

c If you'd (only) speak one at a time, I'd be able to hear what you have to say.

c The speaker is impatient: they're all trying to speak at once.

6a If you were interested, I'd tell you the whole story.

6a *If you were* suggests that you are *not* interested.

b If you are interested, I'll tell you.

b You may be interested.

c If you /would/ /should/ be interested, I'll tell you the whole story.

c I do not wish to presume that you *are* interested.

7 If you (/should/ /happen to/) see George, /will/ /would/ you ask him to ring me?

7 *should* not replaceable by *would* in this case. See VI.29.6.

8a If we had caught the plane last night, we'd have been in time to see Mary.

8a Normal example of Type 3 (IV.19).

b If we had caught the plane last night, we'd be in New York by now.

b If that had happened in the past, this would happen in the present.

c If you /were/ /had been/ serious about finding a job, you would have found one long ago.

c If you were serious, or had been in the past, you would have found one in the past.

VI.21 Conditional sentences with progressive aspect in one of the clauses

Models

If you are looking for that new grammar book, you'll find it on my desk.
If you do that, you'll be breaking the law.

Notes

1a If we catch the next plane, we'll be sitting in Paris this time tomorrow.

b If we were on holiday now, we'd be having a wonderful time.

c If we had caught that plane, we could have been taking part in the celebrations.

d If you hadn't come to our rescue, we shouldn't be sitting here safely now.

2 If I get up in time tomorrow, I'll be waiting at the corner when you pass.

3a If you are looking for that new grammar book, you'll find it on my desk.

b If you are standing at the corner when I pass, I'll give you a lift into town.

4 If I were looking for a job now, I'd read the advertisement columns every morning.

5 If you had been standing at the corner as we agreed, I could have given you a lift.

6a If you lean on that glass, you'll break it.

b If you take that through the Customs without declaring it, you'll be breaking the law.

c If you did that, you'd be breaking the law.

d If you had done that, you would have been breaking the law.

1a Type 1, PROGRESSIVE in MAIN CLAUSE, as in IV.16.1.

b Type 2, PROGRESSIVE in MAIN CLAUSE.

c Type 3, PROGRESSIVE in MAIN CLAUSE.

d If you hadn't done that in the past, we shouldn't be here now.

2 PROGRESSIVE providing 'temporal frame' for *you pass*.

3a If that is what you're looking for now, ...

b If you are standing there when I pass at some future time.

4 Type 2 with PROGRESSIVE in *if*-CLAUSE.

5 Type 3, with PROGRESSIVE in *if*-CLAUSE.

6a Normal example of Type 1.

b That action will constitute a breach of the law.

VI.22 Special uses of the simple present tense and of the present progressive

Models
Astronauts reach Mars.
I'm hoping you can come and have lunch with me.

Notes

1a A tidy person puts everything in its proper place.

b I put my book down and look out of the window.

2 'Tom stands up on the coach and looks back at his father's figure as long as he can see it.'

3 A man comes into a restaurant. He notices a lady who is sitting at a table near the window.

4 *Astronauts reach Mars.*

5 *Parliament reopens today.*

6 Some people are always complaining.

1a SIMPLE PRESENT referring to habitual activity.

b SIMPLE PRESENT referring to an action completed at the moment of speaking.

2 Quoted from *Tom Brown's Schooldays*. An example of the historic PRESENT as often used in narrative.

3 SIMPLE PRESENT used in anecdotes. Note the PROGRESSIVE providing a temporal frame for the chief actions.

4 Newspaper headline reporting an event that has recently occurred.

5 Headlines announcing event due to occur.

6 *always, constantly*, etc, with PROGRESSIVE to indicate an endless process or endless series of acts.

7 I usually get up at eight, but I'm getting up at six every day this week.

7 Temporary series of acts.

8 I won't telephone the Robinsons now. They're usually having dinner at this hour.

8 PROGRESSIVE indicating habitual action in progress, rather than a series of completed habitual acts.

9 *A* Look at this chart. Can you see it?
  B I'm looking at it. I (can) see it.
  A Listen to this. Can you hear it?
  B I'm listening. I (can) hear it.

9 Contrast *look at*, *listen to*, which suggest deliberate direction of attention, with *see*, *hear*, which suggest PASSIVE reception of an impression.

10a That soup smells /good/ /bad/.
   I smell gas. Is there a leak somewhere?
  b This soup tastes /good/ /bad/.
   I (can) taste onion in it.
  c This pullover feels nice and warm.
   I (can) feel a stone in my shoe.

10 In this section, *smell*, *taste* and *feel* are used as *see* and *hear* are used in 9 above. When these VERBS are used in this way, avoid the PROGRESSIVE.

11 I'm /smelling/ /tasting/ this soup to see if it is all right.
   I'm feeling inside my shoe to find that little stone.

11 In this section, *smell*, *taste* and *feel* are used as *look at* and *listen to* are used in 9 above.

12 I'm hoping you can come and have lunch with me. I've been wanting to ask you for a long time.
   I'm forgetting my irregular verbs.
   Are you /understanding/ /beginning to understand/ this better now?

12 VERBS like *hope*, *want*, *think*, *imagine*, *suppose*, *understand*, normally 'STATIVE', can occur in the PROGRESSIVE to suggest that the speaker's hoping etc is tentative or temporary or incomplete: cp VI.23.11b.

VI.23 Unfulfilled or suspended intentions, hopes or wishes

Models
I was going to phone him tomorrow.
I was to have seen him, but . . .

Notes

1 *A* You were going to phone me yesterday.
  B I did phone you, but you weren't in.
    or I was going to phone you but I just didn't have time.

1 See II.12.2. Intentions yesterday.
The intentions were fulfilled.
Intentions not fulfilled.

2 *A* Have you phoned the Bank Manager yet?
  B No, I was going to phone him today.
    or No, I was going to phone him tomorrow.

2

My intentions in the past were to phone him today—or tomorrow even.

3 *A* What were we doing last lesson?
  B You were telling us about X.
   You were going to tell us about X.
   We were (just) about to begin Chapter Two.

3 PAST PROGRESSIVE, as in III.18.
This suggests non-completion.
This suggests plan interrupted.
But we didn't actually start it.

4a I had a few words with Mr Z yesterday.
   He was speaking at a meeting, so we weren't able to talk for very long.

4a
= He was due to speak at a meeting.

b You're not well. You should stay in bed,
   Yes, I think I will (stay in bed). I was
   speaking at a meeting, but I really
   can't go.

c I can see you tomorrow after all. I was
   speaking at a meeting, but it's can-
   celled.

5 *A* I really must have this room re-
    decorated.

  B You've been going to have it re-
    decorated for the last six months.

6 *A* You were to see Mr Z yesterday. Did
    you?

  B Oh yes, I saw him all right.
       or No. I know I was to have seen him,
       but . . .

7 *A* Will Z be here today? I was hoping to
    see him.
    Will he be there tomorrow? I was
    hoping to see him then.

8 I'm sorry I missed you yesterday. I had
   hoped to meet you at the station.

9 Mr Z wasn't there yesterday. I'd been
   hoping to meet him for a long time.

10 *A* Did you call on Mr Z yesterday?

   B No, I $\left\{ {meant \atop intended} \right\}$ to (call on him),
    but . . .

   A Did you send him that letter on pur-
    pose?

   B Yes, I $\left\{ {meant \atop intended} \right\}$ to send it to him.

11a I wondered if I might have a word
     with you.

  b I was wondering if I might.

b Arrangements made in the past cannot
   be carried out now.

c Similar arrangements cannot be carried
   out tomorrow.

5

   You have had those intentions for six
   months, with no result yet.

6 Those were your plans or orders.

   Plans or orders carried out.
   I was to have . . . not carried out.

7 Hopes formed in the past: the speaker
   is not very confident that they will be
   fulfilled.

8 *I missed* = I didn't meet. *I had hoped*,
   but hopes were unfulfilled.

9 PROGRESSIVE emphasising the duration
   of my unfulfilled hopes.

10

   Intentions unfulfilled. Fall-rise
   intonation after $\left\{ {meant. \atop intended.} \right\}$

   Action carried out deliberately. Final
   intonation fall on $\left\{ {meant. \atop intended.} \right\}$

11 Present wishes expressed in PAST TENSE
    or even PAST PROGRESSIVE, as a sign of
    diffidence, deference, etc.

VI.24 *Should* and the subjunctive: see also III.22, IV.18 and VI.5.8

Models
We propose that somebody neutral
(should) take the Chair.

Notes

1 *A* What is Mary's second name?
  B How should I know?
2   We were sitting in the lounge waiting,
    when who should come in but Terry
    Stalk.
3a We [think][1] (that) somebody neutral
    should take the Chair.

1

   Brusque, colloquial fixed expression.

2

   This suggests a surprise appearance.

3a As in III.22.1: *should* replaceable by
    ought to.

b   We [propose]² that somebody neutral should take the Chair.

b   *should*, normal, not *ought to;* but 3b replaceable by 3c or 3d.

c   We [propose]² (that) somebody neutral takes the Chair.

c   *takes* may be felt to be insufficiently formal.

d   We [propose]² that somebody neutral take the Chair.

d   *take*, formal, example of the SUBJUNCTIVE, replaceable as in 3b or 3c.

e   We [recommend]² that a neutral Chairman should be appointed.

e   *should be* replaceable by SUBJUNCTIVE *be.*

f   We [recommend]² that a neutral Chairman be appointed.

f   in formal language, after [*propose*]².

4a   I am [sorry]³ that he should feel that way.

4   *should feel* replaceable by *feels*, though *should* suggests that something has made him feel that way.

b   I /cannot understand why/ /regret (that)/ he should feel that way.

c   I /am sorry that/ /cannot understand why/ he should have been overlooked.

= *I am sorry* etc. *that he has been*, or *was, overlooked.*

5a   It is a [pity]⁴ that he should /feel so upset/ /have been overlooked/.

5a $It + be + $ NOUN $+ that$ ...

b   It is [disgraceful]⁵ that you should /be/ /have been/ left all alone.

b $It + be + $ ADJ $+ that$ ...

c   It is regretted that you should etc.

c   As in VI.5.7b.

6   It [worries]⁶ me that you should be looking so tired.

6   *should be* replaceable by *are.*

7a   It is [essential]⁷ that we (should) have all the facts before we decide.

7   As in 4 above, regard *should have* as normal, *has* for third PERSON as informal, and *have* for third PERSON as formal.

b   It is essential that he /should have/ /has/ /have/ all the facts.

c   It is absolutely essential that all the facts {should be / are / be} examined first.

c   *that all the facts be* would be formal.

9   Why should I /think/ /be thinking/ of Vienna?

9   = What makes me think of it?

Why should I have thought of Vienna?

= What made me think of it?

Lexicon

1   *believe, think* and other VERBS from IV.11, Lex 1
2   *ask, demand, be determined, insist, prefer, propose, recommend, request, suggest*
3   *alarmed, amazed, amused, annoyed, astonished, disappointed, disturbed, glad, happy, horrified, pleased, proud, sad, shocked, thankful*
4   *disgrace, mistake, nuisance, pity, shame*
5   *alarming, annoying, disappointing, disgraceful, embarrassing, extraordinary, (un)fortunate, odd, peculiar, regrettable, remarkable, shocking, surprising, understandable, wrong*
6   As in VI.10, Lex 4
7   *desirable, essential, important*

VI.25 Special uses of *would* and *might*

Models   Notes
Anyone would have thought ...
You might have told me.

1 *A* What is his second name?
  B I (just) wouldn't know.

2 Aren't you tired? I would have
[thought]¹ you had done enough for
today.
To hear him speak, anyone would have
thought he owned the whole town.

3 I suggest we might meet again next
Thursday.

4 *A* Why did the police stop you?
  B I /may/ /might/ have been driving too
fast.
  A This landscape is like California.
  B Yes, we might almost be driving through
California.

5 The landscape was like California. We
might almost have been driving through
California.

6a Be careful. You might get hurt.
 b Where *are* we going? You might tell me.
7a You might have been killed.
 b *I* didn't know you had seen George. You
might have told me.

8 Memories are a chronicle of what might
have been.

Lexicon
1 *imagined, said, supposed, thought*

1
Evasive, sometimes impolite, alternative
to *I don't know.*

2 I venture that opinion. See Lex 1 below.

would think, as in VI.9.5, replaceable by
would have thought.

3 *should*, as in VI.24.3, replaceable by
might, making a more tentative
proposal.

4
Perhaps I was.

It is as if we were; but of course we
aren't.

5 It was as if we were; but of course we
weren't.

6a But of course I hope you won't be.
 b A complaint: I wish you *would* tell me.
7a I'm so relieved you're all right.
 b A complaint: I wish you *had* told me.

8
. . . but of what did not really happen.

VI.26 Special uses of *as*, *so* and *such*

Models
As you say, he resigned, as was right
and proper.
He never so much as said good-bye.
Books such as these . . .

Notes

1 As your lawyer, I advise you not to
write.
2a *A* It's a pity we can't go with you.
  B Yes, it is a pity, as you say.
 b He resigned, as was right (and proper).
 c When the lights fail, as often happens
in our house, we light candles.
3a His teachers [described] John as
hopeless.
John was described (by his teachers)
as careless.
 b Careless as he was, he could never pass
an examination.

1 = In that capacity, I advise you . . .

2

 b = as it was right for him to do.

3a *His* refers forward to *John.*

   Lexicon: *describe, look on, regard, treat.*

 b Because he was careless. Cp VI.30.13.

4 *A* Has the plane landed yet?

4

   B It has, $\left\{ \begin{matrix} as \\ so \end{matrix} \right\}$ far as I know.

= I think it has.

   or Not $\left\{ \begin{matrix} as \\ so \end{matrix} \right\}$ far as I know.

= I /think it hasn't/ /don't think it has/.

5a   /As far as I am concerned/ /As for me/, I am not interested in the project.

5a   Speaking for myself. Prefer the shorter expression on grounds of economy.

 b   /As far as expense is concerned/ /With regard to expense/, there is no need to economize.

 b   See V.22.9a. Prefer the shorter expression.

6   We are for peace, as are all men of goodwill.
     We support it, as do all men of goodwill.
     He resigned, as did every member of the Committee, as everyone else had to (do).
     He must resign, as must all men of good faith, as you must.

6   Inversion (see VI.30) is possible here, but only when the VERB takes the form of a single word, eg *are, do, did, must,* and provided the subject is not a PERSONAL PRONOUN, eg *you.* Normal order, eg *as all men of goodwill do,* is possible in every case.

7a   As to whether we can help financially, that question will have to be considered very carefully.

7a   ie as far as that question is concerned.

 b   A decision as to whether we can help financially will be taken later.

8 *A* Shall I answer this letter?

8

   B Yes, please do so.

do so = answer that letter.

9a   He never so much as said good-bye.

9a   = He didn't even say good-bye.

 b   He went so far as to telephone the Queen.

 b   = He even did that.

 c   He was so naive as to think he could.

 c   = He was as naive as that.

10   He made $\left\{ \begin{matrix} \text{such a strong impact} \\ \text{an impact so strong} \\ \text{so strong an impact} \end{matrix} \right\}$ that
     everyone was fascinated by him.
     The impact of his work was such as to impress even the dullest of his readers.

10   See II.26. Regard *an impact so strong* and *so great an impact* as more literary.

11a Books such as these should be treated with respect.

11a = Books like these.

 b   Only take such luggage as is really essential.

 b   = Only take whatever luggage is really essential.

VI.27 Reported statements, using the past tense

Models

He never doubted that they would succeed.
He doubted whether they would be able to help.

Notes

Direct speech	Past reported speech
1 *A* Mr X came to see me /yesterday/ /last night/ /last week/ /two months ago/.	1 A said that Mr X had visited him /the day before *or* the previous day/ /the night before *or* the previous night/ /the week before etc/ /two months before/.
2 Mr X will come again /this afternoon/ /today/ /tomorrow/ /next week/.	2 A said that Mr X would return /that afternoon/ /that day/ /the next day *or* the following day/ /the next week etc/.
3 Shall I receive a letter about it?	3 A asked if he would receive a letter about it. (*Past equivalent of II.13.5, changed to third* PERSON.)
4 Shall I send them a letter about it?	4 A asked if he should send them a letter about it. (*Past equivalent of II.15.6.*)

5 You $\left\{ \begin{array}{l} \text{can} \\ \text{may} \end{array} \right\}$ go.   5 A said they $\left\{ \begin{array}{l} \text{could} \\ \text{might} \end{array} \right\}$ go.

6 Perhaps we $\left\{ \begin{array}{l} \text{could} \\ \text{might} \end{array} \right\}$ go.   6 A said perhaps they $\left\{ \begin{array}{l} \text{could} \\ \text{might} \end{array} \right\}$ go.

7 I think we $\left\{ \begin{array}{l} \text{should} \\ \text{ought to} \end{array} \right\}$ stay.   7 A thought they $\left\{ \begin{array}{l} \text{should} \\ \text{ought to} \end{array} \right\}$ stay.

8 I am very sorry I was rude to you, B.	8 A apologised for being rude to B.
9 I am very sorry that I shall not be able to attend the meeting on Friday.	9 A /apologised/ /sent his apologies/ for not being able to attend the meeting.
10 I am very sorry that I shall not be able to accept your kind invitation.	10 A regretted that he would not be able to accept B's kind invitation.
11 There is never any doubt in my mind. I know we shall succeed.	11 A never doubted that they would succeed.
12 I don't think we shall be able to help.	12 A doubted whether they would be able to help.
13 Don't worry. I am quite sure there will be no difficulty.	13 A assured B that there would be no difficulty.

14 I must be quite firm about this. The money must be repaid by the end of the week.

14 A insisted that the money $\left\{ \begin{array}{l} \text{must} \\ \text{had to} \\ \text{would have to} \\ \text{should} \end{array} \right\}$ be repaid by the end of that week.

15 Remember you have to go to the dentist.	15 A reminded B that he had to go to the dentist.
16 Why not have the garden party later, when the weather's warmer?	16 A suggested postponing the garden party until the weather was warmer.
17 Be careful. These rocks are slippery.	17 A warned B that the rocks were slippery.
18 Your essay was very good. I am so glad you won the prize.	18 A complimented B on his essay, and congratulated him on winning the prize.

VI.28 Constructions used in reporting the essential points of a dialogue

Models

Asked how long he intended to stay, the Minister was non-committal.

Notes

Dialogue	*Report*
1 *A* Don't you think the story has been exaggerated? *B* I certainly do.	1 B quite agreed that the story had been exaggerated.
2 *A* First, you have neglected your duty. Second, you have been the cause of very serious damage. *B* I am afraid I should have attended to the matter myself; but surely the damage was not as bad as that.	2 B admitted that he had been negligent but argued that the damage was not very serious.
3 *A* I can see how the accident happened. There was too much pressure in the tank. *B* You're absolutely wrong. I won't accept that explanation.	3 B disagreed with A's explanation that the accident had been caused by excessive pressure in the tank, and refused to accept it.
4 *A* How long do you intend to stay here, Mr Minister? *B* Well, that depends, doesn't it?	4 Asked how long he intended to stay, the Minister was non-committal.
5 *A* Would you like to make a statement about your meeting with the Board of Directors? Is it true that you have been discussing fresh proposals? *B* Yes.	5 Commenting on his meeting with the Board of Directors, the Minister confirmed that fresh proposals had been discussed.
6 *A* One more question, please. It is being said that you have asked the Board to resign and that... *B* I've done nothing of the kind. Well, that is all, gentlemen.	6 In reply to a further question, the Minister flatly denied that he had asked the Board to resign, and declined to say more.
7 *A* I should like to move, Mr Chairman, that we make a donation of £1,000 at once. *B* I am against that. There are more reports to come in, and I would urge the Committee to wait until these are in our hands before we make up our minds.	7 Opposing A's motion that £1,000 be donated at once, B urged the Committee to defer its decision until the remaining reports had been received.
8 *A* What is our sales position, Mr B? *B* Very satisfactory. Sales are going up all the time. I can assure you that we shall have covered our losses by the end of the year.	8 B reported that sales were very satisfactory and were continually increasing. He assured the meeting that losses would be covered by the end of the year.
9 *A* I am very hopeful. I can double production within six months. *B* Nonsense. You simply can't. You are completely ignoring realities.	9 B dismissed as unrealistic A's claim to be able to double production within six months.

VI.29 Variations on the form of *if*-clauses

Models	**Notes**
If it weren't for this rain, ... But for this rain, ...	

Had it not been for your knowledge of
the language, ...
Should you be interested, ...

1 *A* I'm not going out because it's raining.

  B Would you go out if it weren't
    (raining)?

  A Oh yes, if it weren't for this rain, I'd
    certainly go out.

2 *A* Where would you go for your holidays
    if you had the choice?

  B If it weren't /so expensive/ /for the
    expense/, I'd go to Florida.
    But for the expense, I'd go to Florida.
    Were it not for the expense I should go
    to Florida.

3a If it weren't for the fact that the nearest
    filling station is 30 kms away, I'd go my-
    self and carry some petrol back.

 b Were it not for the fact that the nearest
    filling station is 30 kms away, ...

 c But for the fact that etc.

4a If I had been able to speak the language,
    I would have enjoyed the country much
    more.

 b Had I been able to speak the
    language, ...

 c If you hadn't been with me, I couldn't
    have made myself understood at all.

 d Had you not been with me, ...

 e If it had not been for your knowledge
    of the language, I should have been
    completely lost.

 f Had it not been for your knowledge of
    the language, ...

 g But for your knowledge of the
    language, ...

5a If it hadn't been for the fact that we
    knew each other so well, I shouldn't
    have agreed to go on that journey with
    him.

 b /But for/ /Had it not been for/ the fact
    that we knew each other so well, etc.

6a Should you be interested, I'll tell you
    the whole story.

 b Should you (happen to) see George,
    /will/ /would/ you ask him to ring me?

7a If we are to do all this today, I shall
    protest very strongly.

1

if it weren't for this rain = if it weren't
raining.

2

But for = if it weren't for.
Formal: *were it not* cannot be replaced
by *weren't it*.

3a See VI.10.2.

 b Formal alternative to *if*-CLAUSE in 3a.

 c Not quite so formal.

4

 b Alternative to *if*-CLAUSE in 4a.

 d Formal alternative to *if*-CLAUSE in 4c.
   Hadn't you unacceptable here.

 f Formal alternative to *if*-CLAUSE in 4e.

 g Not quite so formal.

5

 b Again, *But for* is not quite so formal.

6a Alternative to VI.20.6c.

 b Alternative to VI.20.7a.

7a ie if these are our orders, ...

b   If we are to succeed, we must all pull our weight.

b In order to succeed, as in VI.9.7b.

VI.30 Inversion of the normal sentence order, other than in questions, for dramatic or rhetorical effect

Models

Never have I seen such a magnificent performance.
Only then did I realize the trouble he was in.

1 Were it not, Had I been, Should you ...

2 Away went the car like a flash.
Here comes the winner.

3 At the end of the hall stood a knight in armour.

4 I have never heard such nonsense.
Never ⎱
Nowhere ⎰ have I seen such a performance.

5 Tom /seldom/ /rarely/ writes to me now.
Seldom do we have the opportunity of receiving such a distinguished writer.

Nor do we underestimate the importance of his visit.

6 He little knows how serious it is.
Little does he know how serious it is.

7a He had /hardly/ /scarcely/ begun to speak when I sensed that he was in trouble.
/Hardly/ /Scarcely/ had he begun to speak when I sensed that he was in trouble.

b He had no sooner begun to speak than I sensed that something was wrong.
No sooner had he begun to speak than etc.

8 Under no circumstances can we allow that.

9a Only yesterday George rang me up.

b Only then, only when I heard his voice trembling, did I realise what trouble he was in.

c Not until yesterday did I realise ...

10 Not only have we defeated the enemy, (but) we have captured all his supplies.

11 So strong was the impact he made on us all that we watched him with awe.
So impressively did he speak that everyone listened in awed silence.

12 I agree that it is important that the work should be of high standard. /Just as/ /Equally/ important, if not more important, is the question of expense.

Notes

1 See VI.29.

2 See III.4.8.

3 Typical of narrative style, see V.29.10.

4 Normal order.
Never, making special emphasis.

5 Normal order.
Seldom at the beginning. Note (a) the element of negation and (b) the rhetorical effect in this structure, as in 4.
Nor replaceable by *neither*.

6 In this case, the inversion structure is more normal.

7a Again, the element of negation.

8 = We can't allow it under any circumstances.

9a It was as short a time ago as that.

b My realisation of his trouble was restricted to that time: I had not realised it before.

10 Negation with *Not only*.

11 Normally, *The impact he made on us was so strong* ...

13 Anxious /though/ /as/ I am that the work should be finished, I must consider the rapidly rising costs.

13 Normally, *Though I am anxious.* In such an example, *though* is not replaceable by *although*.

14 America became a melting-pot, into which poured a great variety of new elements.

14 Inversion in a RELATIVE CLAUSE: *a great variety . . . poured.*

15 To this list must be added the following interesting examples.

15 ACTIVE: *To this list we must add* etc.

Summary of Stages I, II, III, IV, V and VI

Stages I, II, III, IV and V, plus the following:

SENTENCE PATTERNS
from the list on page 107, as follows:
A 1, VAR; A 6 c and d; A 7 b and f; B 11b, 11c D 7 and 8
It-sentences, as in VI.5
CLEFT SENTENCES, as in VI.6
Comparison structures, as in VI.8
That-CLAUSES in apposition, as in VI.10
If-sentences, as in VI.20, VI.21 and VI.29
sentences used in reporting statements and dialogue
inversion of normal word order, as in VI.30

NOUN PHRASE
   NOUNS
   formed from PHRASAL VERBS, eg *a break-up*
   DETERMINERS
   Special uses of the articles, as in VI.1–3
   some and *any* as identifiers, as in VI.4

VERB PHRASE
   VERBS
   special uses of simple PRESENT TENSE and of PROGRESSIVE aspect, as in VI.22
   unfulfilled intentions, as in VI.23
   special uses of *should* and use of the SUBJUNCTIVE
   special uses of *would* and *might*, as in VI.25
   the PASSIVE, as in VI.11–13 inclusive
   ADJECTIVES
   of the type *bald-headed*
   ADVERBS
   varieties and position of ADJUNCT, as in VI.14
   adverbs of frequency in negation, as in VI.15
   ADJUNCTS, DISJUNCTS and CONJUNCTS, as in VI.17
   ADVERBS with PHRASAL VERBS, as in VI.18
   MODIFIERS, especially INTENSIFIERS, with PARTICIPLES used adjectivally, eg *highly qualified*

OTHER ELEMENTS
   CONJUNCTIONS
   special uses of *as* and *so*

Appendixes

Examples are given in the appendixes of lexical items that fit into certain structural patterns. The appendixes are intended as a guide to the material which might be included in a performance test at the end of Stage VI.

Appendix A Lexicon for certain verb patterns

1 **Model** *I*[*want*] *to buy a car*. (I.22.2 and III.1.1)

(can't) afford[1]	continue (IV.10.5)	intend (IV.10.5)	propose (IV.10.4)
agree	decide	learn	refuse
appear[2] (IV.15)	deserve	like (IV.10.3)	remember (IV.10.7)
apply	desire	long	seek
arrange	determine	love (IV.10.3)	seem[2] (IV.15)
attempt	endeavour	manage	start (IV.10.5)
(can't) bear[1]	expect	mean (= intend)	tend
(IV.10.5)	fail	need (IV.25.8)	threaten
begin[3] (IV.10.5)	forget (IV.10.10)	offer	try (IV.10.8ˋ
(don't) care[1]	happen[2] (IV.15)	omit (IV.10.5)	undertake
cease (IV.10.5)	hasten	prefer (III.20.5)	venture
chance (IV.15)	hate (IV.10.3)	pretend	want
choose	hesitate	promise	wish
claim			

[1] Use *afford*, *bear* and *care* in NEG and Q only.
[2] For the function of *appear*, *chanced*, *happen*, *seem*, see IV.15.
[3] For *begin* etc + -*ing*, see IV.10.

2 **Model** *I*[*ask*] *you to open this door*. (II.15.3 and III.1.1)

advise (P)	drive (P)	love	request (P)
allow (P)	enable (P)	mean (P)	require (P)
appoint (P)	encourage (P)	need (P)	sentence
ask (P)	entitle (P)	oblige (P)	teach (P)
beg	expect (P)	order (P)	tell (P)
bribe (P)	forbid (P)	permit (P)	tempt (P)
cause	force (P)	persuade (P)	trouble
challenge	get	prefer	trust (P)
command (P)	help (P)	press (P)	urge (P)
compel (P)	instruct (P)	promise	want
condemn (P)	intend (P)	recommend (P)	warn (P)
dare	invite (P)	remind (P)	wish
direct (P)	like		

Notes i. (P) indicates that the VERB can be put into the PASSIVE, thus: *You were asked to open the door*.
ii. Exceptionally, *I promise you to go* = I give you my promise that I will go.

3 **Model** *I'm*[*giv*]*ing James all these books*. (I.28.1)

accord	allow	bring	charge
advance (money)	ask (sby a question)	cause	deny

do	owe	recommend	teach
give	pass	sell	tell
grant	pay (money)	send	throw
hand	promise	serve	wish
lend	read	show	write
offer			

Notes i. All the above VERBS can be put into the PASSIVE as in IV.21.7 and 9.
ii. Also: *Drop me a note. This cost me a lot of money.* No PASSIVE.

4 Model *He's making me a suit.* (I.28.5)

bring (P)	change (money)	guarantee (P)	order (P)
build (P)	choose	keep	save (P)
buy (P)	find (P)	leave (P)	spare (P)
call	forgive (P)	light	write
catch	get	make	

Note (P) indicates that the VERB can be put into the PASSIVE, as in IV.21.8.

5 Models

a I'm looking (at a picture). (See I.25, III.11)
b We're longing for the holidays. (See III.11)

Note that in Model *a* the VERB, *I'm looking*, can occur without the PREP PHRASE, whereas in Model *b* the PREP PHRASE is obligatory.

account (to sby) for stg
act (on instructions)
add to one's problems
agree (with sby) (about stg)
agree (on a course of action)
agree (to a proposal)
allow for stg
amount to a total
answer (for sby)
apologise (to sby) (for stg)
appeal (to sby)
apply (to sby) (for stg)
approve (of stg or sby)
argue (with sby) (about stg)
arrange (for) stg
arrive (see III.11.3d)
ask after sby's health
ask for stg or sby
attend (to sby or to work)
bargain (with sby) (for stg)
believe (in an idea)
belong to sby or stg
benefit (from stg)
beware[1] (of sby or stg)
boast (of or about stg)
call for sby
call (on sby)

care (about sby or stg)
care for sby (= look after)
care for stg (= like it)
combine with stg
decide (on) (stg)
depend (on sby or stg)
despair (of stg or sby)
die (of hunger)
die (for /sby/ /an idea/)
differ (from stg or sby)
dream (of or about stg or sby)
economise (on stg)
embark (on a course of action)
emerge (from stg)
engage in an activity
experiment (with stg)
fight (with sby) (against stg)
gain (by or from stg)
hear (of or about stg or sby)
hope (for stg)
impose on sby
indulge (in stg)
inquire (about stg or sby)
insist (on stg)
interfere (with stg or sby)
invest in stg
join in stg

joke (about stg or sby)
judge (by or from stg)
know (of or about stg or sby)
laugh (at sby or stg)
laugh (about sby or stg)
lean on stg or sby
listen (to stg or sby)
live (for stg)
long for stg
look (at stg or sby)
look (after sby or stg)
look (for stg or sby)
object (to stg)
operate (on sby or stg)
part with stg
pay (for stg)
persist (in stg)
play (with sby/against sby)
prepare (for) stg
profit (by stg)
qualify (for stg)
quarrel (with sby) (about stg)
rank with sby
reason with sby
reflect on stg
rely on sby or stg
reply (to sby)
report (on stg or sby)
resign (from stg)
respond (to stg)
result (from a cause)
result (in an effect)

retire (from stg)
search (for) (stg or sby)
serve (as stg)
share (with sby)
share in stg
shoot (at a target)
smell (of stg)
smile (at sby)
speak (of or about stg or sby)
stare (at sby or stg)
struggle (with stg or sby)
submit (to stg or sby)
succeed (in stg)
surrender (to sby)
swear (at sby)
sympathise (with sby)
talk (of or about stg or sby)
taste of stg
think (of or about stg or sby)
tire (of stg)
trade (with sby) (in stg)
unite (with sby)
vote (for a candidate)
vote (on a proposal)
wait (for sby or stg)
watch (for sby or stg)
wish (for stg)
wonder (at stg)
worry (about stg or sby)
write (to sby) (about or on stg)
yield (to sby or stg)

[1] Only use *beware* in the IMPERATIVE, or after *must* or *should*.

6 Model *We thanked him (for his help)*. (See III.12)

accuse sby (of stg)
add stg (to stg)
address stg (to sby)
admire sby (for stg)
ask (sby) (about a subject)
ask (sby) (for stg)
assure sby (of stg)
base stg on stg else
blame sby (for stg)
bless sby (for stg)
borrow stg (from sby)
change stg (for stg else)
charge sby (for stg bought)
charge sby (with a crime)
cheat sby (out of stg)

claim (stg) (from sby)
clear sby (of suspicion)
combine stg with stg else
compare stg with stg else
concern oneself with stg
confine stg to limits
confuse sby with sby else
congratulate sby (on stg)
connect stg (to or with stg)
consult sby (about stg)
convince sby (of stg)
contrast stg with stg else
convert sby (to a belief)
convert stg (into stg else)
cure sby (of stg)

curse sby (for stg)

defend sby (from stg)

deliver sby (from stg)

deliver stg (to sby)

demand stg (for a purpose)

demand stg (of sby)

discuss stg (with sby)

dismiss sby or stg (from stg)

distinguish stg (from stg)

divide a number by a number

divide stg (between or among people)

divide stg (into parts)

exchange stg (for stg else)

excuse sby (for an action done)

excuse sby (from an action, stg, due)

exempt sby (from stg due)

explain stg (to sby)

forgive sby (for stg)

free sby (from stg)

help sby (with or over stg)

hinder sby (from stg)

honour sby (for stg)

include stg or sby (in stg)

inform sby (of or about stg)

instruct sby (in a subject)

interest sby (in stg or sby)

introduce sby (to sby else)

involve sby (in stg)

lead sby (to stg or sby)

limit stg (to stg else)

mention stg (to sby)

mistake sby for sby else

mistake stg for stg else

neglect sby or stg (for sby or stg else)

pardon sby (for stg)

pay (sby) (for stg)

pay stg (to sby)

pity sby (for stg)

praise sby (for stg)

prefer stg (to stg else)

prejudice sby (against stg or sby else)

prepare sby (for stg)

present sby with stg

prevent sby (from doing)

protect sby (from stg)

provide sby (with stg)

punish sby (for stg)

refer sby to stg or sby

regard (IV.23.5)

rescue sby (from stg)

reserve stg (for sby)

respect sby (for stg)

revenge oneself on sby

reward sby (for stg)

rid stg of stg else

rob sby (of stg)

sacrifice stg (for stg)

save sby (from stg)

search stg or sby (for stg)

sell stg (for a price)[1]

sell stg (to sby)

sentence sby (to stg)

separate stg from stg

share stg (with sby)

shelter sby (from stg)

shield sby (from stg)

steal stg (from sby)

submit stg (to sby)

supply sby (with stg)

supply stg (to sby)

surrender stg (to sby)

suspect sby (of stg)

tell sby (of or about stg)

thank sby (for stg)

threaten sby (with stg)

trouble sby[2]

turn stg (into stg else)

warn sby (of danger)

[1] Sell stg at a price = offer it (for sale); sell stg for a price = exchange it (for money).
[2] *trouble sby with a problem, about a subject, for stg one wants.*

7 Models

  a I enjoy listening to music. (See III.24)
  b I'm tired of waiting.

Note The *-ing* form, not the INFINITIVE, occurs after a PREPOSITION and will therefore occur when a VERB is required after any of the PREPOSITIONS in Appendix A5 and 6, thus: *I object to smoking, succeed in doing stg, thank you for helping.*

admit	avoid	begin (IV.10.5)	carry on
advise (IV.10.4)	(can't) bear (IV.10.5)	burst out	cease (IV.10.5)

continue (IV.10.5)	forget (IV.10.10)	like (IV.10.3)	remember
delay	give up	love (IV.10.3)	(IV.10.7)
deny	go on	mind	resent
dislike	hate (IV.10.3)	miss	risk
enjoy	can't help	need (IV.25.8)	start (IV.10.5)
face	imagine	omit (IV.10.5)	stop (IV.10.9)
fancy	intend (IV.10.5)	propose (IV.10.4)	suggest (IV.10.4)
feel like	keep on	recollect	try (IV.10.8)
finish	leave off	recommend	want (IV.25.8)

Appendix B Irregular verbs

If necessary, use a good pronouncing dictionary to verify forms marked by an asterisk. See notes at the end of the list.

Stem	Past	Past Participle	Stem	Past	Past Participle
arise	arose	arisen*	eat	ate	eaten
be[1]	was*/were*	been	fall*	fell	fallen*
bear*	bore	borne[2]	feed	fed	fed
beat	beat	beaten	feel	felt	felt
become*	became	become*	fight	fought*	fought*
begin	began	begun	find*	found	found
bend	bent	bent	flee	fled	fled
bid	bid	bid	fling	flung	flung
bind*	bound	bound	fly	flew	flown*
bite	bit	bitten	forbid	forbade*	forbidden
bleed	bled	bled	forget	forgot	forgotten
blow*	blew	blown*	forgive*	forgave	forgiven*
break*	broke	broken	forsake	forsook	forsaken
breed	bred	bred	freeze	froze	frozen
bring	brought*	brought*	get	got	got
build	built*	built*	give*	gave	given*
burn[3]	burnt	burnt	go	went	gone*[4]
burst	burst	burst	grind	ground	ground
buy*	bought*	bought*	grow*	grew	grown*
cast	cast	cast	hang	hung	hung[5]
catch	caught*	caught*	have*	had	had
choose	chose	chosen	hear	heard*	heard*
cling	clung	clung	hide	hid	hidden
come*	came	come*	hit	hit	hit
cost	cost	cost	hold	held	held
creep	crept	crept	hurt	hurt	hurt
cut	cut	cut	keep	kept	kept
deal	dealt*	dealt*	kneel[3]	knelt	knelt
dig	dug	dug	know*	knew	known*
do*	did	done*	lay	laid	laid
draw*	drew	drawn	lead	led	led
dream*[3]	dreamt*	dreamt*	lean[3]	leant*	leant*
drink	drank	drunk	leap[3]	leapt*	leapt*
drive	drove	driven*	learn[3]	learnt*	learnt*

Stem	Past	Past Participle	Stem	Past	Past Participle
leave	left	left	speak	spoke	spoken
lend	lent	lent	speed	sped	sped
let	let	let	spell[3]	spelt	spelt
lie*[6]	lay	lain	spend	spent	spent
light[3]	lit	lit	spill[3]	spilt	spilt
lose*	lost	lost	spin	spun	spun
make	made	made	spit	spat	spat
mean	meant*	meant*	split	split	split
meet	met	met	spoil[3]	spoilt	spoilt
pay	paid	paid	spread*	spread*	spread*
put*	put*	put*	spring	sprang	sprung
read	read*	read*	stand[7]	stood	stood
ride	rode	ridden	steal	stole	stolen
ring	rang	rung	stick	stuck	stuck
rise	rose	risen*	sting	stung	stung
run	ran	run	stink	stank	stunk
say	said*	said*	stride	strode	stridden[8]
see	saw	seen	strike	struck	struck
seek	sought*	sought*	swear*	swore	sworn
sell	sold	sold	swept	swept	swept
send	sent	sent	swim	swam	swum
set	set	set	swing	swung	swung
shake	shook	shaken	take[9]	took	taken
shed	shed	shed	teach	taught*	taught*
shine	shone*	shone*	tear*	tore	torn
shoot	shot	shot	tell	told	told
show*	showed*	shown*	think	thought*	thought*
shrink	shrank	shrunk	throw*	threw	thrown*
shut	shut	shut	thrust	thrust	thrust
sing	sang	sung	tread	trod	trodden
sink	sank	sunk	wake	woke	woken
sit	sat	sat	wear*	wore	worn
sleep	slept	slept	weave	wove	woven
slide	slid	slid	weep	wept	wept
sling	slung	slung	win	won*	won*
slit	slit	slit	wind*	wound[10]	wound
smell[3]	smelt	smelt	wring	wrung	wrung
sow*	sowed*	sown*	write	wrote	written

[1] See 1.1, 1.8, 1.13 and 11.3.
[2] But /Where/When/ were you born?
[3] These forms also have regular forms. For lighted, see V.5.11.
[4] See II.9.4–5.
[5] Hang, meaning 'put to death by hanging', is regular.
[6] Lie, meaning 'tell a lie', is regular.
[7] Sim. understand, withstand.
[8] PAST PARTICIPLE seldom used.
[9] Sim. mistake, undertake.
[10] Wound, /wuːnd/, is regular.

Appendix C Examples of the four main types of 'phrasal verb': III.23 and VI.18

(P) indicates that the verbal group often occurs in the PASSIVE as well as ACTIVE.

Type 1 III.23.1. See also Appendix A5

ask after sby (= enquire about his health)

come across sby or stg

do without stg

get over a difficulty (= overcome it)

go into a matter (= investigate it) (P)

live on (eg *He lives on fruit*)

look after (= care for sby or stg) (P)

look into a matter (= investigate it) (P)

run for a post (= seek to be elected for it)

run into sby *or* run into difficulties

run over sby in the street (P)

see to stg or sby (= attend to) (P)

stand by sby (= support him)

stand for stg (= represent it)

take after sby (= resemble him)

take to sby or stg (= get used to)

turn into stg (= become it)

Type 2 III.23.2. No PASSIVE

answer back (= reply, eg to an order)

back down (= retreat from a position)

bear up (= not collapse)

boil over (eg *Milk boils over*)

break down (= collapse)

break off (= interrupt oneself)

break out (eg *A fire breaks out*)

break up (fall to pieces, end)

clear up (eg *Weather clears up*)

come about (= happen)

come to (= regain consciousness)

die away (eg *The sound died away*)

die down (eg *The fire died down*)

die out (eg *The fire died out*)

give in *or* give up (= surrender)

hang about (colloq. = loiter)

look out (= be on watch, on one's guard)

pull up (= stop, in the car)

run out: *see* run out of, *Type 4*

set off, *or* set out, on a journey for destination

turn up (= appear, present oneself or itself)

Type 3 III.23.3 *All expressions in this section can be marked* (P)

answer sby back (see VI.18.3d)

back sby up (= support)

bear sby or stg out (= confirm a statement)

break stg down (= destroy, or analyse)

break stg off (literally, or interrupt)

break stg up (smash or end)

bring sby up (= educate)

call stg off (= cancel)

call sby up (= telephone, enlist sby in the army)

carry stg out (*literally, or* undertake)

clear stg up (**tidy,** *or* solve a mystery)

cut stg or sby off (= interrupt)

draw stg up (eg draw up plans)

feed information back

get stg over (= finish it or have it done)

hold stg or sby up (= detain)

keep stg up (= maintain)

lay stg by

lay supplies in

leave sby or stg out (= omit)

let sby down (= fail to support)

let sby off (= not punish)

make stg up (= invent or compose)

pick sby or stg out (= select)

pull sby up (= stop)

put stg off (= pospone)

put sby up (= give him a bed)

run sby down (= speak ill of him)

run sby over *or* run over sby (*Type 1*)

set stg up (= establish)

take stg on (= undertake)

take stg over (= assume responsibility for it)

try stg out (= test)

work stg out (= solve a problem)

Type 4 III.23.4

do away with stg (= destroy)

fall back on stg or sby (= have recourse to)

fall in with a plan (= co-operate with it)

be fed up with (= be tired of)

get away with stg (= not be penalised for it)

get rid of (P)

go back on one's word (= not keep to it)
go in for a subject or a pastime
grow out of (= become too old for)
hang on to (colloq. = hold, keep a grip on)
hold on to (= keep a grip on) (P)
keep up with (= keep level with)
lead up to a conclusion
look out for (= watch out)
look down on (= regard an inferior) (P)

look up to sby (= respect) (P)
make up for (= compensate)
put up with (= tolerate)
run away with (= escape with)
run out of (= exhaust supplies)
stand in for (= deputise for)
stand up for (= support)
stand up to (= not be afraid of)

Appendix D Structures and collocations with simple verbs, eg *do*, *get*, *give*, *have*, *keep*, *make*

catch a cold, or some other infectious disease; *catch* a bus (III.4.1).

come to an agreement, to a conclusion, to a decision.

do business with sby, one's best, damage to stg, one's duty, an experiment, a favour, good, one's hair, harm to sby or stg, homework, an injury, justice to stg or sby, a kindness, lessons, right, a service, a translation, the washing up, wonders, work, wrong.

earn a living, money, a reputation, a salary, wages.

find an answer to a question, a solution to a problem, time for stg.

follow advice, an example, a procedure.

gain an advantage, a grip on stg, a hold on stg.

get and *keep* both occur in the following structures:

vt + NP (as in I.27.4)	*get* the tickets	*keep* the change
vt + INDIRECT OBJ + DIR OBJ	*get* Mary a seat	*keep* me a seat
vi + ADV PARTICLE (as in I.20.2)	*get* up	*keep* away
vt + NP + ADV PARTICLE (as in III.9.1)	*get* your books out	*keep* your head down
vi + ADJ (as in III.23.3)	*get* ready	*keep* warm
vt + NP + ADJ (as in IV.24.3)	*get* your room ready	*keep* your feet dry

get (+ NP) can be used with a wide range of meanings, some of which are indicated by the verbs in parentheses in the following examples:
I *got* a letter (= received); I *got* the tickets (= obtained or fetched); I *got* £10 for my work (= earned); I *got* a cold (= caught); I didn't *get* the joke (= understand); I *got* breakfast (= prepared).
See also I.15.2, II.6, II.16 and IV.20

give sby some advice, an answer, a blow, a definition of stg, a description of stg, encouragement, an explanation, some help, a kick, a kiss, permission to do stg, a pinch, a punch, a push, a reply, support, trouble, a welcome; *give* stg a brush, a polish, a rub, a trial, a wash.

go for a drive, a run, a swim, a walk.

grant sby admission, an interview, permission to do stg, a request.

have an argument, a bath, a bathe, a dance, /ə/ /no/ desire for stg, a drink of water, an effect on sby or stg, a fight with sby, a game, an influence on *or* over sby, a look at stg, a rest, a sleep, a talk with sby, a swim, a wash.

keep stg under control, one's temper: *See also get*

lose the advantage, control of stg, one's temper.

make an accusation against sby, an agreement with sby, an allowance for stg, an appearance, an application, an appointment, an arrangement, an attack on sby, an attempt, a bargain, a bed, certain of stg or *that*-CLAUSE, a calculation of stg, a choice, a comment, a complaint, a comparison between stg and stg else, a connection, a contribution to stg, a copy of stg, a correction, a criticism, a decision, a difference, a discovery, an escape, an excuse, a fortune, friends, fun of stg or sby, a good job of stg, haste, an improvement, an inquiry, an investigation, a journey, love, a mark, a mistake, money, a move, a noise, a note of stg, an observation, sby an offer, peace, progress, a proposal, a recommendation, a reduction, a reference to stg, a report on stg, a request, a reservation, room for sby, sense of stg, sure of stg or *that*-CLAUSE, a suggestion, time for stg, trouble for sby, use of stg or sby, war on, a will.

offer (sby) an apology, one's congratulations, an explanation, one's resignation, a suggestion.
pay attention to stg or sby, a call on sby, a visit to sby.
put emphasis on stg, a question to sby, stg on record.
reach an agreement, a conclusion, a decision.
submit an application, one's resignation.
take a breath, care of, hold of, an interest in, a measurement of stg, a note of, notice of, a photograph, pity on sby, trouble over sby or stg.

Appendix E Stative verbs and avoidance of the progressive aspect

The PROGRESSIVE aspect (I.18) is normally avoided with the following STATIVE VERBS:

1 be (*except as in IV.28.6*)
2 have (*except as in II.2*)
3 *Verbs referring to states of being and having*: eg appear (IV.15), belong (I.25.5), concern, consist, contain, cost, depend, deserve, equal, fit, happen, (*as in IV.15*), lack, matter, merit, own, possess, resemble, seem, sound, suffice.
4 *Verbs of inert perception*:
   a see, hear; smell, taste (*except as in VI.22.11*).
   b feel: *see the models in* VI.22.10 *and* 11.
5 *Verbs of inert cognition*
   believe, expect, fear (= be afraid to say), feel (= think), find (= conclude), forget, forgive, hope, imagine, know, like, love, mean, mind, realise, recognise, remember, suppose, think (= have the opinion that), understand, want, wish. *However, see* VI.22.12.
6 *Avoidance of the* PROGRESSIVE *aspect in beginning, statements and declarations, eg* I accept your invitation with pleasure. I admit I was wrong. I entirely agree. *Similarly* beg, confess, consider, declare, deny, doubt, expect *and similar verbs in IV.11, Lex 1, 2, and 3, and in V.30, Lex 3, 5, 6 and 7.*

Appendix F Prepositions after adjectives: see III.6

An asterisk after an ADJECTIVE indicates that the ADJ must be followed by a PREP PHRASE, eg *He was fond of me.*

Preposition	Model		Lexicon	
about	*a*	You were right about Jim.	*a*	certain, clear, curious, doubtful, honest, right, uncertain, wrong
	b	I'm /happy/ /sorry/ about Mary.	*b*	anxious, concerned, crazy, delighted, glad, happy, mad, sorry, uneasy, worried
at	*a*	He was good at arithmetic.	*a*	bad, brilliant, efficient, expert, good, no good, hopeless, quick, slow, skilful
	b	I'm surprised at you.	*b*	amazed, astonished, mad (= angry), surprised

Preposition	Model	Lexicon
	c I was angry at his conduct.	*c* angry, furious, surprised
for	*a* I feel sorry for Mary.	*a* sorry (= sympathetic)
	b He's sorry for his actions.	*b* famous, responsible, sorry (= regretful)
	c We're ready for work.	*c* eager, fit, prepared, ready
	d This work is good for you.	*d* bad, convenient, good, suitable, useful
	e There is enough for everyone.	*e* enough, sufficient
	f We're grateful for your help.	*f* grateful, thankful
from	*a* We're far from /home/ /danger/.	*a* absent, far*, free, safe
	b This is different from that.	*b* different
in	*a* He is interested in games.	*a* fortunate, interested, lucky, weak
	b He's deficient in courage.	*b* deficient, lacking
of	*a* He's not afraid of anyone.	*a* afraid, ashamed, aware*, certain, conscious*, envious, fond*, jealous, proud, sick, sure, tired, worthy
	b He's not ashamed of anything.	*b* afraid, ashamed, aware*, capable, careful, certain, conscious, fond*, guilty, ignorant, proud, sick, sure, tired, worthy
	c The room is full of smoke.	*c* full
	d We're independent of Jones.	*d* ahead, independent, north*, south*, east*, west*
on	*a* We're dependent on Jones.	*a* dependent, keen
	b He's very keen on his work.	*b* intent*, keen
to	*a* Your answer is equal to mine.	*a* close, contrary, equal, inferior, similar
	b He has been loyal to me.	*b* answerable*, dear, faithful, invaluable, loyal, obedient, polite, responsible, rude, subject*, true, unfaithful, useful
	c His motives were clear to me.	*c* clear, evident, obvious, plain
	d You will be liable to a fine.	*d* liable
	e He is sensitive to criticism.	*e* indifferent, sensitive
	f Some things are fatal to us.	*f* fatal, harmful, sacred
with	*a* He was angry with us.	*a* angry, annoyed, bored, disappointed, disgusted, familiar, fascinated, furious, generous, gentle, impressed, mad (= angry), (im)patient, pleased, (un)popular, (dis)satisfied
	b This statement is consistent with his previous one.	*b* (in)consistent, identical

NB NOUNS *derived from these* ADJECTIVES *usually take the same* PREPOSITIONS. *Thus* His interest in games, absence from home, loyalty to me, impatience with us

Appendix G Frequently-used prepositional phrases beginning with *at*, *by*, *in*, *on*, *out of*

It is assumed that these phrases will be presented in a suitable context and with the meaning given in a good modern dictionary.

1 *at*, eg *We spoke about it at dinner.*

at breakfast	at all costs	at ease	at first
at church	at dinner	at all events	at hand

at heart	at short notice	at rest	at tea
at home	at once	at school	at a time
at last	at peace	at sea	at the same time
at least	at play	at sight	at times
at length	at present	at first sight	at war
at a loss	at a profit	at supper	at will
at a moment's notice	at any rate	at table	at work

2 *by*, eg *We went by air*.

by accident	by degrees	by no means	by rights
by air	by far	by mistake	by sea
by bus	by good fortune	by name	by ship
by cable	by hand	by night	by sight
by car	by heart	by oneself	by surprise
by chance	by land	by plane	by telegram
by day	by letter	by post	by yourself
by design	by all means		

3 *in*, eg *We have a lot in common*.

in all	in fact	in need	in secret
in bed	in fun	in order	in a sense
in brief	in general	in particular	in short
in case	in half	in pencil	in sight
in any case	in hand	in pieces	in stock
in class	in hospital	in place	in tears
in common	in a hurry	in prison	in time
in debt	in ink	in private	in town
in difficulties	in itself	in all probability	in turn
in danger	in the long run	in public	in two (pieces)
in due course	in love	in reach	in a way
in the end	in name	in reply	in other words

4 *on*, eg *The building's on fire*.

on no account	on foot	on horseback	on time
on average	on guard	on a journey	on vacation
on business	on the one hand	on pleasure	on watch
on duty	on the other hand	on purpose	on one's way
on fire	on holiday	on sale	on the whole

Note the difference between We arrived on time = at the exact hour.
We arrived in time = with time to spare.
and between You're in my way—I can't move.
I'm on my way to my destination.

5 *out of*, eg *I'm out of breath*.

out of breath	out of doors	out of place	out of sight
out of control	out of hearing	out of practice	out of stock
out of danger	out of one's mind	out of the question	out of turn
out of date	out of order	out of reach	out of work

6 *Other* PREPOSITIONS

off duty	under control	up to date

Appendix H Adverbs that commonly occur as modifiers of past participles

Note: The PARTICIPLE *may be part of a* PASSIVE *construction, or an* ADJECTIVE. *See VI.16*

Participle	Modifiers used include	Participle	Modifiers used include
admired	much, greatly	forgotten	completely, entirely
amazed	absolutely	frightened	very, badly, thoroughly
amused	very, highly	furnished	well, badly
annoyed	very, thoroughly, extremely	grieved	deeply
astonished	absolutely	hurt (physically)	slightly, badly, seriously
based	well, soundly, broadly	hurt (feelings)	deeply
bored	very, completely, utterly		
broken	badly, completely	injured	slightly, badly, seriously
built	well, soundly, badly	insulted	thoroughly
changed	greatly, completely, entirely	insured	fully, completely
		interested	very, keenly
cheered	greatly	justified	thoroughly, completely, entirely
confused	very, highly, completely		
controlled	strictly, severely	known	well, widely
cooked	well, badly	limited	strictly, severely
covered	fully, completely, entirely	mistaken	very much, greatly, completely, entirely
damaged	badly, slightly		
delighted	highly	moved	deeply
depressed	very, deeply, utterly	offended	very, deeply
determined	very, thoroughly, absolutely	opposed	completely, entirely, utterly
disappointed	very, deeply, bitterly	organised	well, badly
distressed	very, deeply	overcome	completely
disturbed	very, deeply	qualified	highly, well
dressed	well, badly, fully	relieved	very, greatly
educated	well	shocked	very, deeply
encouraged	very, greatly	trained	well, highly
exaggerated	much, greatly	treated	well, badly
excited	very, highly, thoroughly	upset	very, thoroughly
exhausted	very, thoroughly, completely	used	much, well, widely
		worried	very, seriously
experienced	very, fully, completely	wounded (as for *hurt*, two senses)	
fed	well, badly	written	well, badly

Index

The index is intended to indicate, first, at what point in the syllabus an item is considered as being introduced for active use by the learners: thus *a, an* I.2. Subsequent entries against the same item, eg *a, an* I.5; I.9, refer to different applications of that item.

The first number, in roman numerals, refers to the Stage; the second to the Unit within that Stage.

Parentheses provide the key to abbreviations used in the notes and the index itself. Thus ADJ(ECTIVE) indicates that ADJ is used as an abbreviation for ADJECTIVE.

Lexical items are printed in *italic*. Grammatical terms, and references to semantic notions, are in SMALL CAPITALS.

Terminology and abbreviations used

The terminology used in the notes is in accordance with that of *A Grammar of Contemporary English* (Quirk, Greenbaum, Leech and Svartvik, Longman, 1972). It is *not* suggested that this terminology be taught to learners, whether in English or in their mother tongue, nor that the concepts behind it be explained. The authors assume that what will be taught first of all will be the models, with vocabulary appropriate to particular circumstances; that the models will be presented and practised in context; and that, if grammatical theory and terminology are taught, it will not be done until the learners are already able to make considerable active use of the language.

The terminology used in the notes is listed in the index, with references to examples in the models showing how each term is employed. The index will also provide a key to abbreviations used in the notes.

DET(ERMINER): This term covers ARTICLES, DEMONSTRATIVES, POSSESSIVES and the NOUN MODIFIERS dealt with in II.5. For combination and MODIFIERS of DETERMINERS in NP see IV.4

did, didn't, full VERB and AUX II.6

different II.22

direct, directly V.19

direction I.19

DIRECT OBJ(ECT) I.21; I.28

dis- V.3

DISJUNCT, see ADV

distance II.19

do, does, doesn't, don't
  as AUX in INTERROG and NEG, present I.24; past II.6
  as full VERB I.18; II.6
  collocations with, Appendix D
  contrasted with *make* I.21
  emphasizing AFFIRM and IMPERATIVE II.25
  NEGATIVE IMPERATIVE I.18

double II.27

double genitive IV.4

doubt that or *whether* VI.27

down: PREP I.19; ADV PARTICLE I.20

downstairs I.19

dramatic effect VI.30

drop of I.16

due to V.10; V.22

duration, see *by* a certain time, *during, for, since, while*

during II.3; III.18

duty III.22

each: *ten pence each* II.19; *each*+NOUN, *each (one)*, *they will each get a prize* II.27

each other III.3

early I.23

earn: collocations with, Appendix D

echo question I.10

-ed forms, eg *pleased, bald-headed* III.8; VI.16

eg= for example

either
  ADV, contrasted with *too* I.23; in repeat patterns II.25
  CONJ with *or* II.30
  DET *either (of them), either (boy)* II.27

elder, eldest II.21

else, someone else II.28; *or else* V.17

emphasis II.25

EMPHASIZER VI.14

enjoy ourselves III.3; *enjoy listening* III.24

enough
  ADV eg *eat enough* III.26
  after ADJ or ADV, eg *(not) good enough, well enough* II.18
  DET and PRO-FORM, eg *enough (soup), enough (sweets)* II.5

evasive answer VI.25

even II.26

ever: with present I.29; with PAST II.3; with

PRESENT PERFECT II.9; after *what, who, why* etc V.14

ever since III.19

-ever, see *wh-ever*

every+NOUN, *every one* II.27; *every hour* III.4; *every such case* VI.4

everybody, everyone II.28

everything I.30; *everywhere* II.28

exactly VI.14

except IV.5

exclamation: with *How* II.18; with *What* II.26

existential *there*, as in *There's a dog in the garden*

explain I.27–28

extremely III.7

fact, the fact that VI.10

fair V.19

fairly II.18; V.19

fall I.18; Supplement to III.9/10

family relationships I.2

far (away) II.19; II.23; *farther, -est* II.23; *far more, far too*+ADJ or ADV II.23

fast ADJ and ADV II.23

feel stg I.23; *feel ill* II.1; *it feels warm* II.1; as STATIVE and ACTION VERB VI.22

few, a few II.4; *fewer, -est* II.21; *a good few, the few* IV.4

find: collocations with, Appendix D

finite VERB (A VERB is finite when it is in PRESENT or PAST TENSE, when it is IMPERATIVE, or when it consists of a verbal group beginning with AUX in PRESENT or PAST TENSE or with a MODAL, eg *am writing, have written, may have written, may have been writing*

first, second, etc I.29; *the first three* IV.4; *the day we first met* IV.27

focus in CLEFT SENTENCE VI.6

focusing ADV VI.14

follow: collocations with, Appendix D

fond of III.5

for
  after ADJ eg *sorry for* III.6; Appendix F
  destination or purpose I.27; III.24
  duration: *You've been here (for) three hours* II.9; *I haven't driven for two years* II.10; *pay for stg* II.19
  for NP *to*-INF II.18; IV.30
  SUB CONJ V.17

for all= despite V.22

forbidden to V.11

fore- V.3

forget I.22; +INF or *-ing* IV.10

formal, passim

formula I.2

frankly VI.17

free to V.11

frequency, see ADV

from I.19; III.6; Appendix F

front I.12

full of II.5; *full up* III.6

full VERB= any VERB except AUX or MODAL